C000254649

Sharing Knowledge

Sharing Knowledge

The Why and How of
Organizational Change

François Dupuy

First published 2004 by
PALGRAVE MACMILLAN

Palgrave Macmillan in the UK is an imprint of Macmillan Publishers Limited, registered in England, company number 785998, of Houndmills, Basingstoke, Hampshire RG21 6XS.

Palgrave Macmillan in the US is a division of St Martin's Press LLC, 175 Fifth Avenue, New York, NY 10010.

Palgrave Macmillan is the global academic imprint of the above companies and has companies and representatives throughout the world.

Palgrave® and Macmillan® are registered trademarks in the United States, the United Kingdom, Europe and other countries

ISBN 1 4039 3801 6 hardback
ISBN 978 1 4039 3801 5 hardback

This book is printed on paper suitable for recycling and made from fully managed and sustained forest sources. Logging, pulping and manufacturing processes are expected to conform to the environmental regulations of the country of origin.

A catalogue record for this book is available from the British Library.

Library of Congress Cataloging-in-Publication Data applied for

Printed and bound in Great Britain by
CPI Antony Rowe, Chippenham and Eastbourne

Contents

Introduction

Change is one of the recurrent themes of developed companies in general and management literature in particular. It is present in all books and articles, at the same time as becoming a virtual obsession not just for managers but also for all those who work today in our organizations, whether in the public or private sector. Even political leaders, identified as being conservatives or assumed to be progressives, define themselves in relation to it: being against change, whatever the sphere under consideration, is held to be backward, "out of touch" and, in a word, blinkered.

This trend reveals a phenomenon that is at the same time simple and universally accepted, or at least in developed countries – change exists. This is an indisputable fact and there is little point in spending too much time and effort on expounding it. Even if, of course, we do not yet have sufficient hindsight to really assess the importance and true reach of events which are taking place in front of our eyes, we can still feel, even at the reduced scale of our own lives, that we shall not finish this life in the world in which we started. *The acceleration of this phenomenon means that children today ask their grandparents – and soon it will be their parents – what the world was like in their day. This has not always been the case, but we tend to forget it.*

As far as organizations are concerned – and they are after all the subject of this book – we are now seeing an interesting paradox which certainly merits some attention: it is not so much change itself which poses a problem – it is even valued as a driving force for economic activity, as a source for the creation of wealth – but more the ability to lead it, to steer it, to control it, in brief to be an "active actor" and not just a simple, even if enthusiastic, spectator. Steering change has become one of today's major issues for managers – for reasons that are easy to understand and which have nothing to do with the megalomania which is supposed to have blossomed in Orwell's footsteps.

Why the cost of uncontrolled change has become intolerable

In the conventional industrial world, where we have mass production, Taylorism, Fordism or triumphant management, in that world in which one used to ask for goods and services even before wanting to see the bill, the extra costs of uncontrolled change never appeared to be intolerable since they never appeared at all. The accounting systems themselves did not give them visibility and, at the end of the day, they just ended up buried under "progress", a concept that was general enough to absorb, without too much difficulty, errors that were not necessarily insignificant.

Nowadays, the picture is different. Everything is calculated, everything is measured, everything is assessed: we don't look solely at defects, but also at the costs of non-quality. In more general terms, such measurement focuses as much on what is not as on what is and the accounting systems mentioned above have adapted to this. The result, not only for managers but also for all those with responsibility at any level whatsoever, is a twofold requirement: firstly, change is necessary because it is a condition for survival, but secondly it is necessary at a controlled cost and, where possible, a reduced cost, and hence it is necessary to control the movement. *It is no longer enough to follow or to put up with change, it is now necessary to anticipate, to hold onto the reins. Just being reactive is no longer enough, one now has to be proactive.*

Let's say this right away, some people do not stop to consider that this is an impossible task and that it would be better not to attempt it. Books and articles make their appearance regularly, written by reputed authors who emphasize that "*change programmes don't produce change*",[1] who wonder about "*why transformation efforts fail*",[2] or who state, even more directly and unambiguously, that one does not "*manage change*".[3] And the fact is that, despite all the attempts to predict everything, master everything, control everything, this just does not happen: the phenomenon remains largely unpredictable, produces unexpected effects and leaves those responsible, those in charge of it, to a great extent perplexed if not in a total quandary. It is true that, as Peter Drucker says,[4] our organizations are designed more for stability than for change, rather in the same way that our managers have been trained more to ensure continuity than to manage or introduce disruption.

As a result, there is a real obsession with the "action plan", through which it is attempted to predict everything, organize everything, control everything right down to the smallest detail, and the establishment of which becomes an essential condition for "launching oneself" and, at the same time, an end in itself. This way of looking at things of course leads to a form of paralysis since nothing can be completely predicted or planned. The actual commencement of the process itself always finds itself pushed back until, through necessity, that is, as external constraints become ever more pressing, one no longer has a choice, one is backed against the wall, or, to put it more brutally, placed in a crisis situation. But change through crisis, so well described and analysed by Michel Crozier,[5] and over such a length of time, is even more painful in human terms and, in general, even more costly. It therefore no longer corresponds to the needs of the moment, and only organizations which are not yet entirely under constraints of accountability – public authorities for example[6] – can allow themselves this privilege. *And again, here at the beginning of the twenty-first century, their slow death process appears particularly agonizing for their individual members as well as for the corporate body.*

Seeking reassurance or trying to control events?

Of course, when faced with the random element of any action for change, such hesitation brings a smile to the faces of all those who are "intermediaries of change", those whose work, rather like that of paediatricians, consists of reassuring anxious mothers even before treating their children, in other words, reassuring managers before doing anything at all. This is what creates business for consultancy firms, and one can understand that the more urgent the need is for change, the more their market expands and the more their involvement increases. After all, the primary function of such involvement is to legitimize what has been done, to release the manager from all or part of his responsibility, which finally has no price.

At the same time, it is important to acknowledge that resorting to such a function of intermediation is a first step indicating that there is an awareness of the need to make things evolve. For the temptation often remains to do nothing, to shield oneself, to wait for the storm to pass over, and to cover up such opposition to progress with an impressive smokescreen of sophisticated action plans, skilfully prioritized projects, focus groups, surveys and work. In brief, substituting agitation for action, until the process itself becomes paralysed and loses itself in uncontrollable meanderings about which, after a while, nobody worries any more.

A major European transport company which, in a way, will serve as the guiding thread for this book, is a living example of this: confronted with increasingly vigorous intermodal competition, but at the same time prisoner of an impressive conservatism finally shared by its managers as much as by the union organizations, it initiated over fifty "priority action programmes" which, put end to end, form its "business project", tying up considerable energy, time, money, and so on … but, at the end of the day, producing only an evident opposition to progress and this to the great satisfaction of all those involved: it's so hard to do nothing while moving about so much!

So, one might say, what is the point of another work on this non-event known as change? Why add another stone to this edifice – so hopeless or so well cemented together, depending on the angle from which it is viewed? Can such a book aim for a result other than simultaneously providing food for ambient discussions and conservatism? Certainly, for when one looks closely, one finds a few experiences of successful change: one of their characteristics is that those who conducted them did not seek to control everything nor indeed manage everything, but instead accepted uncertainty and, finally, did not consider it absolutely essential to know where they were going to in order to get there. Maybe they had no choice. But whether or not they were successful, there is always something to be learned and adopted from their approaches. One can start with something that they themselves point out – thus joining the ranks of some of the authors referred to above:[7] they have wagered on knowledge – that is, they did not want to hide from reality – at the same time as on trust – that is, they wanted to share such knowledge with those who were most concerned by change: their workforce.

The importance of knowledge and knowledge sharing

In saying that, one cannot help thinking of Air France between 1993 and 1998, and the famous "method" which took its name from their CEO of that time: we will be using that case a great deal in this book. And one cannot help being struck by how nonconformist and unusual this approach appears in relation to our ways of thinking, our education and our habits. Confronting reality, seeing things as they really are and not just as one would like them to be, in other words listening, is disturbing for managers, who are there because they are supposed to know more than others about how things are, how they must be, and how to achieve this. Such acceptance of reality shows modesty but also boldness, both of which have to be learned as suggested by Chris Argyris.[8]

However, such access to knowledge cannot be spontaneous, unless by exception which is all the more remarkable for being an exception. To be successful, this requires time – but not precipitation, agitation or hyper-activity. It needs true intellectual investment, which presupposes learning and mastering new ways of reasoning, usually very different from those taught to our elites, whichever schools or universities they attend, and whichever side of the Atlantic they find themselves on. In particular, it requires their agreement to do without the models – quantitative, organizational, behavioural, and so on – which give reassurance but also block the view and impede listening. It is not at all surprising that each of us seeks to connect that part of reality that confronts us to a vaster whole that is already known. In a stressful situation, like those which demand the implementation of change, this reduces uncertainty and allows the use of solutions which have been "tried and tested" in circumstances that appear to be similar. But then there is a substantial risk of not really trying to get to grips with the specific reality with which one is confronted. Experience teaches us that we must listen, it does not tell us what we must hear.

Sharing knowledge – we will later return to this more fully – is an even more unusual experience, since it presupposes *trust*, an approach which is as unfamiliar to our organizations as investment in knowledge. Since the industrial world became the industrial world, that is, when work was no longer described by poets but analysed and organized by specialists, efforts have been immense and continual towards reducing the inherent uncertainty in human behaviour. From rules to organization charts, from recommendations to procedures, everything is done to make what people do at work predictable and above all independent of their good intentions or, even worse, their arbitrary nature. Basically, never more than in business have people been judged as so fundamentally bad and unworthy of trust. Hence all the rhetoric on "resistance to change" which so marked the 1970s and 1980s and which served as a windbreak to the ultra-conservatism of a good number of managers. People – but who are these "people"? – would not like change and so it is necessary to impose it on them and to watch carefully that they do exactly what they are supposed to do. It is not particularly important that they know why they are being asked to change: they are just expected to apply the new instructions, to come, to go, to follow, and then everything will be all right.

One only needs to watch one's children to see that military logic, which Robert Reich[9] noted had durably marked our companies since the end of the Second World War, no longer works. If one understands that an organization is first and foremost a structure of human behaviours – of rational strategies as we might say in this book – then one can understand that actors will only agree to modify these behaviours if one shares with them the necessity for change, that is, the final problem that one is seeking to resolve. This is what we mean here by the sharing of knowledge, which puts everybody on the same level and which, no doubt, leaves the king naked but restores a certain independence and margin for manoeuvre to his subjects.

However, while it is true that one cannot control everything, plan everything nor indeed organize everything, it is possible to propose an approach which, while modest, makes it possible to tackle the problems outlined above, those of knowledge and trust. This approach is centred on the organizations, for it is they who are concerned first and foremost with change: under pressure from customers, they need to reappraise, often urgently, their normal "ways of functioning", that is, the way in which their members work, make decisions, resolve their problems, cooperate or, to the contrary, defend themselves.

Using strategic analysis of organizations

The frame of reference will be that of the strategic analysis of organizations, although its use will be extended, in view of the latest experiences of leading change associated with this mode of reasoning. In fact, until recently, organizational analysis has primarily been used as a knowledge tool, of which the relevance today is no longer contested by anybody. It is now important to take another step forward and, in the light of new case studies, look to see what this same tool can contribute in the phases following the initial diagnosis. This, as we will see, retains all its importance since it allows us to highlight the *problems* that an action of change is supposed to handle. However, because the basic postulate of organizational analysis is that of *limited rationality*[10] – therefore of the intelligence of actors – this makes it possible to continue and to work on terms and conditions which favour the behavioural evolution of such intelligent actors.

One should not underestimate to what extent this idea of intelligence, when one has a thorough understanding of all its implications, can be demanding and off-putting compared with conventional management approaches – marked by suspicion, doubt and the necessity for control in the narrowest sense of the term. At the same time, it is easy to anticipate that this is what establishes the foundation and legitimacy of the transition through *trust*.

This transition is made necessary by the increase in independence, information, capacity for choice and therefore intelligence of those working in our organizations. All are not yet *"knowledge workers"*,[11] although the tendency is moving in that direction. We are thus confronted with populations who are more inclined to question the orders given to them, to be more critical if what is proposed does not correspond to an apprehension based on reality – their reality.

The positive aspect of this new requirement lies in the opportunities that it opens. Starting from reality, therefore from knowledge, is a necessity that is even less contestable in that it is so necessary to reduce the human and financial costs of change. But once this investment is made, it can be valorized by associating all parties with such knowledge, and involving them in the search for practical solutions that focus on their own behaviours, and not simply on structures or on attitudes.

All that has been said above in fact dictates the logic and structure of this book. For while there is a necessity to propose an *approach*, a *method* that at least makes it possible to limit the risks inherent to any process of change, to avoid some of its pitfalls, it is just as essential, upstream, to explain *why*: what it is that means that today no organization, whether public or private, can be exonerated from rapid transformations in its methods of operation or, as we will be demonstrating, in the way in which its members work. The revolution in organizations that we will be discussing at the start of this book in order to provide its readers with the necessary landmarks, is in fact a revolution in working methods. We must first and foremost come to understand its fundamental nature if one day we want to be able to make it acceptable to the actors themselves, as will be suggested at a later point.

1. Part I, "The customer's victory: A challenge for organizations", will therefore focus on analysis of the environment which precipitates organizations – and mainly those that we will define as "bureaucratic" – into change and on the presentation of a chart of concepts that make it possible to decipher the incidence of such changes in organizations. An answer to this question of "why" is primordial, not because it allows us to interpret history – one cannot rewrite the past – but because it gives meaning or a sense to what we experience every day, to what we feel we have to endure rather than promote.
2. Part II, "The change process", will focus on the method and tools. It aims to answer the question of "How?" by identifying the approaches and ways of doing things that make it possible to

accompany change, to control it, and even, more modestly, to reduce its cost in human terms.

Lastly, I would like to point out that this book is built around real cases on which I have had the opportunity to work over the last few years. They are therefore used here with the concern that their presentation does not cause any problem to the organizations involved, and so, as a precautionary measure, most of them have been made anonymous. The use of such case studies is a guarantee that only reality – that we will be seeking to understand throughout these pages – will be taken into consideration. As I have already emphasized, assessing reality by means of knowledge tools helps to make it less dramatic and thus an objective for action rather than the subject of biased arguments.

Part I

The Customer's Victory: A Challenge for Organizations

1
An Uncertain World

Globalization, internationalization and their effects on economic systems are at the centre of debates of all kinds in the early twenty-first century. Its consequences are usually discussed at the level of global economies (expansion, recession, massive unemployment), or of individual economies (an uncertain future, unemployment and the related human drama, forced displacement, the redefining of work tempos, and so on). Both the impact of these phenomena on the workplace, on the "company" in the largest sense, and our ability to control and manage that impact have not really been dealt with, no doubt because these aspects are less visible and consequently much more difficult to talk about. These are the issues which this book intends to place at the centre of debate, that is, how the emergence of a globalized, post-industrial society has affected organizations – that is to say, private, public or para-public businesses – organizations which, in the twenty-first century, provide the goods and services which people need, an assertion which many authors are currently debating. Second, through the examination of several recent case studies, we will consider how the transformation of these organizations might best be managed so as to avoid some of the tragic or painful consequences which often result from uncontrolled experiences of change.

After 15 years of teaching executives the world over, the author believes that, beyond the distressing collective and individual phenomena which the world is experiencing such as unemployment, poverty, diminishing wages, reduced social welfare, and so on, it is really in the day-to-day routine of the workplace that men and women are most dramatically confronted with the fact that today's expectations of them are very different from those of yesterday. This increased instability we hear so much about not only affects people on the labour market. It also affects people in the workplace, in their relationships with one another, in the way pressure is applied to them, as well as in the way job tasks and relationships with the company are being redefined. One might object here that from this angle I am limiting my analysis to the most advantaged part of the general population, the employed. This is indeed true, but nonetheless, that segment of the population plays a very important role in the evolution of business firms, and is therefore worth looking into. All the more so since, as most writers on the subject agree, that which I call in this book "the organization"[1] is the factor best able to explain the differences, including the reasons for success, between countries and companies.[2]

There is therefore good reason, in order to track the problematics of change as closely as possible (which is our aim in this chapter), to first place it at its two levels of relevance and complementarity:

- the general situation, which establishes the context in which organizations evolve;
- and that of the organizations themselves, with the upheaval that characterizes them and which the second part of this book proposes to give assistance on controlling and steering.

Let us set the scene!

One principal fact stands out: the emergence of post-industrial society is painful, and this pain can be observed everywhere, both in the literature and in the statistics. Here are a few examples: Edgar Morin warns that "the times are not of hope, but of falling back and despair",[3] and "that from now on, we must confront an historic process which destroys everything".[4] The title, of course, but also the success of Viviane Forrester's *Economic Horror*,[5] demonstrates with emotion and desperation just how difficult and frightening this emergence really is, how it can arouse in certain countries feelings of fear or aversion. Robert Castel, in his remarkable book *The Metamorphoses of the Social Question*, speaks of "disaffiliation" in regard to his "history of the present".[6] On the American side of the Atlantic, even if those who express doubt or reservation are barely audible above the ambient optimism, Jeremy Rifkin puts forth several truths which are worth repeating here. He says:

> the numbers send shivers down the spine: at the end of the 1980s, one out of four young black men was either in prison or on probation. In Washington DC, 42 per cent of blacks between the ages of 18 and

25 are either in prison or are wanted by the police. The number one cause of death among young black males is now murder.[7]

Rifkin is by no means the only one to see in these background trends now shaking the world the reasons for society's problems. Sami Naïr has no doubt good reason to claim that "the emergence of exclusive nationalist and religious fundamentalist movements is not simply the outcome of internal mutations within each society; it is also the result spread through the media of a much deeper set of changes: that of globalization".[8] Finally, whenever there is opposition or attempts to resist these changes, the difficult and sometimes disgraceful result is only the preservation of a few pieces of social protection, although it is likely that these only briefly hold at bay the day of reckoning.[9] To symbolize this state of affairs, Robert Reich points out that in the private sector in the United States, union membership[10] has fallen to levels below those of 1930, estimated at 13 per cent.[11]

These realities, which we have only touched on here, are not temporary. They appear to be here for the long haul, at least as far as modern sociology can see. Among the possible developments outlined by Robert Castel in the part of his book on the crises of the future, "the first is that, starting in the 1970s, salaries will continue to depreciate".[12] The trends, which seem to be taking hold, are very serious indeed. An original way to better understand them might be to look at some of the words which figure in the titles of key works from this period: *metamorphosis, end, death, crisis*. Each one expresses the sentiment, both strong and diffuse, that a world is disappearing before our very eyes, at a speed which we cannot fully grasp because we are so involved in the process ourselves.

Confidence crisis

That this should result in a real confidence crisis in all spheres and all institutions of society is hardly surprising:

> If society has today lost confidence, it is because we have returned to a financially-based line-of-thinking and have not wanted to take this into account. The capital/work relationship has been turned around – money is more productive than industry. In this context, it would be absurd to suggest that work will always be available. The rules have changed, and a new system of equitable remuneration must be invented.[13]

The confidence problem is crucial. It is a topic of current debate,[14] and I have seen that in seminars with executives, lecturers run up against it on a daily basis. The deterioration of the relationship between individuals and institutions brings with it disintegration, especially in companies, which are often no longer able to mobilize their remaining resources. A goal of this book is to show how this issue might well be handled through the sharing of knowledge. Otherwise, Michel Crozier would be wrong in vigorously affirming in *The Company that Listens*[15] that the only real wealth of a company is and always will be the human element.

So as to better understand the situation, note that, contrary to a widely accepted idea, there are really very few who question the basic observation that globalization is occurring. It is only the generalization of this observation which has taken some time, no doubt because quite naturally it first had to be observed that globalization was progressively spreading its effects, even on to those who work: the mechanism was already at work in the Great Depression of the 1930s.[16] Globalization has therefore been observed for quite some time, even before the rapid explosion in technology, even before advances in communications.

This was announced by Alvin Toffler,[17] and we heard at the same time of the end of bureaucracies, of the appearance of new elite groups (financial, planetary, intellectual), holders of knowledge, the "new key to the world", controlling realms in which the outcasts – those who are "disaffiliated" – have decreasing access to wealth, and constitute a threat for the well-to-do.[18] These nouveaux riches would even withdraw from the world – at least from the world which is not theirs – keeping it out with barricades. A visit to southern California would seem to confirm these predictions.

Thus I claim that there is agreement on the basic observation, but disagreement on the interpretation, and especially on the consequences. Between the resignation of those executives whom businesses now readily classify according to their supposed degree of adaptability, and the overwhelming optimism of the pioneers of new industries or services, there is more than a shade of difference. But it will become apparent in this book that not only do these people not work in the same types of industry – something we already suspected – but moreover they are part of very different organizations. Traditional bureaucrats whom we will meet, those in public administration or in the most traditional sectors of production in terms of their modes of functioning, are either worried, losing hope, or are trying to protect themselves the best they can ... They all know well that they will not escape a very profound upheaval, not only in the "technical" ways in which they are protected (their status as employees, their working conditions...) but primarily in the day-to-day manner in which they work together,[19] which is the key to the revolution of organizations which we are going to try to understand through a variety of case studies. Definitely, working is no longer what it used to be.

Cooperation: here then is the keyword for tomorrow's organizations, and thus the focal point of this book. Those who, unlike the bureaucrats in the preceding paragraph, are part of businesses which have already taken the decisive step towards networks, towards a blurring of traditional structure, towards overlapping functions and the drastic elimination of internal monopolies, are perhaps experiencing more difficult working conditions, but in any case are much more optimistic about their future. And of course, between the two extremes lies a kind of tidal basin of businesses which move from one extreme to the other, at times seeking gurus, at others seeking recipes or tips which might help their leaders in their genius to spare the organization a slow and painful revolution, or at least to help the organization understand why and how it must change, and why it should be happy about it.

The anxiety stems from that which we call "the re-proletarianization of the former proletarians". Edgar Morin and Sami Naïr express this very clearly:

> There is...the liberal scenario itself, which postulates that the negative effects of globalization result specifically from resistance to it... And so there are those who, in the fight against unemployment, advocate an increase in "work flexibility", which in fact leads to a widespread decrease in salaries (more closely in line with salaries in the newly industrialized countries), or even job mobility (corresponding to changes in American capitalism, which is itself increasingly deterritorialized).[20]

On the optimistic side, there is a progressive decline of the traditional way to work (industry), and an increasingly important link to society through the "third sector".[21] In short, there are some who see in the unremitting disruptions cumulating over the last few decades, either an inevitability with unpredictable and disastrous consequences[22] or, on the other hand, a source of new opportunity which must not be missed so as to partake fully in the upheaval.[23] It is understandable that, since they were at once decisive players and simple bystanders in this tempest, human beings waver between these two positions. This is part of the short-term nature of the structural phenomenon, and is proof enough that simply being involved in a given reality does not necessarily mean we will understand it better. We will have to bear this in mind later on as we take up the matter of managing change.[24]

Middle Ages or Mad Max?

Nevertheless, if the key facts and the general framework are now disputed by only a minority, then the question has become how this revolution might best be managed. There is a great deal of debate surrounding this question, and not only in Europe. The idea that the United States or Great Britain already reached "the other side" as early as the 1990s, is both ridiculous and might even act as a deterrent.[25] Even though the debate surrounding these issues differs somewhat from country to country, even if the reaction of Anglo-Saxon communities or of associations to the most destructive effects of the upheaval tends to keep public debate to a minimum – Tocqueville discovered this long ago – people are still voicing their concerns. After all, downsizing and re-engineering were first challenged in the United States,[26] as was the notion of an "anorexic corporation".[27] The arguments are sound, not controversial. Everywhere we turn, the debate over the consequences of this fundamental movement which we are all experiencing is the same: "At best the Middle Ages, at the worst Mad Max", writes Edgar Morin.[28] The "forms of progress which destroy work" which Rifkin lists in his book are impressive[29] because of the universality of the domains which they affect. It is not simply, nor even principally, a question of capital funds which are constantly in motion, seven days a week, 24 hours a day, entirely outside of the control of public authority, a fact which undermines the very existence of nation-states.[30] It is a matter of concern, for example, to all food production industries of all kinds, including synthetically manufactured foods, that a new technology could potentially have the same effect on a large portion of the labour force of developing countries as did the mechanization of cotton harvesting on the condition of black Americans.[31]

More differences in this debate appear when we consider how these issues are discussed in different countries. Indeed, what is at stake here is the historic and contemporary place of countries on the global economic and political chessboard. But we also see that they differ – and this is of particular interest to us in this book – in the kinds of organizations which can be found there, as well as the relative ease or difficulty with which organizations can be induced to change. Limiting ourselves to several states or regions, let us take a brief look at America in its triumph, a somewhat arrogant America; at the persistent anxiety in France and Germany; and at uncertainty in several Asian countries.

The American model

The United States has the dual characteristic of undergoing violent upsets which seem to affect the country's economic health – although without seriously undermining it – while at the same time being the country from which "everything starts", the country that, in a way, announces to the rest of the world what its future is going to be. In the long term, this seems to show two possible pathways for anticipating the last days of the bureaucracies.

The first, naturally, we might say, is that of the increasingly precarious nature of the labour market, of salaried employment itself, and of the decrease in salary levels. In 1993 alone, out of 1.23 million jobs created in the United States, 728,000 were part-time jobs, really little more than "side" jobs, accepted by those who were in fact seeking full-time employment.[32]

Robert Reich, for his part, notes that inequalities in revenue increased in America from 1977 to 1990, when average income before taxes of 20 per cent of the poorest Americans decreased by 5 per cent.[33] At the same time, the income of 20 per cent of the richest Americans increased by 9 per cent. Rifkin adds that between 1973 and 1993, working-class Americans lost on average 15 per cent of their purchasing power.[34] Both authors agree that one of the conditions which made these changes possible was the deep, long-term and unprecedented weakening of the union movement.

The figures are cause for neither celebration nor sorrow. It is simply a sign that today, when we see the word "change", and when opposite this word we are presented with examples – "the success stories" – they are best understood in terms of "less", for they have been achieved at the cost of the renunciation of advantages, of security and of comfort. Bureaucracies, whether of the public or private sector, are characterized by the advantages which they have obtained for their members, the "pluses", even if the customer has had to pay the price of these pluses, not only in terms of the basic cost of a given service, but also in day-to-day terms of business schedules, of the speed of delivery, of the quality of the product or service or, to make it short, in terms of convenience.

The result of all this is that "opposition to change" is not an abstract, psychological problem, but in fact a rational strategy,[35] in the sense that the actors who develop such a strategy struggle to hold on to something.

Even if what they are trying to hold on to comes with a price, due either to the association or the customers as mentioned earlier, one cannot naively explain to these actors that their future will be more fair and above all, "better", if only because in the short run at least, this is not true. Clearly, the more that organizations come up with different kinds of benefits for their members, the more difficult and costly it is in human terms to give up these benefits. This will lead to some methods for managing change which take this into account.

The second factor which America of the 1990s considers to be crucial to its success is the organization. Robert Waterman, who might be considered as the primary popularizer of the state of the art in American managerial thought, writes:

> High-performance companies differ from all the rest, I would say, in the ways in which they operate. In particular:
>
> - They are better organized to meet the needs of their employees, and they also attract people who are more effective than those of the competition. These people are more motivated to produce better work, whatever the job might be.
> - They are better organized to meet the needs of their customers, they are more innovative in anticipating customer needs, and better even at producing their goods and services at low cost, or any combination of these factors.[36]

There are of course good reasons why one might question this best-of-all-possible-worlds optimism in which salaried employees, hourly employees and customers are reconciled. We will not defend this point of view here. But what stands out is the crucial role of the organization, in the sense of "organizational arrangements", that is to say, not in terms of structure, but in the way in which people work, arrive at mutually satisfactory agreements, and cooperate more effectively and more actively. In particular, as we will see, bureaucracies are organizations which demand very little cooperation of their members. They in fact protect them from it, and in the case of the most strict organizations, they do away with cooperation altogether. This then explains the other aspect of the discussion of "less" mentioned above: this "less" strikes at the very heart of day-to-day concerns of the business place, on the relationship with others, on the need to share, to cooperate; in short, on all manner of behaviour which we will show is in no way spontaneous or natural.

This much deeper interpretation of the American situation is not meant to make any claims about its durability, its superiority or its success. We still lack sufficient perspective to pass judgement on the situation.[37] Nonetheless, our analysis helps show the extent to which in the 1990s the day-to-day affairs of the workplace are affected by this third industrial revolution. It allows us to formulate a first hypothesis, one which we will attempt to verify throughout this book: not only are executives no longer protected as once was possible, but today, they are all caught up together in the great tempest in which new organizations are being formed. They are the ones who feel the full force of what I call "internal instability".

Many words for a single disease

"Where is the world headed?", asked *Le Monde* columnist Erik Izraëlewicz in 1997.[38] In exploring the alternatives, he contrasted the new economy, one which is built on regular growth and the creation of jobs as in the United States, with the other, which is the "catastrophic approach", that of a great economic depression which has taken hold in France and part of Europe. And indeed, although one must take care not to confuse short-term phenomena with more serious trends, a survey of some of the titles which have appeared in the economic and social literature in France over the last decade is nothing short of striking: *L'horreur économique* (*Economic Horror*) of Viviane Forrester,[39] would certainly head the list, but what about *La concurrence et la mort* (*Competition and Death*) by Philippe Thureau-Dangin,[40] *Les peurs françaises* (*French Fears*) by Alain Duhamel,[41] *La France malade du travail* (*France Sick of Work*) by Jacques de Bandt et al.[42] We would have no problem labelling the literature of this period "morbid", an observation summed up rather nicely by the *International Herald Tribune* under the title "A somber France, racked by doubt".[43]

These fears and uncertainties revolve around two main themes.

- The criticism of the idea that "everything is of the market", and its consequences for human beings. Edgar Morin draws a brilliant comparison between liberalism and Satan, a rather nice metaphor for this trend.[44] Viviane Forrester echoes this theme from a literary and emotional perspective:

  > Time and time again it is the same phenomenon, that of the small group in power which no longer requires the labour of others (did

we ever put them in charge of it?) who can get the hell out with all their uncertainties, their medical bulletins. But alas, there is nowhere else to go. At least not in this life, even for the faithful. There is no spare geography, no other ground to walk upon; these are the same lands, on the same planet, which from time immemorial go from garden to mass grave.[45]

- And whenever emotion gives way to analysis, the question which surfaces time and time again, in one work after another, is that of the end, the last drop of the "always a little more" which employees are asked to give, and which is in fact "always a little less", as I argued earlier. In connection with the idea of flexibility, which we take to be sufficiently general so as to encompass the conditions under which one accepts employment (status of the employee, employee protection such as insurance and other benefits, retirement) as well as the conditions under which one works (schedules, job mobility, and also the organizations), the fear has broken out that this deterioration might be inescapable and that no compensation will be received in exchange.[46] Even the technologies which accompany – or provoke – the breakdown, are viewed with suspicion.[47]

Finally, there is, in the case of France, pressure from abroad imploring the nation to get moving, to "give up" the idea of protecting itself.[48]

In fact, the rigidity of the French system as opposed to the adaptability of the Anglo-Saxon one, which is one way of characterizing the differences between these two approaches to the world, is indeed a matter which it might be worth taking a few steps back to re-examine.[49] But we can already suggest a hypothesis, which we will explore in more detail later on: French bureaucracies – including the French public administration which is at once the archetype and the model which the others have for a long time sought to imitate – are notorious for their skill at spontaneous adaptation, a skill which allows them to keep pace, as best as they can, with changes in the collective fabric in which they are caught up, but never to anticipate them.[50] These modes of adaptation – which include ways of bending the rules, the development of parallel networks linked to the *grands corps* which they are part of, and so on – appear today simply laughable, even counter-productive in light of the great leap which lies ahead. Above all, one precondition for their development was a context of abundant resources, a context which no longer exists today. As long as bureaucracies could "buy" their customers, they survived and adapted. The day that they no longer have the means to do this, their deficiencies, their shortcomings, their excessive behaviour quickly become intolerable. The word "adaptability" has taken on a new meaning, and the line of reasoning of the French bureaucrats provides them with no help in coping with these new realities.[51] In our view, this is why "globalization" carries with it so much distress and fear: the consequences of globalization cannot be handled in the traditional French way.

Germany: escaping the crisis in a different way

The case of Germany will allow us to expand our inventory of the general context in which the bureaucracy crisis is taking place. In Germany as in France, the widespread Anglo-Saxon model of capitalism is not blindly accepted: "Originally", writes Alain Lebaube,[52] "there was nothing more opposed to the strategy of Anglo-Saxon capitalism, of globalization and flexibility than the centralized systems of the socio-democratic models which tend to standardize social relationships." This is no doubt why, when from the end of 1996 to the beginning of 1997, the unemployment rate in Germany went above the 12 per cent level. The worst fears of those who had predicted a crisis in the German model in its entirety were confirmed.[53] Some of the difficulties can be attributed to reunification,[54] but in the framework of this book, let us focus on three main points.

- First of all, whatever the complex causes of the difficulties which Germany is experiencing – and no doubt there as everywhere they are piling up – the German economy is clearly industry-based, orientated towards production. Michel Drancourt makes the reasonable argument that "for a long time Germans went along with the belief that by developing quality products, they could sell them at a high price, something which would permit a high level of remuneration and of social welfare".[55] The choice between cost and quality is and will be each day less feasible. I will make the case in Part I that cost is not what stands in the way of satisfying the customer (this is the classic vision held by bureaucracies which always seek more means through which they might satisfy their customers), but the organization itself, in the sense of a mode of functioning, which will allow reconciling those things which once appeared irreconcilable. To oppose cost and quality – we will turn to the example of the impossible reform of French hospitals – is to maintain one's opposition to change at the customer's expense. At the same time, from the standpoint of change management, such a solution brings us right back to increases in physical production, unimaginative, brute, which can only heighten fear, increasing opposition and conflict.

- From this angle, we arrive at the second point which surfaces in the case of Germany, that is to say, attempts to try to get out of this dilemma with something less than a full-blown crisis. We can learn a great deal from the rivalry between Renault and Volkswagen, regardless of how temporary this may be.[56] It shows that, despite the difficulties, helping technical bureaucracies get through these changes can be managed at a lower cost than was previously the case (Great Britain or even the United States), although the cost is still high in certain countries (France, for example).

- A final noteworthy aspect of the German example – but one could say the same thing about Sweden – the bureaucratic crisis is also reaching, by a sort of ricochet effect, organizations which were traditionally grafted on to these bureaucracies, and fed off them. This is the case of the union movement. We noted earlier, along with Robert Reich, the decline of unions in America, although they are supposedly deeply rooted in the world of work and endowed with considerable means. With regard to this union myth, Jeremy Rifkin speaks of "capitulation".[57] Germany is no doubt undergoing something rather different: union activity has been and remains clearly much more institutionalized there than in the United States. Consequently, if the German model should implode, German unions might well implode along with it. Yet this is not what we find, or at least not to such a degree. Union bureaucracies, like all bureaucracies, stand before a wall and must adapt[58] by reviewing the levels at which they can act (branch, business or institution), as well as the ways in which they can act (from global negotiation to attention given to special cases).

The need for change here does not stem directly from competition, it is rather the indirect consequence of environmental transformation. The main point of the foregoing is this: bureaucracies directly on the market or about to enter the market are not the only ones expected to die out. All forms of bureaucracy will be caught up in this contagious process. This book attempts to pinpoint just how this will happen.[59]

Asia: the frailty of the "dragons"

Moving now to another stage in our discussion, let us take a look at some of the Asian countries (Japan, South Korea, China). The author had the opportunity to present an analysis of the "Japanese miracle", highlighting the market more in terms of the system (its "organization" in the sense that the word has been used here) than in terms of the miraculous recipes and other imaginary exaggerations which Western analysts have tried to import.[60] I identified, based upon the analysis of the white appliance industry, two explanatory facts which still seem today to be rather poorly understood: on one hand the roughly mediaeval organization of the Japanese distribution network, and on the other hand the power and remarkable harmony of their system of production. This system, largely organized into cartels, closely controls the widely dispersed distributors and dependent firms. These base-level units very rarely venture to offer foreign products, whatever the legal measures in place or however the authorities might object in good faith. The way in which the home market is dominated by producers, backed up by the financial control of consumer organizations, makes it possible to maintain a nucleus of loyal workers with guaranteed lifetime employment. This attachment is itself made possible by externalizing its cost on to part-time employees, hired to do their master's bidding. In the end, these are the employees for whom there is no sacred aura to the miracle.

In such a case, the problem of cost is not resolved through new techniques (Rifkin's hypothesis[61]) or through the organization as proposed in this book. It is resolved through pressure on the labour force. It certainly seems simple. But it is likely that the days are numbered for this competitive advantage. The strikes which occurred at the end of 1996 in South Korea drew attention to the social pressure which had been felt there since the 1980s and which now seems destined to reduce the advantages which that country once held.[62] The ongoing sluggishness of Japan, of great concern to Americans, could very well stem from the same source. It could even be suggested that China will follow more or less the very same path a little further down the road.[63]

So what can we draw from the foregoing? That in the end, the triumph of Japan, of South Korea, and perhaps yet tomorrow of China, have been, are, or will be only intermediate successes, their market advantage stemming only from a relatively inexpensive labour force? Those who believe in the end of work might add that "it is only a question of time before this same labour force becomes useless". Perhaps. But at least in an even shorter term the pressure on labour costs will not endure, first because developed countries will adapt to it either by reducing costs of their own labour force as they have already done, but more importantly by seeking their own increases in productivity in other forms of organization; second, because Asian countries will follow the same route, a route upon which the most developed of those countries have already set foot. With just a little imagination Western countries could manage to "think the unthinkable" as suggested in this book, and those who have travelled to the East in search of a model might just turn around and head the other way.

2
The Customer's Victory

It is starting from the debate on globalization, as discussed in the introduction, that one can reach an understanding of what we will be calling the customer's victory, and how this leads to a revolution in organizations. As we saw, the idea of globalization today is no longer contested, but this is not to say that the concept is accepted everywhere in the same way, or that its consequences do not undergo harsh criticism. In many countries, we find two schools of thought. On the one hand, there is the school which, although having observed the unavoidability of globalization, does not take for granted the elimination of nation-states.[1] Instead, a strong state should increasingly regulate the effects of globalization and protect its citizens from the more serious consequences. This would mean voluntarily bowing out, "politically", from the hyper-financialization of the world. This line of thinking is the exact opposite of the one proclaimed on billboards in the United States, such as the well-known slogan "Government is the problem, free enterprise is the solution". On the other hand, there is the school, in the minority, that suggests that we might, by cutting ourselves off from the rest of the world and refocusing our energies on national culture, tradition, morality, and so on, escape the generalized movement towards a global economy.

These are not very realistic. Robert Reich clearly defined globalization, and its consequences on a country, by adopting a distinction between American society and the American economy:

> We are experiencing a transformation which will reorganize politics and the economy in the next century. There will be no national products or national technologies, no national businesses or industries.

National economies will no longer exist, at least in the way in which we conceive of them today. All that will remain rooted within borders are the people who make up a nation ... the underlying question concerns the future of American society as distinct from the American economy, and the destiny of the majority of Americans, who are losers in global competition.[2]

The idea of a dual society returns with, on one hand, those who can participate in globalization, benefit from it and free themselves once and for all from the former local dependencies which have left a deep historical imprint;[3] and, on the other, those who are subject to its consequences, with few means to react and intervene in their own fate.

This winner/loser vision is not wrong, at least in the short run, which is, after all, as far as we can see in respect of the phenomenon of globalization. But what is of interest is that this vision can be found in the workplace and in organizations, starting with what seems to be one of the most immediate and abrupt consequences of globalization: the customer's victory. This is not a new observation, no more than the intuition that this victory must have irreversible consequences for organizations which produce goods and services. It was at the root of the re-engineering process, which many countries, including France, rejected categorically[4] without reflecting more fully on the extent of the preconceived notions from which this movement stems, looking only at the technical aspects, most often only to refute them. "Economic power has been handed over from the producer to the consumer ... mass production, more quality, more for the money, more choice, more service", write Hammer and Champy.[5] This is about as clear as one can get concerning the consequences of such a movement.

From an entirely different perspective, and with quite different conclusions, Sami Naïr says much the same thing:

In its "chemically pure" form, the legitimization of liberal globalization hinges on praising the consumer as king. Since the market constitutes the most effective mechanism for distributing wealth, and since globalization is now helping to tear down all borders – be they geographical, cultural, of the nation or the state – borders which, up till now, have held it back from fulfilling its universal vocation, globalization must now be allowed to run its full course. For the final result will be the victory of the consumer ... If the latter is not the "end of the story", it is at least the "sense of the story".[6]

Rifkin offers yet a third version of this observation:

> The "personalized" consumer is now starting to displace "standard-ized" distribution amid the various forms of competition in which businesses engage in the hopes of winning customers over, one by one, while at the same time attempting to keep costs associated with maintaining a stockpile of products as low as possible.[7]

This is thus the same vision, today commonplace in many companies, built around "disinterested consensus" which keeps us from under-standing the actual consequences in day-to-day life in the workplace. In their heated battle to hold at bay the drastic changes which are on their way, bureaucrats – a term which we will define more precisely in the next chapter – "swallow" the idea of the customer's victory, but see it as little more than a tasteless pill. The idea must thus be explored more seriously in three directions. First, what does it mean that the "customer has won" in daily life, but conceptually as well, in terms of the distri-bution of power? Next, if the customer has truly won, and must be lis-tened to at all costs, then how do organizations react to this new constraint? Finally, why does this victory present a fundamental prob-lem of the organization, as defined in the preceding sections?

From a scarce product to a scarce customer

To more fully comprehend what the customer's victory means in con-crete, day-to-day terms, let us take a simple example with which the author has had first-hand experience. The example concerns a medium-size town (of about 20,000 residents) located some 50 kilometres from Paris. Thirty years ago, there were about as many people. But in those days prospective car buyers in the town had only one vendor to turn to, in this case a Renault dealership. When asked about the availability of an automobile, the dealer would explain that it was a difficult time to place an order, and after consulting his books and calling the manufacturer, would say that with a little luck a vehicle could be brought in within two or three months, provided that the buyer was not too set on a particular colour or horsepower. The customer, delighted by such good fortune, would have celebrated the event that very evening with friends and fam-ily. Along the same lines, some readers might recall how difficult it was to come by tyres, even well after the end of the Second World War.

Today, in the very same town, there are 13 automobile dealerships, each one fighting for a piece of the local market through aggressive advertising campaigns. Prospective buyers, off to test-drive a few models in the early afternoon, could easily be on their way home two to three hours later in a new car, the details of insurance and temporary registration all worked out, credit established in no more than 15 minutes, and a substantial reduction off the base price thrown into the bargain.

This is the revolution. We are moving from a long-standing period in which what was scarce was the product, to a period where what is scarce is the customer. This then is what is happening, the scarcity relationship is being overturned, with far-reaching consequences. When the product was rare, it was costly, a classic economic observation. In fact, this costliness involved three dimensions: the price, of course; the quality, in the most basic sense of the term, that of the product; but also in terms of quality in a more complex sense, that is, the quality of the way the goods or service are produced and delivered to the customer. Here then is what we are interested in, "organizational costliness", for it leads to a first observation, which we will develop fully in the following chapter: "organizational costliness" is the cost which a producer, in a superior position, requires that customers pay, permitting it, the producer, to maintain modes of functioning based on its own strategies, its own human or technical constraints. When, on the other hand, the customer wins out and the scarcity relationship is reversed, power in the relationship is also reversed, and not just economic power as suggested by Hammer and Champy. Power pure and simple, or global power, if you will.

Although the observation that power passes from the hands of the producer to those of the customer is true, it is not very specific. Customer's victory, yes. Victory over the producer, indeed, but actually over the producer's process (the way in which a product is made and offered) and all that is tied to it in terms of the management of individuals (schedules, guarantees, status) which bears a price, once again not only monetary but also in terms of customer "convenience". Later on, as we consider the nature of a bureaucracy in more detail, we will be able to grasp more fully the after-effects of this veritable earthquake.

The hazards of segmentation

It is worth mentioning here that some organizations actually weaken the notion of the customer's victory, especially those for which this victory bears the most severe consequences. These organizations react by developing, on the one hand, a new function, a kind of "listening management programme", one more vertical structure; and on the other, yet more sophisticated traditional marketing tools, so as to keep tabs on the market. These reactions make it possible to work with "virtual customers", customers who can be made to say just about anything through the manipulation of statistics, and who therefore place few real constraints on business since they do not really exist. The religion of numbers, of quantities and statistics, of "segmentation", is moreover the target of growing criticism from all sides. Some point out the chronic inability of quantitative knowledge to comprehend the subtlety of consumers, their real satisfaction and expectations, *a fortiori* their customs, even the complex evolution of their way of life and standard of living.[8] Others viciously condemn the idea of tampering with numbers and the dehumanized nature of the entire process.[9] Beyond the rather emotional arguments, Edgar Morin makes it clear that quantitative analysis takes the place of reality, ensuring the survival of bureaucracy: "there is a depoliticization of politics, which self-destruct within administrative structures, technical considerations (expertise), the economy, and quantification (polls and statistics)".[10]

Numbers set us all the more ill at ease as we realize that there is little real connection between the sophistication of the tools of analysis which are used to probe the customers, and the ability of the organization to satisfy them and gain their loyalty. We can even observe today that "market segmentation", an expression which can be taken literally, has led to a re-segmentation of organizations, built around categories of customers. This has developed just as rigidly as when segmentation was based on tasks, one after another. Since customers now belong to a category – a category that is of course too strict to be able to take into account customer complexity – they are presumed to be satisfied, all because the organization has provided that category with a special division. It is trying to solve the problem by simply reworking the "structural puzzle", as we already pointed out, except that the real problem has not been addressed.

How not to listen

To take this a bit further, let us turn to a simple example, which we will then develop with a slightly more complicated case study.

Take, for example, a European telecommunications firm which, just like its sister companies, will be facing deregulation in the near future. This company grew out of the long-standing management traditions of the public sector. Agent loyalty is not a problem, their status is secure and clearly defines their rights and obligations, as well as how their careers can evolve and how they are to be remunerated. These rights are linked to seniority and not to the business activity of the company. Recall that monopolistic situations have been particularly favourable to the development of these advantages, the cost of which has been externalized on to the customer – the user – who at the time could do nothing about it.

In order to match the growing competition, our company has developed remarkable marketing skills, and has conducted an impressive number of customer profile studies. Similarly, it has developed elaborate methods of measuring customer satisfaction, which it does on a regular basis. The surprising fact is that, despite the quality of the company's products, which are as good as any, its customers, especially those who generate the greatest amount of business, seem ready to take any chance they can get to head over to the competition. In its attempt to deal with this paradox, the company has tried offering more and more products and services, targeting the categories of customers which it has identified, but seems all the less able to keep customers from taking their business elsewhere.

To better understand this situation, let us take a look at one of the company's customers, John Doe, a "professional", according to the company's own system of classification. The company, having identified specific needs for this particular segment of the market, has offered Mr Doe the services of a special department. He was informed by mail that "his" department had opened (the possessive was used so as to create a sense of intimacy), which he right away decided to call up in order to have a fax line installed in his home. John is told by a company representative, obviously well trained in "the customer welcome process", that the company regrets that it cannot accept orders over the phone. Surprised by the lack of confidence in the very medium which, after all, the company is promoting, he asks how, then, should he place an order? He is informed that orders must be placed by mail – and cannot help but wonder whether this company is simply trying to generate some business for former co-workers at the postal service.

In any case, ten days after mailing his letter, our "professional" receives a highly personalized reply bearing the name and address of a "correspondent" on the letterhead. The letter states that the new phone line will be installed that very day, within a window of about two hours, so as to avoid any unnecessary delay. Suddenly faced with the prospect of having to stay home from work (Mr Doe is after all a "professional"), he picks up the phone and asks to speak to his new correspondent. The representative on the line is surprised by his request, and informs him that the title "correspondent" simply refers to the person who entered his file into the computer database. After being transferred to another representative, he explains that he cannot possibly wait at home for the fax line to be installed. The representative is sorry about the mix-up, adding that the company could not foresee that he would be away. Surprised that they could not have simply called to set up an appointment, he is told that of course they had tried to contact him, but that since he was not at home (he is of course a "professional") a time had been set anyway and the letter sent out. At the suggestion that a message could have been left on his answering machine, the employee, who incidentally pays no attention to the customer's remark that the answering machine had been purchased through the very same agency, states that the company does not conduct business in that fashion. Finally, at the "professional's" suggestion that they call in the evening, the representative retorts that the company has not yet resorted to working after hours.

What is going on here? The organization has in fact addressed the wrong problem, or, at the very least, has not understood the scope of the problem. Increasingly forced to listen to its customers, the company first reacts by offering more products. In this respect, which is moreover how the company determines whether or not its customers are satisfied, the company is doing an outstanding job. But, as we will see later on, the product, as a function of demand (its technical characteristics), is decreasingly what differentiates competitors. Competing products are increasingly similar, regardless of their apparent sophistication.[11] The "differential advantage", then, resides more in the way the product is produced and/or the way it is offered. That is to say, in the organization, the one which develops products, the one which manufactures products, and the one which offers them, and in the ability of these three to cooperate.

In the case of this company, the products are technically very good and their prices very reasonable. However, the organization which offers them has in no way "listened" to the customer. It is simply entrapped in its own norms and procedures, in the way it develops its database, in the routine and red tape which are part and parcel of the way it manages public relations and work schedules. Suddenly, the professional customer has disappeared. And the reason he is gone is that the complexity of his needs were not understood. The company never dealt concretely with his daily life, including when he goes to work, when he stays home, how his phone is used by his family during the day and for work purposes at night. He was no more than a *virtual* professional, around which no concrete organization had been set up either for him or for the other members of the organization, nor had a pricing policy been established which could take into account how he really uses the telephone.

All that had been set up was a means of sidestepping the issue, a screen, a decoy – the words are not too strong – which simply stand in as the symbols of listening, but they are not listening.[12] By dealing with listening as a function – an aspect of marketing in this case – the organization spares itself from taking a good hard look at itself, that is, more directly, at how appropriate its own modes of functioning are for the customer which it intends to serve. This is exactly what it needed to see. Listening to the customer, which has become so necessary, so inevitable now that the customer stands as the winner, confronts bureaucracies with very difficult and disturbing problems. Listening simply cannot be reduced to yet another function – bureaucracies excel at that – no more than quality could be reduced to a function in the 1980s, despite many attempts to do so.

Much more than a function, it is a mode of functioning, organization. Listening is a set of behaviours, of arrangements, of cooperative efforts; it includes how employees' careers evolve, and through this their status in the company, their benefits, their privileges. In order to truly listen to the customer, one must begin by taking a closer look at all of these various domains. In many cases, listening can be quite painful.

The case of a British catering company

The case of a British catering company provides a good illustration of what is meant by listening. The company in question is a world leader in its domain which includes providing food service in various institutions: schools, businesses and offices. Its structure is simple: the country is divided into regions, each of which is headed by a regional director, assisted by a small team which is responsible for human resources, marketing support of base-level units, and the development of quality control strategies. In turn, each region is divided into sectors, which are under the direction of sector supervisors, who are generally young graduates of business schools, and who themselves put pressure on the restaurant managers, who are responsible for the day-to-day production and delivery of meals. Note that a considerable part of the salary of the regional heads is variable, their bonuses related to two criteria: on the one hand, the profits achieved within their region; on the other, the number of meals served, so that the top of the line (restaurants and business clubs, for example) will not be overdeveloped to the detriment of restaurants with low profit margins. The variable portion of the sector supervisors' salaries is calculated in the same way, but represents a considerably smaller part of their total earnings. Lastly, the manager is paid a fixed salary, which increases with seniority and according to the relative clout of the restaurant for which he or she is responsible. Finally, we should point out that the regional director appoints the sector supervisors in the different regions, knowing that some of them have better reputations than others in terms of their profitability or "risk", which boils down to customer loyalty.

As we focus on the day-to-day activities of this organization, we find several interesting facts:

- Relations between the regional directors and their sector supervisors are courteous and convivial, although it is fairly rare for them to meet given the expanse of each region. Overall, communication between these levels is fairly superficial. There is quite a bit of talk, but not much is said: there is often more discussion about daily life than about daily work.
- Sector supervisors themselves have few occasions to get together. Their territories cover a lot of ground and they are responsible for a large number of restaurants. When they do meet up, once again we see conviviality; food is often served, for example, and once again work is not the major topic of discussion.
- Sector supervisors and managers seem to be subject to very intense pressure. The former are constantly complaining about this, to the extent that company directors are concerned and talk seriously about tackling the problem, although they do not have a clue how to go about it. Restaurant managers also suffer from pressure, but are less willing to discuss it openly. The reason is that they are the scapegoats within this organization: the regional director and sector supervisors agree that managers are not very competent and are therefore generally unable to take an objective view of the situation. Management laments having to fire a certain number of them on a regular basis.
- In last place, there are the customers: those who, it is important to note, sign the contracts and not those who eat at the restaurants (whom we might call the guests). The customers express great satisfaction. They feel that the company, and more specifically the sector supervisors who are their real contacts, take good care of them, listen closely to their problems, and seem always to do their utmost to satisfy them. The customers and sector supervisors meet, moreover, outside of the workplace, in gatherings organized by the latter. The regional director, who deals only with several of the more significant clients, is not associated with these events. Finally, the customers

share the negative opinion of the restaurant managers, whom they consider to be the weak link in the chain of this organization.

Satisfied customers, people who have been "listened to": what differences are there between this and the case of the telecommunications company which might explain these relationships? Certainly not the people involved and their loyalty, but the organization itself. Let us try to understand how it functions: all the young sector supervisors express a desire for autonomy, freedom to organize their work and their "rounds" just as they see fit. They work within a large region, which they know well, and are in contact with customers whose concerns they have identified, and which they try to address. Any intervention into their operations by the regional director is viewed negatively, even as a kind of sanction. In any case, the directors have neither the time nor the training to keep a close eye on the supervisors. They leave them a great deal of freedom (autonomy) so long as everything runs smoothly. What might be a "problem" for this organization? Most certainly the loss of a customer, which can easily happen in this very competitive environment, and which translates into a rapid drop in the number of meals served, thereby affecting the regional director's bonus. A decrease in profitability as well, which has the same effect. So, by reconstructing the triangle of the regional director, the sector supervisor and the customer, we have a good model of how the organization operates: the regional director yields full autonomy to the sector supervisor, according to the latter's own wishes, so long as the two criteria on which the director is evaluated and paid are not jeopardized. Should this happen, the director intervenes immediately; to avoid such a scenario and remain autonomous, the sector supervisor almost literally "hangs on to" the customers, attempting to anticipate their needs and satisfy them. This is the classic model of an organization operating within a highly competitive market, in which armed peace between the travelling sector supervisors and the sedentary regional director works to the advantage of a customer who holds the key to the relationship: the contract.

The limitations of this mode of functioning are of course easy to identify. It is based entirely on the fact that one of the participants pays the price: the restaurant manager must work out the agreement struck between the sector supervisor and the customer, the conditions of which almost always border on the impossible. From a certain point of view, restaurant managers "pay for" the sector supervisors' freedom, and whenever the latter complain about being under pressure, whether they know it or not, they actually transfer most of this pressure over to the restaurant managers. It is thus a system which carries a heavy human cost – this is the cost of the customer's victory, a point which I intend to get back to later on – a system which every day wastes a great deal of know-how, focused on the short term, much more reactive than proactive. But let us consider it first and foremost as a reaction to the advantage now held by the customer, a reaction involving constraints, in a sense. The system is not very sophisticated, implying a physical environment in which work is hard and uncomfortable. But after all, since when does a customer worry about the well-being of a company?

Getting off the beaten track

Other businesses have found more elaborate ways of listening to their customers, but in each case they proceed in terms of their own mode of functioning, and not in terms of a function. Richard Normann and Rafaël Ramirez have outlined the path chosen by Ikea which consists in getting the customer to help co-produce real value. They summarize what they consider to be the strategy of the future as follows: Companies create value not only by making more intelligent product offers, but by developing more intelligent relationships with their customers and suppliers. To do this, the businesses must continuously re-evaluate and redefine their abilities and their relationships so as to maintain the flexibility of these value-creating systems, keeping them new and reactive. In this new value strategy the ongoing dialogue between the company and its customers can explain the success and the survival of certain businesses, and the decline and failure of others.[13]

It is interesting to consider L'Oréal's answer to the problem, which is beyond doubt one of the most original since it is so far removed from traditional management models. In this high-performance corporation, strategy is the number one "intangible asset". To put it briefly, within the organization there is no internal monopoly. By this we mean that in its primary domains – those of marketing and commercial activity – no one decides anything all alone, and more importantly, knowing just who should decide what is never perfectly clear. The launching of a product, for example, involves the director of international marketing, the director of marketing of the brand name under which the product is to be sold, the director of marketing of the country in which the product will be tested, and so on, all at once. Everything must be negotiated, each participant must "confront" the others, using the in-house expression. In this confrontation, one's position within the hierarchy matters very little. This is no doubt why there is no organizational chart, and why no one has even bothered to create one. The decisive factor in a confrontation – and one must know how to win a confrontation in order to make a career within the organization – is the knowledge of a given market which one can contribute to the negotiation. This knowledge carries with it personal involvement in the outcome and is thus a constraint, but it is at the same time the argument which causes others to give in. The loose structure of the organization – the exact opposite of a bureaucracy, as we will see in the following chapter – is not a sign of disorganization, as some of the American executives in the corporation seem to fear. It is really a kind of "political" system, in which the market is the players' principal resource. Once again, but in ways that are quite different from those of Ikea, the border between the company and its market fade away, beyond theoretical organizational charts. This being the case, in order to function in this way, several conditions must be met. It is worth stating these here if only to temper some of the enthusiasm of those who wish to follow the example.

First, a system of sanctions must exist to put the dream that everyone has "the right to make a mistake" back into proper perspective. In a system which snaps its fingers at hierarchical structures, the need for a code of ethics is obvious. By "code of ethics" read "a set of unwritten rules" – a culture, some might say – which limits the unpredictability of the participants' behaviour. This means making any dishonesty in negotiation, in regard to the market and its possibilities, for example, very costly. Participants must rely on real knowledge, which is why there is personal commitment. Otherwise there would be "no holds barred", which is not the case in this company. Over time, the lack of a code of ethics would break the organization apart and lead it to ruin.

Similarly there must be some kind of arbitration, generally seated at the highest level. This guarantees that a decision can be made carefully, within reasonable time limits, and at the same time encourages the local actors to make the decision themselves: indeed, recourse to a third party, as in any organization, implies a price to be paid, in this case objectives which are generally more difficult than those which the actors would have settled upon themselves.

So as to keep the human cost of this kind of operation within reason, and it is high, there must be a human resources strategy which is flexible and individualized, able to move individuals about, taking them off the battleground when they are worn out, giving them a chance to recover. The strategy must compensate employees in a way that is fully linked to their success in the markets and business activity for which they are responsible even early on in their career.

Finally, within this arrangement, production can in no way dictate its own constraints. Not that production is of no importance: on the contrary, a great deal of energy is invested in production; not that quality is not as good here as elsewhere: the company could not survive under such conditions. But in the context of day-to-day running, production is akin to what supplies management was to General Charles de Gaulle – it has to follow.

Human resource management, as an essential counterweight to the customer's victory

Taking a few steps back now, what have we learned from this first look at the consequences of the customer's victory for organizations? First and foremost that an appeal is being made to the organization itself and not just a few of its members (the marketing division or the front office). It is not enough to send a few good soldiers off to the front lines to face head-on the ever-increasing demands of customers. Bravery and loyalty are quickly spent if the organization does not follow, or if the soldier deserts to join the army of consumers: this is a classic mechanism which has been with us for some time now.[14] Whenever members of an organization are in contact with the environment and the organization does not allow them to satisfy that environment, they then become its representatives, its lobbyists at the heart of their own company or administrative structure, which they will then criticize even more vehemently than the customers themselves, proving in this way how flexible they are when faced with a sclerotic bureaucratic body, insensitive as it is to the expectations of the general public. In this relationship, these members "sell" themselves against their own organization. For a long time it was believed that this model worked only for administrative structures, especially those in France, but today, in fact, we see that it is spreading as a result of the pressure which customers are exerting on organizations in the competitive sector, organizations which do not understand what it is they are being asked to do. Further on in this book, we will re-encounter this problem in the air transportation industry, as well as in banking and insurance.

Furthermore, organizations differ in the way in which they manage problems, for they are not all equal in their ability to confront them. This observation is central to this book. However they might deal with these problems, we might add, there is always a human cost which companies are more or less able to reabsorb. Although we have yet to discuss the profound nature of this cost, its presence is a sure sign that the worlds which are being rebuilt around the customers, attempting to meet their needs, are *de facto* more uncomfortable than those which were in place when customers were of relatively little concern, or when solutions were sought in ways other than a major organizational change. This is not a disinterested observation: it brings up the issue of opposition to change, not as a psychological problem – that would be a natural, "cultural" tendency of individuals to resist change – but as a practical and very concrete behaviour, calculated in terms of the cost-benefit relationship. The "less" we are involved, at least in the transitional phase which we see today, is also a "less" in terms of advantages, comfort and possibilities to live in a world where there is much pressure.

When this idea is taken a little further – less comfort in the most general sense of the term – we begin to see just how important the management of human resources is in an organization's struggle to adapt to the customer's victory.

First, since the environment is increasingly hostile, if the company does not want to settle for "squeezing the lemon" and then throwing out the rind, it must manage careers as a function of this new deal. If not, the human cost becomes quite considerable, and even if the cynicism of those involved – and we know how corrosive that can be for organizations – allows them to accept this human cost, it will in time have serious repercussions on the business itself, whose members experience the company exclusively in a utilitarian mode. There are many today who are quick to point out the dangers of such a relationship: Robert Waterman's advice to "put your people first" is by no means at odds with customer satisfaction, it is rather one of the conditions for it.[15] This is echoed by the words of a particular human resource director, who, at a meeting with his company's board of divisional directors, compared the work environment to a sporting event between professional athletes under constant pressure, who must, by definition, be even better during an actual event than in training. One participant in this meeting asked the human resource director for how long one might expect to remain a top-level athlete, and what one would be expected to do later on in the company.

The second major aspect of human resource management concerns the criteria for the management of individuals – how they are evaluated, promoted, remunerated, and so on. These become, as in the case of the British catering company, keys to behaviour modification, and it is always surprising to note just how many businesses have still not bridged the gap between their overall corporate strategy in the matter and their ability to generate business and serve their customers. Make no mistake: this is not meant as a throwback to the old Taylorian observation that individuals at work are motivated exclusively by monetary concerns. There are many other things which can be offered to make the new constraints more acceptable. The catering company was a good illustration that the actors' autonomy, when properly regulated by the organization – here by profitability and the number of meals served – can be a powerful lever in getting the company to meet the needs of the customer.

One might object that it is precisely this quest for unbridled autonomy which keeps public bureaucracies from learning anything new. This is true, but those bureaucracies are characterized by a large gap between how careers, salaries, and so on, are administered, on the one hand, and the business outcome, on the other. Hence there is no compensation for autonomy here. It is not a constructive term of exchange at the heart of the leader–customer representative–customer trilogy.[16] We have finally begun to glimpse the problem of the "fuzziness" of certain organizations, an aspect which it is not worth contrasting with clarity, in which there seems to be no special virtue, but with monopolies instead. This explains our hesitation to follow the pundits of re-engineering in their passion for processes. Of course, on careful reading, they themselves reveal this hesitation. Hammer and Champy write:

> The fourth key word in our definition – of reengineering – is "process". It is also the most important word, the one which presents the most serious problems for company directors … An operational process is a series of activities which, based on one or several entries (inputs), produces a result (output) representing some value for the customer.[17]

Two hundred pages later, the authors back off from this, enumerating the errors which lie in wait for a re-engineering programme: "[one of the errors] is to look only at the processes, to not take into account the new systems of evaluation, the redefinition of hierarchical powers, the transformation of the relationships with personnel".[18] In fact, behind processes, even with the slightly different meaning offered here, there is cooperation between the actors, which escapes precise definition, which is an unstable equilibrium, a policy within the organization itself. Cooperation cannot be decreed, nor can it be codified into a set of rules and procedures which would form "the layman's guide to the appropriate method of cooperation between members of the association".

Conversely, it assumes that once a favourable environment has been created (through personnel management, or exchanges in autonomy, for example), the organization will agree to go no further in defining itself, nor even in attempting to understand its own mechanisms. Now we understand why these fuzzy organizations very rarely accept that their "culture" should be rendered explicit. They fear the reification of that which must remain implicit. And they know just what they are doing.

3
What is a Bureaucracy?

To take an interest in bureaucracy is not to look back at the past, but towards the future. The central hypothesis of this book is that the end of bureaucracies, as they will be defined in a few moments, is the number one hell to face in the transformation of companies and organizations in coming years. It is no secret: there is not one management textbook or analysis of world trends that is not keenly interested in the end of bureaucracies, regardless of the author's point of view: "Today in the realm of organizations we see and suffer from cumbersome bureaucracies which, more than ever, are signs of the poor management of meaning."[1] To which Waterman adds a more precise definition: "The problem is as follows: the bureaucracy, our most traditional form of organization, was created to manage the day-to-day problems of organizations: the sales department sells, manufacturing manufactures, and so on. So long as economic activity does not change too quickly, bureaucracies get along fairly well. But things are changing quickly."[2] So why has this disjointed, compartmentalized mode of functioning taken the upper hand over other forms of organization? Robert Reich explains it as follows, based on the American situation:

American bureaucratic companies were organized around the model of military bureaucracies for the efficient deployment of plans developed well in advance. It is perhaps not by chance that war veterans who entered the major American companies in the 1950s very naturally re-created at the centre of these companies the military model of a bureaucracy. They were set up along the lines of a military hierarchy, with chains of command, control methods, rank, divisions with division leaders, and procedures outlining the decision-making process. If you have a question, check the manual![3]

After presenting Reich's thesis, Rifkin adds: "The managerial system of business organization is a giant oaf, a powerful producer capable of creating sizable quantities of standardized commodities, but lacking the flexibility to make nimble adjustments so as to adapt to rapid fluctuations in domestic or global markets."[4]

The story of an evolution

One key idea stands out in these quotations: the bureaucratic form of organization belonged to a moment in history during which products (either goods or services) were scarce. In this sense, a bureaucracy is intimately linked to mass production and, no doubt, to a democratic way of thinking. It corresponds to the arrival of a new age in the evolution of humankind: in economic terms, by making available to the greatest number the goods and services to which they may legitimately aspire; and in politics, by setting up a state of human rights which presupposes rules and procedures and their application.

This is why for Max Weber as well as for Henry Mintzberg,[5] bureaucracy designates a collective order, a legitimate state of domination based upon a set of rules and procedures, a professional and process-based organization. From this perspective, one could define the bureaucracy as an organization whose responsibility it is to produce both general and impersonal rules and to apply them.

Furthermore, this "mode" of doing things must apply as much to the people the bureaucracy serves as to its own members. This is the opposite of the "organic" mode, that of the artisan class as defined by Burns and Stalker.[6] It can similarly be found in the works of Henri Fayol.[7] Virtuous towards its subjects, bureaucracy in this paradigm would also be good to its members, ensuring equality for all in law, acting as the *de facto* guarantor of civil rights, whether it be with respect to a political state (rights of the citizen), or an economic state (rights of the customer).

Yet as time passed, doubt began to cast a shadow over virtuous bureaucracy. Although some authors were able to demonstrate how these organizations have a tremendous ability to adapt from day to day, in particular by betraying their "Weberian" mission to apply rules and procedures,[8] it has become increasingly clear that the bureaucratic way of doing things primarily serves internal concerns related to the protection of the organizations' members, rather than the establishment of a form of government working on behalf of everyone's happiness. Or at least that is how bureaucrats have evolved! Michel Crozier was the first, and, in the author's opinion, in a quite definite manner, to identify the key characteristics of a modern bureaucratic organization[9] as it existed in the 1960s – centralization, stratification and its method of human resource management – by bringing to the fore systemic aspects as opposed to an individualized view of the "bureaucrat". He described centralization in a way which still today makes leaders of large international corporations jump because it comes so close to what they observe but dare not admit. Centralization results from an imbalance between the centre which is supposed to decide everything although it is caught up in endless petty decisions and lacks the information to do so, and an outer sphere which is all the more free and uncontrolled as a result of having to apply the inapplicable rules established by the under-informed centre. The author does not share Michel Crozier's view that "the bureaucratic phenomenon" owes its success in the United States to the fact that it helped explain French bureaucracy; it simply helped explain the American businesses whose functioning is described by Robert Reich.[10] Similarly, he identified in a decisive manner "the fear of face-to-face interaction", which for our purposes we will reinterpret in terms of non-cooperation, as well as the gap between what employees do and how personnel are managed.

Taylor, or the sole rationality

From the standpoint of this book, we have to go one step further and shed light on an analysis of bureaucracy which is less endogenous and which can reveal effects on the environment, which we denote here by the generic term "customers". To do this, we must go back to the idea mentioned earlier of the customer's victory over the producer, its process and its human resource constraints. With this in mind, I would like to propose the following definition for a bureaucracy:

> A bureaucracy is an organization which translates its technical constraints (the task), its human constraints (personnel), or both, spontaneously and systematically into its mode of functioning (that is to say, without wondering whether there are other alternatives).

This definition is valid for industry as well as the service sector, for both companies and public administration. It underscores that the most fundamental trait of a bureaucracy is that the criteria upon which its organization is based are endogenous and considered to be universal, unavoidable and unquestionable, including of course by its customers, to whom they can possibly be explained in a learning context. This definition will allow us to begin where Taylor[11] left off and work our way up to the customer's victory.

It was indeed Taylor who proposed that an organization can be built around technical tasks, underscoring the universal nature of this kind of organization.[12] Jeremy Rifkin summarizes Taylor's principle as follows:

> With the help of a chronometer, Taylor reduced the different tasks of workers to their smallest identifiable operational parts, then measured the latter to obtain the minimum amount of time required for a given task under optimal operating conditions. His research permitted calibrating worker performance to within almost a fraction of a second. By calculating the average and optimal lengths of each part of workers' tasks, Taylor was able to make recommendations on the most minute details of the execution of tasks, so as to save precious seconds, even fractions of a second.[13]

Each and every word is important in this reading of the logic of time and movement, but clearly the one word which appears most frequently as the base unit of scientific management is "task".

Let us stop here a moment, and make a rather simple observation: we are not asking whether an organization set up around tasks is possible or even desirable, it is simply what we observe. This kind of organization represented a significant step forward, and has been thoroughly discussed in the literature. It made possible both mass production and lower product cost, thereby making products available to the greatest number. It likewise made possible "mass management", one of the conditions of Weberian democracy; it was even a source of inspiration to the founders of total quality approaches, such as Taïchi Ono. But to conclude from all this that it is the only possible form of organization would be a serious mistake, a fact made clear by the customer's victory. Taylorian thinking, then as now, makes the same mistake. It jumps from a hypothetical phase – organization around tasks is the best way of assuring mass production whenever the product is scarce – to a universal proposition: it is the only possible way (an approach in terms of "one best way").

This mode of reasoning which is built not only around the primacy of technical constraints but also around the idea that there is one and only one way of running an organization, is still today the dominant model, probably because we are aware of so few alternatives. Once this model has been accepted, we lose the ability to distance ourselves from technical constraints, and require others to suffer the consequences. Why? Because the responsibility lies not with us, which would clearly be self-serving, but with science, which is above special interests. By claiming that the primacy of the producer is scientifically based, we can set up such unquestionable organizations that to dispute them would be nothing short of revolutionary. But what can lead to such a revolution, or, in other words, how and for whom is such reasoning a problem?

The professor, his map and the bureaucracy

So long as the customers have no say in the matter, since they are the "losers", they agree to give in to the whole set of bureaucratic constraints. A "set" because the loose thread which appeared with the task has been pulled and the bureaucratic bobbin has come unwound: tasks lead us to procedures, procedures to geographic segmentation, segmentation to schedules, schedules to job status: and thus, step by step, we begin to see just how big the monster really is. The customer who has to give in to the producer is also the one who has to send his or her child to a given state school, the one who has to run to the local retailer not when there is a pressing need, but when the store is open. This is the customer who has to follow a complex process of rules and procedures, running from one place to the next, all because the system was not designed for the customer's convenience, but for the bureaucrats who have certain tasks to do, while other tasks which are not part of their job responsibilities are not accomplished. The key symbolic word in the Kafkaesque world of bureaucracies might well be "file": "I have your file", "Where is your file?", "Do I have a good file?", "Your file is incomplete", "Your file was not sent over to me", and so on.

Let us turn to a simple illustration. When visiting professors arrive in a state university in the United States, right off the bat they need to get hold of two important "tools": a bank card and a university identity card (which provides access to various campus services). The two cards look alike: they are about the same size and shape, have a magnetic strip with a picture and signature of the holder printed on the back and an identification number of about the same number of digits on both cards. How are they obtained? For the bank card, it takes about ten minutes at the bank, during which time different accounts are opened. The bank employee offers the bank card, suggests getting a picture ID, snaps the picture in a little room set up just for this purpose, and delivers the card. In a short span of time, one person carries out a set of tasks revolving around the customer. This is a case of "seamless service", as we will see later on. The employee is friendly and courteous, but more importantly, we see that the organization is itself built around the customer, and to do this, the very job description of bank employees was redefined and enlarged: they must be photographers, printers, and of course able to open accounts!

As for the university card, the courtesy or dedication of employees, their obvious desire to be of service are not a problem here either. But the intent of the organization is another matter altogether! After a visit to the Office of International Services, seekers of an identity card have to run over to a health insurance agency to pick up several important papers before returning to the first office. They must then return to their own department, where they might find out that it will take several days for the necessary paperwork to be approved by the dean and the department head. When all of the paperwork is in order, the journey ends at a final stop with the photographer, who asks new faculty members to stop by a week later to pick up the magic card.

The first organization is built around the customer, the second around the tasks and their segmentation. The first offers one location, the second several journeys from one specialized office to the next. Given a choice, we can easily imagine that a customer would prefer providers, public or private, to reorganize around customers and their way of thinking, which is by definition very different from that of the bureaucracy. This calls into question not only the "organization" in the largest sense of the term, including here what employees actually do on the job (their job descriptions), but also its rationale. To better appreciate the full scale of this revolution, let us consider in the following pages three sectors of the economy, each one having undergone some degree of upheaval: the air transportation industry, the automotive industry, and hospital healthcare. A comparison of these case studies should help emphasize the universal scope of the problem.

The airline industry

The case of air transportation is interesting for two reasons. First, from a macro-sociological point of view, it is a sector which has undergone relatively rapid deregulation, which in Europe came to completion in early 1997. Deregulation has brought profound change to the industry, including the elimination of some of the key players (Pan Am for example), economic and social tragedies (Air France lost roughly $1.6 billion in 1993, and Iberia also faced a tough financial crisis), as well as fierce struggles on the part of airline personnel trying to avoid what they felt was a general decline in the conditions under which they are hired, and under which they work. In early 1997, the President of the United States had to intervene to head off a strike at American Airlines, which everyone thought would be a catastrophic event for the American economy. At the same time, mergers and joint-operating agreements have reconfigured the global air transportation industry: an environment in which each company is in a battle to survive.

From a micro-sociological perspective, we are dealing with a business in which technical constraints have always been the number one concern. This is due to the nature of the business and of course for safety reasons. While the planes are on the ground, there are carefully codified maintenance procedures carried out on a precise schedule by ground crews; in the air, there are very specific security guidelines – nothing is left to chance. A large company would have a hard time surviving a catastrophe for which it is to some degree responsible. As a result, safety is never a part of an air carrier's sales pitch; it is simply taken for granted throughout the industry.

This fact has had far-reaching effects on the organization. If we just consider flight attendants, their traditional role was more focused on safety than on customer service – even if these two roles are not contradictory – and this focus has structured their relationship with the customer, just as in the earlier case of the railroad company. It puts the flight attendant in a position of superiority, somewhat like a doctor, whose symbol is the seatbelt: passengers are requested to remain seated with their seatbelts fastened, although they may not really understand the soundness of this reasoning.

At the same time, this focus has provided for the attendants a certain number of advantages in terms of rest, rotas, even salary, which is scaled to compensate for the difficulty of their work (jet lag, negative effects of altitude on health), and the pressures of the job (there is no room for careless mistakes). An entire realm of mythical proportions has thus been built up, and airline operations have gone unquestioned for a very long time, operations which force customers to run from this place to that, not unlike what we saw in the case of the university identity card: reservation, check-in, long hours in the terminal, boarding, deplaning, possibly a return to the terminal, the baggage claim. Generally speaking, these tasks are not usually carried out by employees of the same departments within the airline, or are even dependent on different organizations.

Let us now try to disturb this seemingly perfect order by asking a simple question just as we did as we began to explore this branch of the industry: "How are you organized to manage your passengers (your customers)?" In response, people arrive quickly at the distinction between ground and flight personnel. It is a distinction which surprises no one, probably not even you as you read these lines. And yet, if you ask why there is such a distinction, it will be explained with a smile – at least at first – that since aircraft spend part of their time on the ground and part in the air, it is perfectly normal and hardly questionable that there should be ground personnel and flight personnel. Yet if you push the issue a little further, you will notice that people get a little irritated, a sign that it is truly difficult for bureaucrats to imagine a mode of functioning that is not built around technical constraints. If you really push the matter, people will ask whether you know much about flying, and whether you understand that planes spend part of their time on the ground and part in the air. How will you answer that? That there is no question about that, it is self-evident. Yet you can still dispute the logical jump which was made which seemed perfectly normal and natural to everyone, the jump from the technical constraint that planes are sometimes on the ground and sometimes in the air, to how airlines organize their operations: there are therefore ground and flight personnel. This jump from technical constraints to how things are done lies at the heart of the bureaucracy as we have defined it: and this is what customers are challenging today, not for theoretical or ideological reasons, but simply because, if they can, they will try to get away from any imposed segmentation which costs them in terms of convenience.

Two observations stand out as we consider a real customer rather than just a statistical one. Do customers enter a travel agency asking to buy a little ground, a flight, then a little more ground to retrieve their luggage? Although putting it this way may sound a bit childish, it allows us to emphasize that technical segmentation is not devised by the customers, who from their perspective are buying a trip, a concept which would integrate the different technical aspects. Even better: in air travel, the points at which the customer is particularly nervous or anxious occur precisely at moments of abrupt change between the ground and the flight. Although the segmentation of tasks is the company's solution, it becomes a real problem for customers: the trip to the terminal is slow and unpleasant, there are delays at the baggage claim area and fear that bags might be lost, travellers experience anxiety over missed connections, and so on. In a classic airline bureaucracy, when a customer asks a flight attendant "What do I do next?" the response is at best "Our ground personnel are there to help you", and at worst "That's not our job."

To take this image even further, consider passengers boarding a French domestic airline, an airline which does not book seat reservations. As they wait to board the plane holding passes bearing a letter corresponding to the order in which they board, passengers are so anxious – worried about finding a good seat in an uncomfortable plane – that they lose all notion of civility. They glare at each other, hiding their passes, and jostle the passengers in front of them; in short, they undergo a mini-nightmare which, ultimately, will cost the company a great deal. Since the company did not listen to its customers, many of them will switch over to the competition.

Is it possible to think differently about these issues? At the start of the new millennium, one airline, British Airways, stands out for its outstanding financial success. Indeed, the British airline began its revolution well ahead of its European sisters. Interestingly, British Airways' revolution was not just about cutting costs. So that cost reductions would not impact on overall quality, which would in the end have had a negative effect on the company, it redesigned its way of doing business around a concept – specifically, around a careful analysis and understanding of the many contradictory demands of its customers – a concept which is at odds with the bureaucratic segmentation around tasks. So-called "seamless travelling" is an attempt to erase as much as possible the abrupt changes in air travel discussed above. The company first had to understand what the customer was experiencing, then had to learn to go beyond the contradictions and the fact that the customer always wants more (more comfort, more space, better meals, and so on). It could thus get away from its strict form of management control.

Next, the concept had to take shape, not in advertising, which is a simple matter, nor even in the behaviour of individual company representatives, which is also not difficult, but in the whole range of ways in which the company operates, its modes of functioning, which is another problem altogether. Let us turn to a few examples which are perhaps not limited to the company in question, but which show the clear link between listening to the customer and a company's mode of functioning.

Until quite recently, what remained of air travel regulation in Europe prohibited an airline from offering service between two third-party nations (which is still the case in the United States). In concrete terms, then, British Airways could not offer potential French customers a direct flight from Paris to Hong Kong. In order to woo these potential customers, the airline would not only have to offer attractive perks (an upgrade in one direction on a round-trip ticket) but would also have to provide service from Paris to London and back at no additional cost. That would mean accepting a loss on one profit centre (Europe) so as to make an even greater gain in another (Asia). This kind of gamble would be almost unthinkable in the compartmentalized scenario in which individuals focus on their own profits with little concern for the overall organization, and with neither the interest nor the ability to cooperate with each other.

Furthermore, for the French customer to be willing to travel the extra distance, the connections in London must be as quick as possible. To save time during the connection, passengers will have to register their luggage at the initial departure point (Paris), and will consequently worry whether the airline can handle transferring their bags to the second plane in perhaps as little as 30 minutes. They will not be satisfied by some oral confirmation: "There's no problem, your luggage will make it." Customers need some kind of follow-up, some proof before boarding the second plane in the connecting airport that their bags have been transferred. This is an extremely delicate matter to handle, for it presupposes that bags will be loaded into the plane's hold in Paris with the knowledge that they will have high priority in London; the ground crews must be able to get the bags quickly from plane to plane; and there must be an efficient computerized system which, as the passengers head towards the gate, will inform them that their suitcases have been safely transferred to the second aircraft. "Seamless travelling", then, is this kind of operation, relying both on cooperation between people, on methods of working which are based on the customer's way of thinking (the loading of baggage as a function of the connection and not some technical or bureaucratic criteria), and on a uniform, high-performance information system which makes real and tangible for the customer the integration of services and employees, who, by the way, might work apart from one another physically.

Just for comparison, let us briefly consider the very different case of an airline in continental Europe. One employee of this airline suggested that passengers concerned over the whereabouts of their bags should glance out the window and try to spot them as they are being loaded. Focused on helping passengers board the plane, this employee felt unconcerned by an activity that was not within his remit, and with which, in any case, he had no real connection.

One more point: the coordination of these operations, which is the "soft" solution devised by bureaucracies so that each person might be able to remain within his or her own frame of reference, fails to deal with the problem. Liaison employees given the task of coordinating the various activities, whether or not they are part of the company's hierarchy, would not have at their disposal the necessary means to integrate and distribute all the information coming from diverse sources. The customer needs cooperation, that is, each employee must be able to enter another's territory, so as to be able to anticipate what is going to happen next, while following up with what has already occurred and eliminating abrupt breaks in the task at hand. We are beginning to glimpse here how the idea of cooperation, which is the focus of a "customer-based" orientation, is hardly compatible with our fascination with clear, precise, well defined structures.

The automobile industry

An analysis of developments in the automobile industry will allow us to proceed even further in two directions: first, how the customer has "climbed the ladder" to higher levels of bureaucracy, including those which are apparently the most distant; and second, that of the cost of development or of the production of goods (or services), often seen as a constraint on the ability to satisfy customers, even though lower cost is an integral part of what they want and is a matter of concern to the organizational revolution discussed throughout this book.

Some years ago, the author had several young automobile executives in his seminars, both in Europe and the United States, and he asked them at the start of the session to explain how their business was organized to develop, produce and sell vehicles. The typical response began, "Oh! It's easy." This simple utterance is quite significant, in that it came naturally to the lips of these engineers, and tells us that there is only one way of doing things, that the organization is predetermined by, of course, the sequence of tasks to be accomplished. And the description which usually followed fully confirmed this "ease": the vehicle must first be designed, and so there is the department of research and development. Next, it must be put into production, which gives rise to centralized or decentralized production methods; next follows the vehicle's manufacture, a process which lends its name to the corresponding department, and finally, there is the network in charge of sales and after-sales services.

This rough sketch does not take into account the other services (the "product", market studies, human resources), it simply describes the most obvious faces of the organization, which for a long time stood unquestioned, inevitable, logical. The design department is the product; methods, the process. How would it be possible to imagine a process for an as yet unknown product? The product/process distinction is sometimes just as intangible as the ground/flight distinction. One of the large French auto companies provides a good example, where for a long time the product/process distinction has translated into geographical separation (the two entities were located as far apart from each other as possible), and a difference in prestige as well. The distinction has even given rise to vocabulary expressing just how poor the relationships between the two divisions are: those in charge of delivering files (*sic*!)

from one to another are called "mailmen", who are supposed to deliver the mail without being in a position to know or explain the contents.

Of course, the division of departments is reproduced within departments as well. If a vehicle has an engine and a body, reason enough to subdivide the methods accordingly. And to the degree that the body is in sheet metal which has to be stamped out and then assembled, there is necessarily a stamping department and an assembly department. Were we to give each one of these a number, some kind of code which would have meaning only for the system's insiders, we would have an ill-sorted set which we could call "bureaucratically vague", in which, as we will see, the job of coordinating the different units is so difficult that only an external supplier is in a position to do it – at a high cost, of course. In light of this, one begins to see how bureaucracy, apparent clarity, compartmentalization, and so on, are responsible in a big way for increased, excessive costs which customers refuse to pay whenever they have the chance.

Hell is everybody else!

Taking a few steps back now, let us refocus our analysis of this kind of organization on two points:

1. We are dealing with a classic technical bureaucracy, as defined in the preceding pages. There's no point in hiding the fact that we like bureaucracies, provided that we do not run up against them, but are part of them. There are many reasons for this. First, it is a kind of organization that has a clearly visible structure, and we like clarity and security. Behind the idea of clarity, there is protection: if my territory is clearly defined, no one can encroach upon it, it is mine, I have a monopoly over it. I do what I am supposed to do, and I need not worry about the overall consequences, insofar as the organization's underlying principle is that if each person does his or her job properly, the results can only be positive. But above all, the actor is protected from the very thing which is least natural, most difficult, and most costly in human terms: cooperating with others.

   Over the years sociologists have come up with various images or expressions for this idea: they speak of "beehive structures", and of the "fear of face-to-face interactions".[14] However it might be described, the observation is still the same. Jean-Paul Sartre put it brilliantly: "Hell is everybody else!" In the Sartrian sense, cooperation leads people into hell, confronting them forcibly with another way of thinking, leading them into conflict, bringing them to accept conflicting interests and compromise, whereas the rhetoric of daily life (the business place) promotes a "shared vision", consensus, common goals and common means. This is a harrowing paradox, and is precisely the reason why bureaucracies are, from the point of view of their members, a wonderful solution to the universal question: "How can we live together without having to cooperate?" And thus instead of troublesome cooperation there is the process, the procedures, the rules, the sequence of tasks, and one time-consuming coordinating meeting after another, something in which bureaucrats excel.[15]

We have already glimpsed that the abundance of means is itself a means of escaping cooperation. If, back at home after a long day's work, a married couple want to watch different television programmes, there are two ways to resolve the problem: either through non-cooperation, in which case they need two television sets, and the abundance of means does away with the necessity of negotiation and thus of conflict; or through cooperation, although of course that will be more "costly" in human terms. However surprising, it is a perfectly natural result that an organization built around the customer, that is, in which people cooperate (as we saw earlier in the case of the air transportation industry and as we will again see later on in the case of the automobile industry), is more efficient in the use of means than an organization built on the segmentation of technical tasks, which allows its members to avoid cooperation. Not only do customers ask that we operate at lowest cost, but they provide us with the means to do it! It should now be evident why for our third example we will turn to hospitals and the management of the high cost of healthcare.

2. But that is not all, especially in terms of the problem of cost. If the division of tasks, accompanied by procedures which clearly specify what employees must do, is supposed to provide customers with the goods or services which they have the right to expect,[16] in reality, this is not at all the case. With less cooperation, employees come up with their own rationales, always justifiable given the specialized technical angle from which they view the situation, and the more it will be necessary at some point to make adjustments.

This is what in the automobile industry and elsewhere is called "modifications". These become more and more frequent as a weakly integrated process goes on, sometimes attaining simply astounding proportions. They run right through the organization, up to the point where they involve the customer either directly, in which case they are called "weaknesses" in the system, or indirectly and are then translated into a price increase and/or delays in production. Quality, cost, delay (QCD): these form the "concept" of the automobile industry, just as seamless travelling was that of British Airways. Clearly, so long as customers have no choice, they are given to accept the degradation of this trio (QCD), but as soon as they can, they ask for more, that is, higher quality at lower cost.

What does this mean? What is a modification, not in the technical sense, but from a sociological perspective? It is the cost which an organization requires its customers to pay so as to permit its members to avoid cooperation. A modification is a way of regulating this system, that is, the key element around which employees adjust their strategies of autonomy and avoidance, the cost of which they pass along to the customer whenever possible.

It should be clear that we are not speaking here of those who work directly with the final consumer, but of all those who produce value for this consumer, under the terms specified above (QCD), regardless of where they might be located within the organization, even as high up as the research department, for example.

In this scenario, listening to the customer means the end of the bureaucracy as a way of doing business characterized by the pre-eminence of a technical rationale over cooperation. Whenever it is said or written that the customer must and will climb high within the organization, it is not just an abstract figure of speech. What good would it do to convince employees that the customer is important, which would amount to little more than a rhetorical exercise with little practical impact? We must identify in concrete terms the consequences for each person involved, that is to say in terms of how people work (modes of work). This was done progressively in the automobile industry, first by setting up cross-functional operations, called "projects".[17] These consist in giving a project leader the job of integrating the work of everyone involved in the concept or production of a vehicle, part of a vehicle, or of a component. Freed from their "occupations" in the "projects", engineers, executives and technicians were supposed to work together towards a common goal. This first breakthrough towards complexity over the expensive simplicity of a sequence of technical tasks nevertheless ran up against an obstacle. The initial assumption was that cooperation would result naturally through individual goodwill, through employee interest in working on a project, and/or the project leader's ability to win everyone over by his or her charisma or conviction.

This somewhat naive vision has not stood up to the facts. Cooperation, like any other human behaviour, cannot be decreed, it must be created. I will try in the second part of this work to offer several possibilities for making cooperation possible. For the time being, let us just say that it was necessary as time went on to bestow on project leaders real means for getting work done, in particular in terms of controlling how budgetary resources are distributed, and how project members are evaluated, so as to get them to work together.

At the same time, as we have said before, the organization has today become more complex, more vague according to its members: the vehicle or component projects are intertwined and encroach upon "occupations", repositories of technical expertise. It has also become more subject to conflict, less comfortable, but at the same time much more lively and "negotiative". This conflict was difficult to accept for a long time, especially in France, a country in which open confrontation over differing interests is considered incompatible with the defence of common interests.[18] Elsewhere, on the contrary, this confrontation has been considered not only as one of the conditions of success, but even as one of the keys to its continuance: "the best businesses have good results because they work hard to build coherence among widely differing and often conflicting interests. It is like a good marriage: a couple enjoy lasting happiness because they have worked to build it: a labour of love, but labour all the same."[19] Today, accepting this conflict is no longer questioned on principle. It is simply a consequence of customers' presence within bureaucracies which had traditionally kept them on the outside.

Integration and cost cutting

Similarly, new problems have arisen which traditional bureaucratic methods of management have been unable to handle. This is especially the case in people management – human resource management – a mainspring in the transformation of bureaucracies.[20] The distribution of resources between different projects and occupations, the methods of evaluating employees – key factors in cooperation, as we said – and career management, have all had to be reanalysed. Organizations have had to learn to manage their crucial problems more openly, more "opportunistically", and with less planning. Employees for their part have had to accept greater risk, more unforeseen events, and have had to be more mobile than they would have had they been able to continue along more familiar paths.

Finally, and without suggesting that we are at the end of the journey, we have had to think the unthinkable – again – and bring together what up till that point belonged to separate, compartmentalized worlds. At Renault, for example, on platforms designed for the purpose, design and methods plan the product and the process simultaneously instead of one after the other. This is nothing but the most visible and meaningful face of the very deep revolution which is affecting companies' modes of functioning. Of course, what we really want to know is how this affects the customer. There are two possible answers: first of all, exact figures held by car manufacturers clearly show that the number of modifications decreases considerably as an organization becomes more transverse. As we said, the "modifications" – those that correspond to a lack in cooperation – are detrimental to QCD.

Moreover, and perhaps more convincingly, the integration that brings together different ways of thinking provides a company with greater control over its suppliers. In the traditional compartmentalized context in which there is no communication, the only ones who in the end have a view of the whole are the suppliers. They are the ones who play the role of "integrator", taking the place of cooperation. But they play this role only for a price – the price of manipulating information, the modifications game – which allows them, in the end, to send the company an invoice which is well above what was first negotiated in the contract. And of course, there is no way of pinning responsibility on suppliers for these changes. The new modes of work, which bring with them the integration of suppliers at a very high level, today allow them to be more closely controlled, and restores, we might say without fear of exaggeration, freedom within the company. Once again, one can see in this example the unnecessary cost of "false clarity". When we try to foresee everything, plan everything, "define" everything carefully in advance, we condemn employees to verticality by helping them avoid worrying about others. Others, such as the customers, may worry about this integration, but even this may come at a price. From this standpoint, the way costs are transmitted in organizations is more a problem of functioning than a question of "savings", in the most basic sense of the term. To say suddenly "We are cutting 20 per cent off everything" is in a way admitting that we have been unable to implement a real organizational strategy for controlling cost. It is a kind of "figure it out yourself" mentality, which is only possible when individuals are subjected to pressure which substitutes for a carefully thought-out plan of action.

The hospital: less spending, more cooperation

To close a chapter on bureaucracies with a discussion of the healthcare industry might seem surprising. What can this highly specialized field which is about devotion and real concern for humankind have to do with the pencil-pushing routines of technical organizations forging ahead with their own way of thinking without concern for customers? The link is this: in nearly every nation people are involved in a heated debate over the problem of rising health costs.[21] Yet very few people realize that there is an organizational dimension that must be addressed.[22] Hospitals – which generate the majority of costs in question – can in fact be viewed as the most perfect form of what we have called a technical organization. Because of a need for specialization, which "customers" are all the more ready to submissively accept since their own health is at stake, a hospital does not really deal in terms of sick people, but in terms of illnesses and body parts, so to speak, and this way of functioning has become quite naturally the hospital's guiding principle. Edgar Morin and Sami Naïr write:

> High tech medicine, while producing wonderful results (liver, kidney and heart transplants, the restoration of injuries or war wounds, the reversal of many infectious diseases), suffers from and makes patients suffer from hyper-specialization, according to which the body's organs are viewed as separate from the body, and the body separate from the overall being, be it biological, psychological, or social.[23]

This hyper-specialization does not just pose a human problem, that of "dissected" patients, as if they were automobiles on the assembly line or in for repair. Hyper-specialization poses the problem of cost for reasons which we have already seen in this chapter. The technical rationale, pushed here to the extreme, allows doctors to avoid cooperating, even getting the patient to help them in avoiding it. The anxiety-provoking nature of the doctor–patient relationship leads the latter to accept and even approve of repetitious exams or treatments. In public debate, whenever people begin to criticize the high cost of these treatments and seek to control them through a purely financial approach – such as forcing doctors to cut down on treatments and prescriptions – practitioners cry wolf and warn of the imminent degradation of public health. Those who are currently sick or potentially sick are quick to join in this outcry. In the end, there is more and more disagreement over solutions, if only because no one has really understood the problem, and there are precious few who actually see the link between the care which they receive and the deficits of a system as abstract as Medicare in the United States or social security in Europe.[24]

Thus healthcare is really no different from the other organizations we have already seen. Cost and quality are not really at odds, but so long as they are viewed as such there will indeed be a decline in benefits in a game in which the stakes are high and everyone loses: as a whole we will only partially be able to control costs, patients will receive care of lower quality, and doctors will experience a drop in their standard of living. The latter, just like everyone else we have encountered, are going to have to learn to work differently, in a less segmented fashion, thus less comfortably. They are no doubt going to have to get used to a little less prestige in their particular area of specialization. At the same time, their relationship with patients is going to have to change just as radically as the relationship with the customer in any kind of bureaucracy: this is, no doubt, where the stakes are highest. This will affect what people actually do at work (their "occupations") on a daily basis. Readers who find this argument difficult to accept should reflect back to the days, now past, when doctors, by being systematically late, made patients feel all that much more dependent on them. To rebuild the hospital around the patient is not a dream. Not only can it be done, but it should be done, for it would result in improved care at a lower cost. Why would we not treat this particular sector the same as all others, regardless of how difficult it might be for the producers, in this case the doctors?[25] Certain countries have already taken the first steps in this process, either for budgetary reasons as in the United States, or because they are involved in national reconstruction, as in Lebanon, and thus have a chance to rethink the functioning and structure of their healthcare system.

There is no question that once again we are dealing with a real revolution. For, in countries such as France or Belgium, not only is there the medical bureaucracy, but there is now a bureaucracy that manages healthcare. In Paris, for instance, women are taken to special hospitals for the birth of extremely premature babies; the premature babies are cared for in entirely separate hospitals. Premature infant delivery and premature infant care are two different "practices", so to speak, so that in the Institute of Infant Care in Paris, there is not a single maternity bed. The segmentation of healthcare is thus based on the rationale of the hospital's organizational chart; but as it respects the various specialists, it increases both cost and risk.

More generally, what is being challenged here is the way bureaucrats and politicians go about trying to reduce public expenditures. We had a good example of this way with the case of public transportation. An exclusively financial approach which favours actual "gross" gains in productivity by simply reducing identifiable costs can only wind up hurting the overall quality of services provided, or might force them to be eliminated altogether. The artificial view that cost and quality are irreconcilable, which stems from a complete misunderstanding of the organizational dimension of the problem, leads many to take a hopeless view of reducing public expenditures, and results in disagreement after disagreement in the debate over how best to go about it.[26]

The lack of real debate on these issues, but also the particularly violent reactions which they cause in France, Belgium and Italy, are clear signs that citizens are aware, however vaguely, of the erroneous path on to which they have been lured. In fact, wiser than their own leaders, they cannot understand why the public sector is the only one not to offer improved services at lower cost. From this standpoint, they have entered into the same struggle with government as the customer with the producer. What they want is reform of the state and of the way it operates. Their leaders have yet to make it part of their agenda. Generally speaking, they do not understand what such reform would mean in terms of the organization of public or para-public services. Thus they make do with traditional approaches to the budget which resolve nothing and displease everyone, and sadly miss a wonderful opportunity to give real meaning to an initiative that would change the way the state and its agencies function. That is unfortunate, since we will all pay for it later on.

4
A Requiem for Bureaucracy

We enjoy bureaucracies. Those in which we work, that is, not those which we have to confront and which bind us with constraints. We are, in fact, both the bureaucrat and the customer: we apply pressure and we resist it, we demand change and yet we cherish the advantages that are already ours. There is no real contradiction here, as a number of writers have already pointed out.[1] Our ability to play both roles is to a large extent the result of how difficult it is to identify, or "flesh out" bureaucracy, so to speak, when it is defined in terms of the line of thought governing the implementation of its modes of functioning, and in terms of the employee benefits associated with them. So long as this definition remains relatively abstract and general – the ability to produce general and impersonal rules and to apply them, for example – so long as it underscores the trivial, day-to-day aspects of bureaucracy, just as Balzac[2] described the bureaucrat – paperwork, drawn-out procedures, little contact with others – bureaucracy resembles any large organization, a military model[3] or a form of public administration. And so bureaucracy is referred to as "them", even for bureaucrats themselves, who are all the more ready to point out the ungainliness of the world they work in, since doing so allows them to point out their own flexibility.[4]

This is misleading, and it allows businesses in the private sector to preserve a good image by distancing themselves from the public sector. In fact, this distance is not as great as they would like us to think. In order to prove this, I will begin by showing, through several simple examples, that there are as many small bureaucracies as there are large ones, that bureaucracy is not defined by size, that the basic problem is how an organization is conceptualized. From this standpoint, knowing that the elite of the private and public sectors overlap both in the United States and Europe, the modes of thinking are both here and there more or less the same.[5]

Task segmentation

Why not begin with a humorous, albeit striking example of a small bureaucracy as defined here. Step into any ordinary hairdressing salon – in America or France – and ask for a haircut. Regardless of the kind of salon, the procedure is the same just about everywhere: we are first seated in front of a sink where someone – often a young woman – washes our hair. Then we are asked to get up and walk over to the stylist's chair. The procedure is so much part and parcel of getting a haircut that we do not even question it, regardless of how ridiculous we might feel about moving from one place to the next with wet, dishevelled hair, a towel around the shoulders. This very simple organization illustrates one of the most characteristic traits of a Taylorian bureaucracy: movement is applied to the product – in this case, the customer's head – rather than to the workers, who remain at their post.

Let us now attempt to "interfere with" bureaucracy to see just how firmly anchored it is in the minds of those who never think of questioning it.[6] Instead of acquiescing when asked to get up and leave the sink area, what if we were to refuse, saying that, for goodness' sake, we are quite comfortable right where we are and would rather not have to get out of our chair? The employee will be somewhat bewildered, wondering whether or not we came to the right hairdresser. He or she will explain that in this shop, this is where customers' hair is washed, so that it can then be cut. Well, in that case there's no problem, since that is exactly why we are here. Relieved, our guide will point out that haircuts are given in the chairs, over in the stylists' area. At this point, we explain that we would rather have the stylist join us over here. Increasingly worried, the employee will cite the technical constraints: all the styling tools are kept by the technicians. When we suggest that the technician bring them along, our interlocutor, at his or her wits' end, will hurry over to the reception desk to tell the owner that a "nutcase" is getting a little out of hand in the shampoo area.

What is a "nutcase"? It is a customer who does not understand the technical constraints, who asserts that they cannot be taken for granted as universal, scientific principles. Here we are again in fully fledged Taylorism, despite the organization's small size, which like all bureaucracies "breaks the customer up" as a function of its own tasks and the sequence in which they must be performed. The shampooer's sink and the stylist's chair, two distinct areas of the hairdressing salon, are the ground and flight operations of the airline, the product and process of the automobile company. And the fact that today many salons are organized differently, either with technicians who handle a whole set of job tasks in one place, or with small teams who work around customers who stay seated in one place, is but one simple confirmation that along-side the segmentation of tasks lies another way of thinking, another possibility, revealed only if we start with the customers themselves. It is worth noting that this alternative results in a change in the duties of a given job (the stylist is now involved in shampooing), or in new modes of cooperation between members of the organization (small teams work within one area of the salon).

The problem of cost is no different in micro-bureaucracies either. Here is another light-hearted example, which occurred in the United States. A European customer leaves for California where he has been sent for six months. Shortly thereafter, he is joined by his wife and children. Just before returning to Europe, his wife decides to purchase a comforter (duvet), which in her view are of better quality in America than in the Old World. The two head for a small specialty shop advertised in a local newspaper to make a purchase. Upon entering, they are greeted with a smile by a young woman wearing a name badge. She introduces herself and asks what the couple might be looking for. The prospective buyers explain what they want, and, with the help of the very sincere and considerate employee, decide upon a particular brand and make. Unfortunately, the duvet in question is out of stock, and so the sales-woman explains that they can have it delivered. Learning that the couple plan to leave the country in a short while, which becomes a deci-sive condition for delivery, she has them fill out three forms – one yellow, one green and one pink – which, according to the employee, will ensure timely delivery of the quilt. The customers and saleswoman say good-bye, everyone in a good mood and quite pleased with the transaction.

Yet the fateful day arrives and the delivery does not take place. The couple, a little concerned, hurry back to the store where they are received by a different young lady in precisely the same manner as the one before: a sign that the warm, friendly welcome is little more than standardized company protocol. The Europeans interrupt the welcome, stating that they have had a problem with a delivery, the very thought of which, in a country where lawsuits and lawyers reign supreme, could pose a serious threat. After hearing the customers out, the employee regains her smile and almost childishly suggests that they must have made a mistake in filling out the delivery papers. Upon presentation, these papers turn out to be in perfect order, which enables the sales-woman, increasingly relieved, to again declare that there is no problem. The customers, on the other hand, increasingly worried, respond that there is a very serious problem indeed since they have not received the order and are leaving the country the very next day. The saleswoman explains that as far as she is concerned everything is in order, and, of course, the situation is all the less resolved.

What can be gleaned from the preceding sketch? The employee's responsibility clearly ends with the sales order, and, so long as everything has been taken care of in that respect, everything having been done according to the specific procedures governing her functions, there is indeed no problem. Of course in this case the term "problem" does not apply to the customer, but to the organization; and, insofar as each task is distinct from any other, and since no one cooperates nor has in the short run any common interests with anyone else, it applies to the employee herself, who can relax, since she is free from the worry of being penalized. Even if the rules and procedures which she uses lead to disastrous consequences for customers – and thus to the loss of their business – she is herself covered by this set of procedures, which, as in any bureaucracy, safeguard her more than they secure a positive outcome for the customers. The saleswoman is therefore not responsible for the end result which is a problem only for the customers. Once again, they have been "divided up" by the mini-bureaucracy between the ordering process and delivery, and it is their job to integrate these two distinct parts of the organization. In the end, they will succeed, of course, but just like the automotive suppliers we saw in an earlier example, they will make the organization pay: afraid of a possible legal battle, the company agrees to ship the item to Europe by express mail, an arrangement which costs the small company almost as much as the original quilt. The shop's loss is twofold: on top of the direct cost which is now almost double and which one way or another winds up increasing the cost of other merchandise, there is the cost of lost business.

Small bureaucracies therefore operate just like large bureaucracies, be they public, industrial or service producers: they are organized around a succession of tasks (here product orders and delivery) and not around the customer. They seek to govern their relationships with the latter through company regulations and a friendly smile rather than through cooperation. The end result is that costs rise, as shown in the preceding example. What is more, these practices wind up "protecting" members of the bureaucracy, watering down their responsibilities, and no form of management control can resolve the situation. In the end, they "dissatisfy" their customers, who, if they had a choice, would seek an organization built around them, an organization that would go beyond simple individual service, which is increasingly taken for granted anyway. Once again, even within small organizations, which are often thought to be adaptable and flexible, the determining factor is the mode of functioning: small is not necessarily beautiful in the land of the bureaucrats.[7]

The better a teacher you are, the less you teach!

From the outset, I have tried to draw a distinction between a technical way of thinking and the customer's way of thinking. So be it. But are they really contradictory, or, at the very least, is there not a way to reconcile them, in a final attempt to ward off the coming revolution? The answer to this question will show not only why we are so attached to bureaucracies, but also why our attachment to them is a lost cause.

Let us begin with the extreme end of the spectrum. Some organizations are built so rigidly around their own way of thinking, around their own technical constraints and/or the advantages provided to their own members, that their functioning, the ways they compensate employees – their modes of management in general – act directly against the needs of the customer. A quintessential, rather light-hearted but useful example of this is the French national education system.[8] This huge "company" employs over a million people, which to the author's knowledge makes it, along with its Italian counterpart, one of the largest organizations in the world since the dismantling of the Red Army. The teachers who make a career in this system get there by taking national exams which, in anyone's judgement, are extremely difficult. From this point of view, the French education system is a highly selective bureaucracy. After exams, those who succeed are granted privileges, rewards of all kinds which are greater as a function of the difficulty and thus the level of the hurdles which were overcome.

Now, contrary to what one might expect, these rewards are rarely monetary: salary differences within the organization are relatively small. Instead, the most highly prized benefits are to have a reduced teaching load and to be able to choose one's own courses. Although the system has not always functioned in the same way, in general, whereas a young, unqualified teacher yet to take a major exam (and thus still only an auxiliary teacher) has to teach 22 hours a week of the most difficult classes, a tenured colleague with high-school certification enjoys the lighter load of only 18 or 17 hours. The *agrégé*, who has successfully completed a prestigious national exam (the *agrégation*) faces students only 14 hours per week and may even be allowed to select among courses. Typically, these teachers almost always choose to teach preparatory courses for the French *grandes écoles* – often under the pretext that these are the most interesting classes (for themselves of course), but more realistically because the student–teacher relationships in these courses are tempered by the prospect of very serious exams. At the university level, teaching loads drop to seven or even three hours per week, and at the end of the long journey there is even the possibility of not teaching at all, at which point successful professors can finally enjoy hearing colleagues speak of a "truly successful teaching career".

Here then is an organization which offers its members the ultimate reward: never having to face the customers and their needs. In classes where one ought to find the most highly qualified, the most seasoned teachers, they are young and inexperienced. Whereas experience should be the guarantee of quality instruction, it is nothing but a way out of the "front office", seemingly in accordance with a universal principle of elitist organizations: direct contact with customers is to be avoided. And yet the students have no choice. The teachers they receive are not the ones they need but the only ones the bureaucracy can offer once its own internal procedures for selecting employees and allocating resources have been established. No doubt that the bureaucracy in question has come up with a good deal of unquestionable rhetoric which accounts for its own functioning to those on the outside:[9] the necessity of conducting research, involvement in administrative tasks, and so on. But clearly, if one wanted to redesign the organization around its actual mission rather than around the needs of its members, the resulting system would bear little resemblance to what is seen today: the assignment of classes, of teaching hours, of localities would be based on different criteria and would result, like the "night of August Fourth" during the French Revolution, in the end of privileges. This would be a real revolution, although it would not be all that surprising since it occurred in an organization whose official mission is to teach, rather than to offer its most qualified members the chance to teach less with each successive promotion.

It is also interesting to note that in the world of teaching, whatever or wherever it is, we find the same drive towards specialization and compartmentalization as we did in the health system. The current example of French national education may seem humorous or hopeless – but at the other extreme, can we be sure that an American business school is any different? The top professors – or at least those considered to be the best by their peers – where are they sent? To schools offering MBAs, the "cash cows" of universities, but these programmes are difficult to teach because of the expectation of young students who will grade their professors. So they usually turn to the so-called "tailor-made" programmes which are geared to provide a much more informal relationship with participants, and which allow a better grade. Once again, in these American or European institutions, there is a remarkable balkanization of disciplines which forces students to learn about reality bit by bit, subject by subject, knowing that the only way to achieve global understanding is to give in and follow this piecemeal process. Joint teaching is quite rare, difficult to lead, and most are too afraid to even attempt it. Just like the mythical "multi-disciplinary case studies" about which many speak but rarely teach. In short, in business schools as well, cooperation is nothing but a farce. People speak to one other, but everything takes place in a thick layer of fog. It is up to the student – the customer, in the true sense of the term as far as the business schools are concerned – to integrate it all, to piece the whole picture together as a system.

This explains our fondness for bureaucracies: they offer their members the opportunity to work in predictable environments – by following the rules of the game you will be protected from the outside world. They make it possible, at least in the most sophisticated and high-tech bureaucracies, to barricade oneself behind hyper-specialization, so as not to have to worry about the rest, everyone else, neither one's customers and their needs, nor one's co-workers and what they do. This explains why in these new bureaucracies people are so very fond of technology which provides some substantive grounds for specialization, and which, in a way, legitimizes non-cooperation. Protected by their job status, their entrance exam, their hard-earned tenure, glued firmly to their computer screens through which they have access to a world without having to ask anything of anyone, bureaucrats are building a world where there is no more need to sit down face to face with customers to iron out the most obvious problems caused by compartmentalized functioning. Everything – courses, grades, exams – is automated, making it impossible to argue, and even if it were, there would be no point in it. There are those today who see looming on the horizon new bureaucracies based upon advances in technology, and it looks like they are right.[10] Just how customers might be able to resist these is as yet unclear.

The contradiction between these two ways of thinking – the technically driven organizations and the market-orientated ones – is not always as obvious as in the example presented above, which almost everyone takes for granted, whatever the explanation. Often, the contradiction more ordinarily appears as a series of actions which, although they seem perfectly natural and justified, even insignificant, when placed end to end so as to make up the concrete "organization", wind up producing the opposite of what the customer wants. In such a case, the struggle against bureaucracy usually runs up against two obstacles: first, behind the daily routine there are "privileges", as defined earlier, that is, in terms of the emphasis placed on an organization's own constraints rather than those of the customer; second, to do things differently means that we will have to change the way we think, accepting that there can be several ways of handling a problem, of accomplishing the same mission, a change which, at least at first, is not natural for people caught up in technical, pseudo-scientific routines, and which they fear might weaken them.

The client held as hostage

Let us take a clear-cut example, once again from the airline industry.[11] Say certain customers wish to travel from one European capital to another on a flight which takes about two and a half hours, departing around 6:00 pm. Say they choose to travel with the national airline of the country of their destination. In making the trip, there is a chance that the plane could be on time, but they themselves could arrive late. Such a statement would seem at first to make no sense whatsoever for the airline's technical staff. If the customers' plane is on time, they are on time; if their plane is late, they are late. It is difficult to grasp the difference because, scientifically, there can only be one working definition of an "on-time" flight. Consequently, we have hit upon one area, at least, where the customers and the provider could be reconciled.

Let us think about this somewhat differently in order to shed some light on the differences between these two ways of thinking and how they affect the bureaucracy's functioning. How does the airline calculate whether a flight is on time or not? It uses the departure time of the aircraft rather than its arrival time. This is a purely internal technical standard, of little interest to customers. They would gladly take off a few minutes late if, for example, a favourable jet stream enabled the plane to make up the delay in the air. Let us go a little further. As we saw, we are dealing with the national airline of the country of destination. The plane touches down around 8:30 pm at the airline's hub. Now, let us suppose it will not take off again before the next morning, and for technical reasons – above all, safety – it needs to undergo a daily inspection. Servicing is not done in the boarding area, but some distance from the terminal building. Insofar as the entire organization is built around the succession of tasks, it follows that this plane, having departed and arrived on time, instead of heading straight for the terminal, will go to the servicing area, taking its passengers with it. Once there, they will wait for a bus which usually belongs to the airport rather than the airline. Getting these two to work together is probably more difficult than working just within the airline. And so "It is not our fault, but theirs" is what the impatient passengers will be told by the flight attendants, who themselves can do nothing about it, but who are the only visible link, responsible *de facto* for the entire trip in the eyes of the passengers. Once the bus or buses are full – at the cost of an "abrupt break" in travel which, as we saw earlier, is a real problem for customers – passengers have another wait as the company verifies that a gate is available and that luggage can be quickly transferred.

According to company standards, for the bureaucracy itself, its statistics and self-satisfaction – the plane has arrived on time. Mrs Jane Doe who says to the pilot "You landed on time, but I'm late!" is clearly just as much of a nutcase as the customer who questioned the procedures of the hairdressing salon. She is appealing to a global vision which the segmentation of tasks prevents members of the bureaucracy from having and applying. The passenger is late, in concrete terms, but not statistically, since she will get home perhaps a half hour later than expected. To regain those 30 minutes, that is, to make her somehow more "on time" than the company, implies an alternative, although not necessarily more complicated, way of thinking. What does it mean to be "on time" for the customer? Obviously not when the plane takes off, nor even when it arrives. More likely it corresponds to the moment the passenger arrives in the terminal building. Some American companies have understood this, and, when necessary, ask their pilots to announce the time passengers can expect to deplane, rather than the time when they think the plane will touch down on the runway.

In fact, the problem for those who like bureaucracy so much is not only in making the definition of an "on-time" flight work for those to whom they provide services rather than for themselves; there is the greater problem of putting this new definition into practice. For the airline, how it calculates being "on time" will determine its mode of functioning. Focusing on the customer rather than on the producer means that the succession of tasks will have to be entirely revised (going to the terminal before the servicing area), along with the description of each task (who does what, who announces what, who is responsible for what), perhaps even in how these tasks overlap. This could mean new work schedules, new definitions of rest periods, as well as new methods of employee assessment and review, different forms of compensation, and so on. In other words, just as bureaucracies have been able to take advantage of a system based on their own constraints, customers are going to be able to do the same with a system based on their constraints. Fondness for bureaucracy may soon be little more than a memory.

The end of monopolies

Incidentally, the end of monopolies is really what will seal the fate of this affection. Of all organizations, they are the ones most capable of projecting their own constraints, or the consequences of working arrangements set up among their own members, on to their environment. The simple reason is that in their case customers have no choice, they have nowhere else to go, whatever price they would prefer to pay. They cannot win since there is no contest. The situation is even more acute if the monopoly has a captive clientele: not only has it cornered the market, but in addition its "services" are essential. Doing without them is not a valid option. In theory, this is what distinguishes government healthcare services (European or Canadian social security or American Medicare) from tax services: a well-off beneficiary of social security who is dissatisfied with the programme can choose to opt out and seek different forms of healthcare. Although the choice may be expensive, the beneficiary can still escape monopolistic bureaucracy. There is no chance of this with the IRS: taxpayers cannot choose not to pay taxes simply because they are dissatisfied with the way the programme is run.

I will soon modify this statement somewhat, but even here, we can go beyond the economist's simplistic, somewhat archaic definition of a monopoly (a single vendor and several buyers) and propose a sociological interpretation using the concept of outsourcing, which was developed in the case study of the French ground transport system. A monopoly is an organization – or a system – with the almost unlimited ability to project on to its environment the burden of its constraints and the cost of arrangements set up among its members. It is a little as if, in going out to eat with a friend, you were to ask someone else to pay, a third party who does not partake in the meal. This would make it much easier for the two diners to agree upon a restaurant, since they do not have to foot the bill. In a way, they do not have to cooperate, that is, to negotiate their different interests. This is exactly what a monopolistic situation makes possible. That is why this kind of organization encapsulates one of the most perfect forms of bureaucracy, and its members never give them up with a smile.

At the same time, what we have just said goes against received ideas and rapid assumptions: bureaucracies appear to be present only in the public sector precisely because this is, by definition, a monopolistic state. This last statement has already been qualified. But one now needs to go further and show that seeking this monopolistic state is a feature of all organizations and that when an organization achieves it, it distances itself from the customer in its everyday methods of functioning – in just as radical a fashion as the French national education system which we have observed to be almost a caricature. Such distancing is not the intentional result of any particular actor but is of an eminently *systemic* nature, as illustrated below.

New economy, old bureaucracy

A "global" company – a symbol of inventiveness and success in different sectors of the changing world economy as well as being a world leader for software[12] – was (and, in fact, at the time of writing, is still) enjoying an undisputed but nonetheless paradoxical success: it was seen, from the beginning, as a real "money-making machine", based on a strong performance culture, while at the same time its customers and "partners" – in fact its distributors – have an ever-growing sentiment of having been taken hostage, not to say mistreated and disregarded: the content of contracts linking the company to its customers is defined in a standardized and centralized manner without any possibility of negotiation, and in daily life it is virtually impossible to reach anybody at all by telephone or to obtain reliable information and *a fortiori* any assistance whatsoever.

Normal, one is tempted to say. On a closer look, the only difference between this company and a public body is that the latter benefits from a monopoly that is established (*de jure*) while our company profits from a monopoly that is gained (*de facto*) through the ability to innovate and manage demonstrated first by its founders and then by its managers, not without the repeated occurrence of legal problems. As a general rule, and no matter what country is concerned, public authorities do not have any great liking for monopolies that are not under their control...

But the result, in terms of operating methods and therefore of quality as perceived by the customer, is the same – an organization turned in on itself and made up of members who seek above all to meet endogenous (and for the most part implicit) criteria which influence their careers.

This relatively "pure" example of the "bureaucratic vicious circle" can be described as follows: the French subsidiary that was the subject of our study is in the classic situation of "go-between" between the corporation in the United States and its own customers and partners locally. It is the corporation that decides everything, in terms of contracts and pricing (logic of mass), guaranteeing margins that are more than comfortable (logic of success). However, the local contacts, frustrated by a relationship in which they feel dominated, without any say in the matter and, by definition, without access to the corporation, turn towards the subsidiary's teams which themselves have only little room for manoeuvre. These then develop two well known strategies – either they take sides with the customer, thus reinforcing that customer's resentments, or else they try to restrict the relationship between them. To achieve this, employees benefit from a valuable resource – the organization's traditional compartmentalization (we are indeed in a bureaucracy!) and the very strong internal autonomy that they possess (model of the organization in crumbs). Such autonomy is reinforced by "what has to be done" in the company in order to be "spotted" and therefore develop a worthwhile career path: one needs to be active, mobile, demonstrate that one is capable of adapting very quickly to a new job or a different "function". This ability to adapt is essential since it has a considerable effect on the value of employees on the internal job market. At the same time, autonomy is what makes it possible to select the priorities that help to make this adaptation successful: one therefore needs to "manage one's life" without being intruded upon by the customer or, even better, according to a very typical concept in administrative bureaucracies, use the influx of requests coming from one's surroundings to increase one's own freedom. In return, this increases the incidents with customers and partners: we are indeed in the presence here of an absolutely classic bureaucratic vicious circle – so frequently described except that, in this case, we find it in a company for which the image is the exact opposite, operating on a market that is theoretically open without restriction to competition and where the customer should therefore be triumphant.

At the end of the day, what will actually distinguish this company from a public administration service is precisely its ability – nonetheless observable – to anticipate that such a situation can only be transitory and make the necessary adjustments quickly, vigorously and without any qualms, especially with regard to the relative organizational "comfort" in which its employees live – or used to live. Here, the willingness to adapt to changes in market conditions – complexification of what is available, need to offer services on top of products, arrival of newcomers – is one of the conditions – first of all for maintaining results but also for survival – experienced and assumed by all actors involved in the company.

But, at the same time, it would be a mistake to think that a monopoly is nothing more than one company or one administrative body operating in a real or virtual market. There are monopolies within almost every organization. They are created each time individuals or parts of the organization attempt to clearly define their functions, making sure that they are the only ones to carry out a given task, under the pretext, however false, that if this were not the case, costs would skyrocket. Whenever this situation arises, when, under the pretexts of "clarity" or of avoiding duplicate functions, internal monopolies in fact appear, they behave just like their market brothers or sisters: they externalize on to the rest of the organization the costs of their internal functioning. Clearly, civil servants are not the only ones fond of bureaucracy. All kinds of "rational" people also like bureaucracy – the defenders of job definitions of all kinds, zealots of the "perfect" organizational chart who want to put each part of the organization in a separate box so that once and for all it can be manipulated by its members, even if such a perfect arrangement would never work out.

The preceding discussion also says something about why it is so difficult to change bureaucracy – people are reluctant to give up the advantages of making a third party pay – and why for this reason bureaucracies can only be changed by necessity. For bureaucracy, the customer's victory is a victory because it has extinguished the opportunities for externalization and forces members to find other solutions, which are by definition more difficult insofar as they will now have to split the costs among themselves. This is why the last bureaucracies to initiate their revolution will be those in charge of the kingly functions of the state, and are therefore unlikely to be put on the market. This is, in any case, what they think, but it is all very theoretical, for three reasons.

1. First, because once again it is important not to confuse market and economic market: the public organizations we are dealing with here are on the political market. Their customer is the politician and they can impose their way of thinking on to their environment provided it has a minimal negative effect on the elected official, who in the end is accountable for public administration in the eyes of the electors. The political market is clearly capable of exercising control, as demonstrated in a somewhat callous way by President Reagan, and more discreetly, but firmly, by President Clinton.
2. Next, there are contact, or what one might call capillarity, effects. Customers are increasingly bothered by the fact that they have to pay for the modes of functioning and the lack of cooperation in traditional bureaucracies since many of the organizations they deal with in their daily lives have undergone profound change. What

they once thought was acceptable, legitimate, even natural, becomes intolerable. Above all, they have seen that things can be done differently. They have become critical thinkers; they are more educated, in a way, and it is increasingly tough to get them to believe in "scientific solutions" which are in fact nothing more than partisan deals.

3. Finally, the very concept of a market is changing; it is broadening, providing new avenues of choice to customers who had seemed captive. Let us take a closer look at what is going on in the Internal Revenue Service, a government bureaucracy which up till recently seemed off limits. By way of "loopholes", advantages granted to this or that taxpayer, exemptions applicable in this or that situation, a fully fledged "tax market" has been created which, needless to say, only benefits taxpayers in the highest tax brackets. These fiscal delocalization phenomena, however limited in respect to the number of taxpayers who actually use them, are nonetheless signs of the effect globalization has had on "taxpaying" customers. They are clearly not yet signs of a victory. They show that the battle has begun, and that even those bureaucrats who thought themselves among the most secure are going to have to change their modes of functioning, that is, the ways in which their organization treats those who little by little will no longer be "slaves" but fully fledged customers.

Coordination and cooperation

The most significant characteristics of bureaucracies which we have seen up to this point are, first, the lack of cooperation among members (they protect themselves fiercely from cooperation since it comes at a high human cost), and second, the way bureaucracies project the cost of non-cooperation out on to others (outsourcing). But what is meant by "cooperation", and in particular how does it differ from simple coordination? As we have already seen, coordination is often little more than part of bureaucratic rhetoric with few real consequences for the way they function. Let us return for a moment to Rifkin, who explains how the terms differ in meaning, and points out that one (coordination) is destined to disappear in favour of the other (cooperation):

> No group is hit more harshly than mid-level executives, those traditionally in charge of the coordination of ascending and descending exchanges ... Time-cutting measures force people to react more quickly and to make hasty decisions so as to remain competitive.

In the new realm of the nano-second, the traditional functions of management control and coordination seem unbearably slow and completely unable to respond, in real time, to the speed and volume at which the organization absorbs information.[13]

Further on, he adds: "The arrival of production technologies makes it possible for information to be dealt with horizontally rather than vertically, which in effect brings down the traditional pyramid of the company in favour of networks functioning in one plane." This goes back to an earlier, more general comment by Robert Reich: "The core of a company is increasingly little more than a façade behind which one finds an abundance of decentralized groups and sub-groups which are in contractual relationships with other equally diffuse work units, throughout the whole world."[14] Even production and operations specialists, who no doubt remain implicitly attached to the product-centred way of thinking, make the jump, even if, as we will see, there is a great deal of hesitation. In regard to the management of a "lean production" project, Christer Karlsson and Pär Ahlström write:

> Different aspects of the project are integrated rather than coordinated. Rather than coordinating different activities and diverse groups of personnel from several functional spheres, employees work together. Direct contact and meetings replace the particular functions and resources related to coordination…The team is integrated, which is the result of physical proximity, something which takes place whenever individuals work together in developing a new product.[15]

From these excerpts,[16] we can formulate a better definition of cooperation as opposed to coordination, and even understand why it is such a threat to bureaucracies. Cooperation and coordination have in common that they concern both macro- and micro-organizations. The size of the group in which they are operative is therefore not a distinguishing factor.

Two features of cooperation work together as a cost-reduction mechanism by changing the way in which the organization's members work together.

- First, cooperation does not require a specialized governing body to put it into practice, whereas coordination does. It implies direct contact between the different parts, the face-to-face negotiation of decisions, of choices, of action to be taken. Here we go back to the controversy over markets and hierarchies, as first mentioned by

Oliver Williamson,[17] and, using his distinction, we could say that cooperation depends on the market, whereas coordination depends on the hierarchy, that the first is an adjustment among members, whereas the second is the application of bureaucratic procedures behind which members protect themselves and each other, and which in the end enable them to continue on in their own line of thinking: using specialized vocabulary and transforming every meeting into what Sainte-Beuve described as "a place where one waits for the previous speaker to have finished before taking the floor".

- But the principal difference is this: coordination is sequential, whereas cooperation is simultaneous. Coordination implies that tasks will be clear (in appearance, at least), they will take place in succession, and they will be subject to modification as time goes by. So, going back to the example of the airline industry, there is an attempt to "coordinate" the activities of ground and flight personnel insofar as they occur in succession, one after the other. But, in the end, this coordination actually prevents individuals from cooperating, from confronting one another, enabling them to remain secure in their verticality. We saw earlier, in the case of the automotive industry in particular, that this approach either wears itself out, causing the system to fail, or requires an ever-increasing number of resources to maintain quality products or services.

The simultaneity of cooperation could be a solution – even if only partial – to this problem. It gets individuals to sit down one on one, or more specifically it means that a flight attendant will have to leave the plane when necessary and assist passengers in the waiting room. It means that the pilot will have to get increasingly involved in ground operations, just as the luggage crew in Hong Kong has to take into account how luggage was loaded many hours earlier in London. At the same time, simultaneity compels the different parties to come to an agreement right then and there. It tears down *de facto* all protective barriers, be it those provided by the clarity of tasks, those created by job descriptions, and perhaps in time, those offered by conditions of employment and job benefits. This description is the exact opposite of bureaucracy, which explains why bureaucrats are so opposed to such changes, but more importantly why cooperation is not the usual mode of functioning. As I said, it is not 'natural' for anyone, because it entails confrontation and conflict, and because in general people prefer avoidance and disinterested consensus. We also see why cooperation cannot simply be proclaimed, it cannot be obtained by some simple proof that it is better to cooperate. It has to be understood by each and every individual. It has to be made possible, rational for those involved, as will be argued in the following section. This is more or less what a Japanese manager meant when he said:

> One of the essential tasks is to create an environment in which all of our employees want to cooperate freely and to make them want to constantly improve themselves. With this in mind, it is essential that we provide them with all kinds of information, regardless of their rank or title. Every employee has the right to consult "all" information available through our computer networks.[18]

This is a very Japanese approach to getting people interested in co-operation, but it serves as a good starting point for creating a favourable environment for the implementation of new ways for employees to work within their organizations.

Since they do not understand this dimension, some organizations skip the creation of a favourable environment and attempt to use some more or less sophisticated form of pressure: this is to try to change bureaucracy by force, using bureaucracy against bureaucracy, and in the long run such a practice seems doomed to failure.[19] This is what Edgar Morin and Sami Naïr describe with zeal in their chapter entitled "Libéralisme, démocratie et avenir" (Liberalism, democracy and the future):

> Since the start of the 1980s, in both the private and public sectors, the system has tended to impose increasing harsh forms of "management" ... This is why we are experiencing the very real destabilization of methods of leadership and human resource management.[20]

The human resource director cited in Chapter 2 wanted to turn his executives into Olympic heroes ...

Indeed, these are the issues facing us, and it would be foolish to claim that it is going to be easy. We know that giving up bureaucratic forms of organization comes at a high cost to individuals, or at least that is what they fear whether they are confronted with the idea or it is forced upon them. In the author's view, this explains to a great extent the severity of change phenomena, as well as the tendency to back away from these challenges, which only increases the ultimate cost of change. Finally, we see that the lack of a methodological approach and the lack of an understanding of human behaviour within organizations, lead us to draw solutions from draconian and stressful forms of management, which in the end only raise the human cost of the process, therefore solidifying resistance a little more, which in turn requires more pressure, and so on.

A vicious circle is created through resistance to change in which everyone is a loser. If this is the case, is there some other way of approaching the problem, some way to lessen the human cost and create conditions in which change is "workable" for those involved? The author's response is yes. The approach offered here, as we will see, begins with knowledge and the sharing of knowledge, and culminates in the opportunity to "think the unthinkable". I will illustrate the process with examples – case studies – which demonstrate as best as possible how it might be applied in the real world. They will help us see that nothing is predetermined, and provided that we are able to think about reality in new ways, that we can show others how to do likewise, and that we can be more confident about everyone's ability to come up with solutions, then even the most "case-hardened" bureaucracies should be able to generate and put into practice their own possibilities for change.

5
Change, Yes, but Change What?

The characteristics that we have seen for a bureaucracy – or more precisely a technical bureaucracy – make up a system. This means that they have developed coherence in relation to one another, that they mutually reinforce and strengthen each other and make it extremely difficult and perilous to define and implement a controlled process of change. This explains the quantity and diversity of literature on change (we will return to this later on) as well as the ever-renewed quest among executives for a "philosopher's stone", a recipe that allows one, with a minimum of risk-taking, to find out what one needs to do in order to have it accepted by the social structure and put into operation while at the same time controlling its effects. For a better understanding of the problem that this poses, let us take a quick look at the five points which today form the nucleus of such bureaucracies when forced to change under pressure from the customer, if they do not want to disappear or implode and at the same time produce a pointlessly high human cost:

1. compartmentalization and verticality, constructed in line with the technical logic of speciality and task;
2. clarity, perceived as virtuous in itself, but where one has seen that it ends in the creation of internal monopolies, and finally by the organization's manipulation by its members;
3. non-cooperation, which resolves the individual problem of difficulty in facing others, but at the same time dramatically increases the cost of running the whole system;
4. endogeneity of criteria for personnel management, that is, the fact that such criteria are defined in relation to the constraints of an organization's members themselves, and not in relation to the tasks that such an organization is supposed to accomplish;

5. lastly, the outsourcing phenomena that encompass the four above characteristics and render them possible by placing the cost – and not only in financial terms – on the "environment", that is, in more concrete terms on the customer.

To conclude, let us once again emphasize that these characteristics are found in all types of organization, as soon as this has a total or partial monopoly in place, whether this is *de jure* or *de facto*.

Changing a winning team

Here, the question that arises is this – can one reasonably hope to "unravel" a bureaucracy other than at the time of a major crisis that is important enough to legitimize change and allow bold innovations that would be unthinkable in the normal course of events? The use of the word "unravel" is intended to highlight the complexity of the task, since the systemic nature of bureaucracy, the cohesion of its structures, its methods of recruitment, its principles of appraising, remunerating, promoting its members, its collective capacity to resist attempts to produce change "smoothly", as well as its skill at digesting reforms and thus rendering them without real effect,[1] give the image of a skein of wool. Where do we start? Paradoxically, this is a question that bureaucrats themselves are asking with a great deal of seriousness. Most of the time, it leads them to a global vision of change – one can only change things by changing everything, by an overall plan, preferably after having anticipated everything and sewn in all loose ends. However, this line of action condemns one to immobility and finally cynicism – why should one be successful one day where so many have already failed? One might as well give up, deal with first things first and let the succession of managers do the rest. Bad luck to whoever is in the job when everything goes up in flames!

At the same time, this strategy of lying low inevitably leads to using a crisis as an opportunity for change. This can show itself in many ways – either a drama which fundamentally challenges the running of one or more organizations (cf. the health-check system in France during the summer of 2003); or successive failures that make it impossible to implement a strategy and thus penalize the market. We will be returning to this in Chapter 10, which focuses on the "moment of change".

Executives often believe that their own desire for change is opposed by the hopeless conservatism of their troops[2] or their representatives; meanwhile these troops are shouting that for as long as the summit is proof of such immobilism, it will indeed be difficult to envisage the slightest evolution. It is while on the subject of such mechanisms that Chris Argyris speaks of "defensive organizational routines".[3] Indeed in these endless discussions on change, certain people, whom one might consider to be very optimistic, see its necessity as well as the resistances which oppose it – the very start of the process: "A change of direction often starts when enough people talk about it, before really knowing what it is", write Waterman, Peters and Phillips.[4] Experience makes one sceptical when faced with such a statement.

More generally, the diversity of literature on the subject is a record of such debates and hesitations on how to proceed. We will not be going over that here.[5] We shall content ourselves with inventorying a few terms of discussion, emphasizing a certain number of deceptive illusions, and highlighting the point of agreement that gradually reveals itself – the importance of knowledge – listening and sharing of knowledge – as soon as one really wants to take action on organizations.

And first of all, what is it that legitimizes change, the nature of which most authors agree to be unnatural? In a word, we have already said it – "crisis", difficulty, malfunctions and, very often, urgency. Erhard Friedberg writes: "In brief, change is always 'impossible' in big and not so big organizations, and there are always a thousand good reasons for not changing, for not destabilizing the pillars of the existing way of doing things."[6] This is echoed by the metaphor from the sports world, "You don't change a winning team." One only starts making adjustments if the team has lost, if there is no other choice. It is enough to emphasize the reactive rather than proactive nature of change. It is rarely a process of anticipating or even accompanying transformations in the environment. It is always a reaction to symptoms where one must wait for them to become extremely serious before they trigger an action. "You don't change a winning team" really means that even if the team plays badly, even if it shows obvious signs of weakness, victory – however provisional it may be – legitimizes its continued existence.

"One continues to govern solely in urgency", points out a top French civil servant[7] and former trade unionist, who was at the heart of the restructuring of regions in decline and sectors undergoing change. When sometimes this is not the case, when one wants to overturn something that does not appear to be experiencing any particular problem, one provokes astonishment and circumspection. And when the manager of the French judo team – an Olympic discipline in which France has been a brilliant example over recent decades – exclaims "You don't change a winning team!", the headline is shown across seven columns in the national daily sports paper.[8] To the question that managers throughout the world ask themselves every day and that is put to him by the journalist, "French judo is successful in the very long term. Do you have a miracle recipe?", he answers:

> Never being satisfied with anything. If something works, it must be broken, otherwise one settles into routine. Unlike many federations, we have no hesitation in changing a winning team. That's judo. We have a continual culture of combat. If you let yourself fall into routine, you're dead. You're already behind.[9]

Basically, Rosabeth Moss Kanter says the same when she invites the American giants to make the effort to reappraise things before it is too late.[10] This issue of the legitimacy of change was part of the writer's personal experience when asked by the director of a big internationally successful company – a world leader in its market – to work on its organization in order to adapt it to what he saw as the future for its business. However powerful this executive may have been at the time, he had never succeeded in motivating his management people – even those who were closest to him – to accompany him in his approach. Everybody used the excellence of the company's results against this.[11]

Nonetheless, any discussion on the difficulty of change, any implication of other people's responsibility in order to explain immobilism – and therefore the need for a crisis to make things possible – cannot form a blockage to the following concept, which I am convinced will be at the heart of future debates and therefore also at the heart of future difficulties: at the start of this new century and across a large part of Western Europe, organizational change (that is, actually trying to change what people do[12]) is perceived as a threat and indeed often as a step backwards. Since the resource became scarce concurrently with the customer's victory, incessant recourse to the word "reform", including where it is used to impose the observation that it is no longer possible today to offer what was guaranteed yesterday in terms of welfare protection, retirement or, more seriously, general working conditions, has made the actors involved, and in particular the most deprived or weakest, extremely distrustful and cautious. Setting against them a simple economic fatalism is not – or not any longer – enough to convince them, in the same way that denouncing their conservatism, their exaggerated attachment to their "acquired benefits", only serves, as shown by experience, to make them more radical.

As we will be seeing later on, it is in that sense that the teaching effort – which cannot be reduced to a communication effort since communication is a weak version of teaching – is crucial. This is so, in order not only to make the "necessities" more acceptable, since their legitimacy can always be disputed in terms of organization (for what, for whom does one work? What is the true end-purpose of the work and hence the organization?), but also to negotiate the terms and conditions of application with the actors themselves.

It is thus understandable how the necessary anticipation of the future in order to legitimize change, the difficulty in undertaking and implementing it even before the storm clouds are seen or understood by anybody else, can feed the current fascination for a leader and his "vision". I will return later on to this approach which I consider to be partly illusion. But it clearly highlights the paradox of modern organizations, in which nobody has the necessary room for manoeuvre for adjusting things while the "indicators" are good, at the very time when they should be getting ready, anticipating and even benefiting from the company's healthy situation in order to undertake in peace and quiet what will have to be done later in storm and tempest. Since there is nothing "concrete" to justify such action, one counts on that quality of "vision" which is literally impalpable to common mortals. And one could even say that counting on the executive's "vision" or leadership in this manner goes against the trust that one might naturally place in the organization's members, in terms of initiating a process of change as well as – why not, after all? – helping to achieve it successfully. Unfortunately, trust is not part of the culture of elites nor even, through the system, of that of the troops. Everyone is used to looking towards the executive and his know-how, in normal times, or his vision, in times of crisis. And yet who has not noticed, only looking at the example of Air France, the necessity of long, hard and painful strike action, with occupation of runways, that is, affecting the work tool, in order to legitimize the first true process of change undertaken by this company? And, from having been at the heart of this process, I would like to emphasize how much the unions contributed to the definition of "doing things differently", the acknowledgement of its necessity and likewise its implementation, and was in fact a key factor for its success. But things had to be pushed by events to actually get there!

Even when the necessity for change is recognized and accepted, the problem is still a long way from being resolved. Must one, as suggested by Michel Crozier, start by acting on the summit – although this deals specifically with the French situation – because of the difficulty here in understanding that what is happening penalizes the overall evolution?[13] Must change, to the contrary, be undertaken "in plants or departments a long way away from general management", as suggested by a number of other writers,[14] in order to then be transmitted via capillarity? The answer is of course largely contextual. However, the question suggests taking one step further – observing that change also is systemic. We will be seeing, further on in this book,[15] that this can be thought out not only in terms of priorities but also in terms of levers, that is, points in the system on which one can act and where one can reasonably assume that, when combined with others, they will strengthen each other in order to produce change.

Is this the business of individuals or of organizations? In other words, does one need to change people, their "psychology", their "mentality", in order for organizations to evolve, or else does one first need to transform the organizations – here largely assimilated to structures – in order for individuals to adapt to them? Beer, Eisenstadt and Spector think that the first strategy is bound to fail, and that it is even one of the principal identifiable factors of immobilism. They write:

> Most change programmes do not work because they are based on a fundamentally false premise. In fact, the theory explains that a change in individual attitudes leads to a more general evolution of behaviour. A change in behaviour, repeated hundreds of times by different people, ends up by having an effect across the whole organization. According to this model, change is like a conversion experiment. It is enough to inculcate the "right religion" in people for behavioural modifications to immediately follow ... This theory is an accurate description of the other side of a change process. In fact, individual behaviour is very strongly fashioned by the role that the individual is made to play in the company. The most effective way of modifying behaviour is therefore to place individuals in a new organizational context.[16]

Experience has shown me that these authors are right and I will try, in the following pages, to provide tools for constructing this "new organizational context".

Other approaches recommend a combination of both levels – that of personal transformation and that of organizational transformation[17] – emphasizing that it is the transformation of individuals that leads to the transformation of organizations. It seems to me, however, that the less understanding one has of the complexity of the situations in which they are evolving (that is, systems), the greater the burden for necessary change that is placed on individuals, on their psychology or their good-will, as described by Fitoussi and Rosanvallon:

> It is also essential to understand the entanglement of situations and positions for different individuals in order to appreciate what may look like resistance to change. What is described as blockages in the company refers, in many cases, only to an insufficiently close analy-sis of the conflicting characteristics of individuals.[18]

Even if this can shock or surprise, it is less a question of asking the var-ious people involved to change their attitude or mindset and convinc-ing them to do things differently, than of finding the organizational levers for persuading them to behave differently. If change – in organ-izations, it is understood – were a matter of individual psychology or mentality, its implementation would be even more likely to be left to chance or indefinitely postponed. In the next chapter, when I show that actors do what they do because they are intelligent (in the sociological sense of the term) and that, at the end of the day, we have no problem with human stupidity but only with intelligence, this is not proof of a blissful optimism. Instead, it will emphasize the difficulties involved in change (since one can no longer tell meaningless stories to people), while at the same time demonstrating the possibilities.

If we listen and understand the rationality of actors – together with its systemic dimension – we will open out some paths for action. And yet such points for action, in order to be found outside of the global and megalomaniac plans that we were discussing earlier, presuppose the ful-filment of two conditions that our experience leads us to think of as essential. The first of these is a shared diagnosis of the problem or, to put it differently, the existence of a minimum of consensus between the organization's members on the real nature of the problem that is revealed behind the symptoms. This shared diagnosis cannot only result in spontaneous discussion, simply by bringing the actors together around a table. It must be fed by what we will later describe as a "listening" function by the organization and indeed its members. This paves the way for real discussion and helps to avoid the controversies and feelings of guilt which immediately block the process of change. The second condition, as I have already said, is to have enough trust in people to be able to ask them, once agreement has been reached on the problem, to play an active and dynamic part in drawing up solutions. How can one think that a meeting between the CEO and a consultant, even when they are the most intelligent people in the world, could possibly take the place of the creativity of an organization's members, provided they have been given the appropriate information? What is more, such an approach will subsequently give legitimacy to decisions that management will be called on to make with a view to establishing the implementation of change.

If the observations drawn up in preceding chapters are correct, then our organizations must make profound and continual changes if they want to adapt to a world which has revolutionized them and will continue to do so. No doubt this is why management literature produces every day an impressive catalogue of "new organizations", new structures, new concepts which interpret quite clearly the proliferation of initiatives virtually everywhere in order to face up to the ever-increasing number of challenges. Even businesses in the "new world economy" do not escape this movement – between 1999 and 2000, eBay, Amazon.com and AOL announced deep-seated reorganizations, intended to adapt their organization to a market that was undergoing substantial changes. In 2003, Microsoft did likewise – noting the erosion of its monopolistic position and trying to assess the consequences. From practice communities to cooperation, presented as the key factor for cost cutting and continual improvement of quality, not a day goes past without the appearance on the market of new ideas and practices in terms of organization. This consensus and proliferation result, at one and the same time, in pressure exerted on the organizations and hesitations in the responses made to such pressure. There is no longer a place today, as there was in the good old days of mass production or, more recently, in the times of triumphant Toyotism, for a dominant model that imposes itself and provides a key guaranteeing performance under optimal conditions.

In fact, there is no longer any model at all that really focuses on the nature of the organizations that need to be set up, nor on their structures, nor on how to steer them. At present, caution and good sense seem to have won the day by giving priority to the methodologies of steering change rather than to the substance which predefines what must exist.[19] This position, although at first glance less reassuring for managers, is nonetheless far more realistic. It formally acknowledges the fact that organizations are now infinitely more varied than in the past, because they are no longer in a position to impose methods of operation on their markets, allowing them then to resolve their own problems, whether technical or human, rather than resolving those of their customers. They can no longer impose uniformity on an environment which now insists on individuality. The response to this individuality is even more difficult to provide because the universes have themselves become more complex, the number of "individualities" to be taken into consideration has never stopped rising alongside the simultaneous appearance of increasing numbers of contradictions between the end results that are needed in order to satisfy everybody.

Even "best practices", so popular because they make it possible to learn from the experience of others, have become more methodological than substantive: in an article published by the *Harvard Business Review*, Jerry Stermin and Robert Choo[20] show how, in terms of change, companies could benefit enormously from the experience of non-profit organizations. Analysing what they call "the power of positive deviancy", they tell the story of an association working to reduce malnutrition in Vietnamese children: having seen that the children of one village community seemed better fed and more healthy, they tried to find out why. They quickly realized that this community had different behaviour patterns, with regard to both what they ate and how often they ate. They therefore tried, with some success, to extend these deviant practices to the surrounding villages. However, they concluded that it was not the types of food – eating more or less fish or greens – which formed the basis of the problem, but the reasoning, that is, the demonstration that it was possible to do things differently from what tradition seemed to have established once and for all. In modern business language, we might call that experimentation.

A theoretical debate: to centralize or to decentralize?

Organizations are all in the same situation, whether public or private. They are desperately trying to find out what is best, most of the time in terms of structures, and yet are unwilling to invest in methodology – which can indeed be more demanding but so much more rewarding. This is how it has been for years – and still is today – in the theoretical debate on the choice between centralization and decentralization. This debate has marked the industrial world for many long years, often in Manichean terms, opposing the two alternatives in a way that makes it obligatory to choose either one or the other, under pain of being accused of incoherence or muddled thinking.[21] And yet …

In a big European industrial glassmaking group – we are talking here about flat glass – eight factories are handling production based on a strictly identical formal organization, a prime example of the irresistible search for coherence which has just been mentioned. Under the apparent authority – or leadership, we might say today – of the factory manager, three deputy managers share out the day-to-day tasks: the technical manager looks after everything relating to the factory's core activity, that is, production and maintenance, which he controls so jealously that even the factory manager himself thinks twice about going round the workshops; the administrative and financial manager watches over compliance with management rules in force within the group, which he is expected to see applied in a manner that is strictly identical for all production units; finally, the manager in charge of human relations manages labour relations, within the scope of a national collective agreement and a company agreement covering day-to-day administration – agreements which were negotiated at branch level for the first and at group level for the second – without the factories having been particularly involved in these negotiations between partners who already knew each other well and didn't have to spell things out for each other.

In this context, it is clear that it is the technical manager who really holds the reins of power.[22] He is the one with exclusive control over what is the factory's reason for being, over how it is evaluated and therefore over the conditions for its survival. And even more so because this example is seen at a time when, faced with the group's need to adapt its technical resources, head office still has the prerogative of privileging sites which it considers to be the most cost-effective. Like all actors, the technical manager uses this power with a view to career management which, after all, is the driving force for any organization: in order to achieve what he wants, that is, carrying out production under optimal conditions while ensuring the full development of industrial equipment, he needs to "buy" all his teams or, in other words, obtain for them dispensations from the group's rigid rules, whether in terms of promotion, grading or remuneration. In order to reach his goals, he applies constant pressure on his colleagues whom, at the end of the day, he considers more as subordinates than equals. Meanwhile, they have no intention of allowing themselves to be "manipulated" in such a way, and so, although they understand what is going on, they hide behind central procedures, thus making things ever more complicated, ever more difficult to achieve and negotiate – an autonomy which the technical manager is always seeking to put through as profit or loss. In brief, this is a classic example of the "bureaucratic vicious circle" that we are able to observe.

Systemic reasoning enables us to understand the consequences of this game, at the end of the day without any great surprises, at the level of the flat glass division itself: central management "functional staff" feed on these local conflicts which help to legitimize their action, and find that their correspondents "on the spot" are partners who are always looking for more of these rules and procedures which protect them from the absolute power of technical logic. To put it briefly, each level reinforces the next without anybody, throughout the progress of each particular decision, anticipating the overall effect of all the micro-decisions.

Added to this is an inflationist drift, linked to the dissociation between *real power* and *formal power*. The factory manager's position of extreme weakness leads him to seek compensations elsewhere than in the effective management of a unit from which, to all intents and purposes, he is excluded. In order to legitimize his role, he has virtually no other means than to always be asking central financial management for more investment, more financial resources, which will allow him to demonstrate that he is capable of playing a positive and active role in the day-to-day running of the factory. However, there are eight factories in this division, which means eight managers all developing the same strategy of asking for additional financial resources.

We should note here that this is a constant in the life of organizations: *when a line manager lacks the organizational resources to be a relevant actor in the universe that he is supposed to be directing, he always asks for more physical resources, whether in financial or human terms.* This is why the dissociation mentioned above, between real power and formal power, poses a problem that is not aesthetic or moral, but entirely practical: it leads to an ever-growing need for resources – not for objective reasons of real needs, but for reasons that can only be qualified as systemic.

In the case that we are looking at, it is thus the eight factory managers who are placed in the same situation and thus develop the same strategy of "always more". To get what they need so as not to disappear completely from the game, they manipulate the information that they transmit in support of their various and varied requirements. But the actors who are in charge of allocating resources have finally ended up understanding the game. Incapable or perhaps unconcerned about carrying out the necessary corrections and arbitrations themselves, they allocate resources in line with a bureaucratic logic which enables them to minimize their own risks. At the end of the day, more has been spent without the resources allocated being suited to real situations and without anybody being really satisfied.

The organization "consumes" huge quantities of resources without in fact seeing an increase in its efficiency. This simple observation helps to anticipate to what extent it is a change in the methods of functioning, that is, the way in which the actors "play", which will become the crucial factor in the process of transformation.

Many will see themselves in the quick presentation which has just been made: there's nothing original about this example. However, incidentally, it helps people to understand some of the very real mechanisms behind the non-control of costs that management accounting tools do not always allow them to grasp. But going beyond this observation, if one investigates possible solutions, one might well reach the conclusion that this universe needs centralization *as well as* decentralization: centralization, because breaking out of the inflationist vicious circle that is revealed would presuppose transferring control over the factory's "core activity", in this case responsibility for servicing and maintenance; but decentralization as well because, while central departments are padded out to such an extent, they will always need to produce more standards and to find allies who will use them as resources in their local strategies.

Here are two useful and amusing anecdotes to illustrate the above. When the technical manager at the biggest factory was himself made factory manager, he immediately requested, and was granted, that the job of technical manager be abolished in his new unit. In the same way, when the results of this diagnostic work were shown to the group's CEO, he showed himself to be dubious about the need for drastically reducing staff levels in the central human resource department ... until the day when he saw, under the windows of his own office, situated in a well-to-do suburb in the capital, twenty or so workers from a factory located somewhere far away in the distant provinces fiercely demanding an increase in their job grading coefficient, for the reason that the person in charge of such questions in the factory had led them to understand that such a decision could only be made at the highest level. You might call this active learning.

It is not therefore mainly through the use of substantial models, which are nonetheless very popular among managers and directors, that one can manage the problem of change. In any case, it is common knowledge that most of them have already fallen by the wayside, although this does not seem to stop people from suggesting new ones. Their therapeutic value, which comes close to how paediatricians describe their role – that of reassuring mothers – cannot be denied. But that is not enough on its own to legitimize its exclusive use on a daily basis. We will therefore be forced to turn towards *methodology*, that is, reasoning, and accept that progress will be slow and sometimes hesitant, without the hope of covering all aspects of a process of change, and without the possibility of escaping from all those lucky or not so lucky surprises that this process is certain to hold.

Change by acting on structures

But perhaps, first of all, we should avoid putting the cart before the horse and try to reach agreement *on what needs to be changed,* once we decide our organization must evolve. With regard to this aspect, the first temptation has always been, implicitly or explicitly, to give an answer in terms of structures, and to see the driving force of change in the modification of organization charts, in the rearrangement of responsibilities, in the amendment of rules and procedures. Many debates have nurtured this vision of things, if only those focusing on the advantages and disadvantages of "flat structures" as opposed to more hierarchical structures, on the merits and drawbacks of "matrix structures", and so on... These cause directors and the consultants that they hire to continually redefine the "processes", the job descriptions, the organization charts – based on the belief that all these things will in fact correspond to the reality. And yet, when one looks closely, there is a curious paradox hidden behind this way of doing things.

It is commonplace to assert that an organization cannot be reduced to a structure and/or set of rules and procedures, to the contrary in fact of a belief that has always been firmly anchored in companies and, *a fortiori*, in administrations where legal state rhetoric vigorously maintains the illusion of legislation. If the organizations were functioning in accordance with their procedures, one would have a great difficulty in explaining phenomena such as the work-to-rule or zeal strike, which consists simply of applying them to their fullest extent.

Similarly, one might conclude that this abundance or even, *a fortiori*, overabundance of procedures, makes organizations even less predictable even though its purpose is to instil clarity and transparency. This is what one might call the "paradox of regulations"[23] which, in the most bureaucratic organizations, produces reversed hierarchies, that is, situations in which the managers manifestly depend more upon subordinates than subordinates upon managers, to the extent that the inapplicability of rules forces the latter to call increasingly upon the goodwill of the former... who themselves expect ever more regulations, on the one hand to cover themselves and, on the other, to increase their own freedom.

This assimilation of the organization to the structure also leads to an entirely static and abstract vision of power, according to which power is seen as the equivalent of the official hierarchy. Outside of any theoretical discussion – and there is more than enough of that – if this was true, it would become very difficult to explain why, in so many organizations, when one wants to get rid of a troublesome actor, this actor is given a promotion and, what is more, is usually under no illusion as to the meaning of the reward that he has just received.

But there is more, and even more serious. The distinction between organization and structure has direct consequences on the *strategy* of change. In particular, it legitimizes the preference for a participative approach, which will be the case throughout this book. For, if an organization was able to reduce itself to its corpus of rules and written standards, then changing it could be effected by injunction, based on an extensive use of consultants commissioned to redefine and redesign the new entity, after a rapid analysis. If, to the contrary, one understands that there is a great deal more to change and that one must look towards real behaviours – or strategies, as we will come to say – then one must rely far more on trust, on the development of capabilities, on the inventiveness of all those involved.[24]

Paradoxically, this idea is relatively well accepted intellectually but little used in practice. A big company, a world leader in its market, came to see us with the following question: over the previous year, with help from a large and well known consulting firm, it had redefined a new structure that was better suited to the perception that it had of its market. The past twelve months had been devoted to setting out the new principles in terms of management rules, accounting rules, reporting rules, human resource rules, and so on … Our contacts told us that this now involved putting in place the methods of functioning, that is, the actual way in which actors would use what had just been developed at huge expense. In brief, it was now finally necessary to look closely at the organization, and those responsible were well aware that this would not only be more difficult than the preceding phase and in quite different ways but, even more importantly, could not be conducted in the same manner. Already, the troops were grumbling against the ambient *authoritarianism*, and pressure was mounting more and more strongly for everybody to be called on to participate in the next phase – the only one that really counted in the eyes of all those concerned.

What has just been recounted through this example appears to be a matter of common sense, especially as, when told like this, in simple terms, it wins everybody's support. And yet the consequences in terms of change are only rarely deduced, and companies continue to prefer approaches focusing on structures, once they have accepted the need to modify their organization. In so doing, they have control over neither the *process* that they have implemented, nor the *results* that they achieve, thus increasing the unwillingness of managers to take action, as well as the phenomena of resistance from those who, rightly or wrongly, feel that their territory is under threat.

An outside observer is sure to be fascinated by the amount of time, energy and, of course, money expended in this way on laboriously defining the "new structures", new processes, new rules – and all this for results that are inadequate if not diametrically opposed to those that were officially expected. Surprisingly, this can open up room for action: a manager's biggest worry, when he has just exhausted his political talents in implementing an organization chart acceptable to everybody, is that he will be expected to rework it. In a confidential manner, his colleagues let him know that they can take "anything, but not that". Which means that everything is possible! More, even – it also signifies greater freedom for working on the day-to-day reality provided the end results are acceptable. Sometimes directors themselves call for this work that they vaguely feel the need for.

This is what happened in a major North American company in the food processing sector. In order to cope with expansion and diversification, it needed to rapidly develop one of its factories, until then in single production, towards a capacity for rapid changeover of brands or products in line with market requirements. To this was added the necessity for a fast improvement in quality together with the eradication of delays in terms of product availability. That was a lot to ask. A new factory manager was appointed and the project for change was put in his hands. Seconded to him were a number of young and ambitious managers, of good level, with whom he formed his executive committee. These young managers, looking on their stay in this factory as only a minor step in their career paths, represented the group's functional management divisions on the site, such as the industrial division, all of which were big producers of regulations and procedures intended to harmonize the overall procedures for doing things in all of the group's factories.

Nothing worked as planned. The executive committee never managed to reach an integrated vision, and each member took refuge in his own particular logic without worrying about the rest. As a result, procedures were seen as too complex, obscure and contradictory, piling up one on top of another. Payroll costs rose because of the need for new recruits to manage the increasingly complicated dealings with the rest of the group. At the end of day, the manager was given to understand that his true job consisted of bending the rules, and that it was his ability to adapt which would be evaluated in priority. It was from that moment on that he was able seriously to get to work and instigate the necessary changes.

The declaration of good tax conduct

Here is another example of the mechanisms that we have described above, which, in this particular case, takes place in the public sector and shows that nobody has a monopoly on blindly following rules. In the French tax administration office, there is a conventional – although not legally defined – distinction between the "certifying officer", who calculates the amount of tax payable, and the "accountant" who deals with its collection, even if such separation suffers from a certain number of exceptions depending on the type of taxation. The result of this, of course, is a huge complexity for the taxpayer, who, even if sometimes able to use the situation to his advantage, is generally shunted from one department to another, from one person to another and watches, powerlessly, over the improbable routing of his increasingly "virtual" file. Of course, the people in charge of this administration are not unaware of such difficulties and, under the pressure of public opinion, conveyed by the spur of political power, it was decided to try out the idea of a "single tax representative" who would be available, in a single location, to respond to questions and requests from taxpayers. This happy initiative was tried out on a single specific case – delivery of the "declaration of good tax conduct".

Under this fancy name is hidden a simple mechanism – that of the usual technical bureaucracies – which can be described as follows: when an individual or a business decides to take part in a public invitation to tender, they must demonstrate that they are in order with regard to their payment of taxes and social security contributions. The intention is certainly praiseworthy, and it meets a need from businesses themselves which would like to be able prevent competitors from being able to put in lower bids than them through not paying their various liabilities to the state and social security bodies.

So there are in fact three different documents that are needed: the first stating that one has properly paid one's taxes, obtained from the French Inland Revenue; the second certifying that one has paid one's value added tax, delivered by their local tax office; and the third confirming that one is up to date with filing one's tax declarations, obtained from the tax office. It is easy to see all the difficulty and time involved in such procedures. This was why a ministerial circular ruled that, as of a given date, it was the paymaster who would deliver this precious document, with the responsibility of obtaining the necessary papers from colleagues in other departments concerned and within the required time limit for responding to the invitation to tender.

The result is easy to picture: it rapidly became apparent that delivery of the notorious declaration was proving extremely difficult, if not actually impossible in certain cases, causing the unfortunate paymaster in charge of delivering it to provide whoever applied for it with a "default declaration", which in fact states the *organizational* impossibility of delivering the document in question, a declaration which is even more useless in that it does not authorize participation in the invitation to tender, even when this is issued by one of the bodies which has contributed to the above-mentioned default. This situation might well be qualified as grotesque.

Why such a stalemate in what was indeed an attempt at change focusing on a real problem which arises frequently for the customer/taxpayer? Are those who made the decision unaware and are those who applied it irresponsible? Certainly neither one nor the other. Quite simply, each side believed that what was written into the rule would actually happen, and that action is produced by the text which defines it. This is a vision of action which can be described as bureaucratic or linear, as opposed to a strategic and systemic vision which I will define later and which is often very far removed from how managers reason, whether in the public or the private sector.

In reality, things turned out rather like this. Between the different organizations involved, there exist traditional rivalries which we will not be expanding on here, but which result in each side watching jealously over their autonomy and, if given the opportunity, with no hesitation in complicating the other side's task in order to really convey their situation of dependency. To this can be added the jealousies linked to differences in official or non-official remunerations. The paymaster, in the system which has just been described, arouses a certain amount of animosity because the others, rightly or wrongly, feel that he is in a privileged position. From the moment that he is asked to be the sole point of contact for the requester, *in a situation where he is dependent on others in order to reply to the request,* these others will not be prepared to put the necessary enthusiasm and speed into the task. Even worse, and here the example invites reflection on the perverse effects of uncontrolled action, from the bidding company's point of view, one finds a situation far worse than the one which was hopefully being remedied: in the earlier situation, however painful the procedures might be, the requester still retained a certain level of control over the process. He could go to the offices, pressurize or even plead. In this new situation, not only is it more difficult to obtain the necessary papers, but the requester cannot even have access to those who deliver them.

His degree of control over the situation is singularly affected and finally the *quality* of the service provided has deteriorated. This is not a mechanism affecting only the system which has just been described.[25]

What is really at stake, therefore, is not the "right rules", those saying how things *ought* to be. We should always bear in mind that, when talking of action, the conditional tense has only negative virtues. It is used more for self-protection than for getting things moving. This does not imply that rules are pointless – after all, what is an organization without rules? – nor that they cannot be used as *levers*, but rather that one must get away from visions that are mechanistic, simplistic and blinkered. And the same can be said for the "right structures", those defining where each person should be and what they should be doing. This approach to change as a mechanical exercise ends up in the same dead-ends, one might almost say the same lottery, so random is the final result with so much remaining to be done for whoever wants to control it.

Formal organization and real organization

Michael Hammer and Steven Stanton give a very illustrative example of this observation in analysing the reasons for failure in the transition from a conventional organization to a process organization. They observe that this change was conducted, at least to start with, by "redesigning" the company's structures, and that this strategy resulted in a dead-end to the extent, as they put it, that, even when the design was good, the real organization was opposed to it. They observe that "the problem was not the *design* of the process, but the fact that the power continued to be held by the former functional departments".[26] The simple fact of distinguishing, as do these authors, between *organization* and *real organization* tells us more than all those sophisticated theories on the extraordinary abstraction of structures and organization charts.

Despite their appearance of solidity – no doubt relating to the fact that they are relatively easy to understand, to put into writing, and therefore to develop with a mere stroke of the pen; at least in theory, since we then arrive at the problem of implementation – they are still a long way away from the reality of those involved. The fact that such theories are preferred can have dramatic consequences to the extent that managers feel that by working in this way they are doing something useful, while those directly concerned are convinced that nobody is interested in what has meaning for them, that nobody is really listening to them.

In fact, action which focuses on the priority of structures relates to intellectual routine, and does not therefore in itself produce change.

On the one hand, we know perfectly well that we can give an organization 20 different structures and finally have a high continuity in the methods of functioning; on the other hand, as we will see further on in this book, modifying the structures is not in any way a preliminary to true change: usually, it makes do with being the statement *ex post* rather than *ex ante*. It relates far more to "active inertia" than to a true action of change.[27] Such inertia means that one is only interested in what one is used to seeing, hearing or talking about. A memo, a follow-up letter, the publication of a new charter, are all part of the routines to which people no longer pay great attention but which fulfil the function of action, satisfying everybody until they are suddenly awoken by the principle of reality: for example, "profit warnings" in the United States plays the same role as sudden and uncontrolled strikes in France.

This is what a major insurance company tried out when, at the time of a merger, it wanted to group together into a single entity the banking activities which, until then, had been split between four different establishments, operating in several European countries. In one of these countries, already marked by language and cultural problems, this involved merging two banks which were apparently totally opposed: bank A was perceived as being a "bank for the wealthy", in which actors at all levels had wide margins for manoeuvre, allowing free rein to their entrepreneurial leanings; bank B, on the other hand, formerly a public savings bank, was looked on as a "bank for the poor", displaying a management that was far more standardized, which its own members described as military.

In appearance, however, the structures of both banks were almost the same and resembled the picture that can be seen across Europe: division into regions, into areas, into districts and into branches. The objective drawn up by the person responsible for the merger and his team was, in a relatively short time, to arrive at an organization that functioned in a uniform fashion, which was expected to legitimize the adoption of a new trading name, a new logo – in brief, a new image. These managers therefore threw themselves into drawing up a single structure, ironing out the few differences that existed between the two initial establishments and, above all, they started the development of a package of strict, complex and detailed procedures, intended to produce the uniformity of operation that they sought. The outcome was the development of a multitude of working groups, each created whenever a new problem arose. The energy involved was considerable and nobody had even thought about calculating the time spent on the process, so distant did this seem from everybody's preoccupations. Meanwhile, successful completion of the merger – that is, harmonization, bringing everything into conformity with the general model – appeared to be the guarantee for the success of the operation.

After a few months, the first anxieties came to light: first of all, nobody seemed able to ensure overall coherence across all the projects and sites which had been started up without anybody knowing either the exact number or topics; and also the few on-the-spot observations that were carried out from time to time demonstrated that everybody had their own individual way of doing things, so that what should have been a procedure of integration finally turned out to be a disintegration of the new entity: the more rules were made specific and restrictive, the less the local actors appeared to care about them, except to highlight their abstract and inappropriate nature to their managers.

What had happened? Once again, the real organization had raised its head. A survey carried out as requested by the managers rapidly brought to light the fact that, in the traditional system, particularly in bank A, the key duo, which in fact shaped the bank's reality, was that formed by the district manager and the branch manager. The first, responsible for the application by the second of directives and policies drawn up by the bank, in the conventional system had a few margins for manoeuvre which were quite useful in negotiations of the operational manager. Not only was he involved in appraising the branch manager, but he also had a function of supporting him with regard to commercial policy and, even more important, a possibility of adjusting the objectives fixed for the branch in line with his appraisal of specific situations. The relationship between these two partners was therefore deep, but at the same time varied and thus in contradiction of the path to uniformity followed by the new team.

When the new organization was put in place, with its package of structures, rules and injunctions intended to produce the *non-differentiation* that was so sought after, the stakeholders had not accepted without grumbling the move from the situation of *actors,* which was theirs in the previous system, to that of *factors* to which they now found themselves reduced. Everybody took hold of the new standards and used them, not in the way intended by those who had issued them, but in line with their own situation in the local game. Identical rules only ended up creating different systems and, as the bank's general manager remarked philosophically after the presentation on the results of this work, "For the mechanics, we were good; but perhaps we neglected the human aspect." The problem is that one does not exist without the other, and that an action for change focused on the first does not make it possible to anticipate or control what the second proceeds to do with it. Never has the expression "putting the cart before the horse" had so much meaning, never has the reversal of priorities been so blatantly obvious with all its related consequences in terms of wasting human and financial resources.

Change through play on attitudes

So does this mean changing *attitudes,*[28] *in the most usual sense of the term, that is, the way in which people express themselves and behave individually in organizations*? For example, when it is a question of adapting the organization to the new demands of customers who are increasingly in a position to impose their wishes, is it simply, or even principally, necessary for those who are in contact with these customers, and who rarely even represent a majority of the organization's members, to change their way of being?

This vision of things, described in this way, reminds us of Courteline.[29] One would switch from agents, from uncommunicative and disagreeable employees, to actors who were smiling, quick, devoted, above all wanting to render service. Such an approach, which could easily be described as naive, is nonetheless omnipresent in modern organizations. Of course, for certain of these it represents a necessity, a first essential step towards a different conception of the relationship with one's surroundings.[30] It sometimes interprets the transition from apprehension of such surroundings in terms of threats from which one must protect oneself, to acceptance of a more open, more trusting relationship with one's contacts. To be brief, it may express the organization's "sense of service", which we will also observe is very different from country to country.

But at the same time, such a vision of change does not lead very far, and it aims above all at laying the responsibility for adapting to new constraints on the only members of the organization in contact with its surroundings. In the same movement we see the appearance inside organizations of familiarity, use of the first name instead of the surname, doors left open and relaxed dress, as if the *container* of interindividual relationships could determine their *content*.

There's nothing like that, of course. The effects can even be reversed, so much does this confusion place responsibility for the necessary changes on the only personnel in contact with the public, thus further increasing the pressure on them, but without the organizational mechanisms that would help them in this. Staying with this case of relationships with one's surroundings, there is little chance of the smile becoming a competitive advantage, so much has courtesy become the universal norm and aggressiveness the exception. However, there is nothing in this way of changing attitudes to indicate that the organization has changed *in its reality,* in its methods of functioning.

A quick example, bringing us back to the tax administration mentioned above, allows us to check this. During the period of tax declarations, the offices of an organization are crowded with taxpayers seeking help in writing their declarations. But they only open at nine o'clock in the morning and, as we have been able to observe, even when it is raining, people queue in front of the offices. When the door is opened at the proper time and some taxpayer or other shows his irritation, he is told – politely – that the office was not able to welcome them in! The individual attitude is faultless, the result in terms of quality perceived by the "customer" is catastrophic.

The negative attitude of inspectors

But we need to go further than this simple anecdote, and show in what way the reduction of an organization to the sum of the individual attitudes of its members, or of some of its members, can produce the paralysing and perverse effects that we have just talked about. Let us return to the transport company which was mentioned in the introduction. It now finds itself faced with growing competition, mainly inter-modal, especially in relation to its high contribution customers. In answer to their continual demands for more speed, more punctuality, more efficiency, the company has developed a technical tool that the whole world sees as providing remarkable performance. It has even "adjusted" its office hours so as to offer its customers a regularity and reliability to which they attach a great deal of importance. And yet everybody seems united in acknowledging, both inside and outside the company, that the service which accompanies this technical excellence is poor and in any case nowhere near the expectations of passengers. In particular, the level of personnel accompanying customers on their journeys – the inspectors – who, as their name indicates, check that everybody is in order, show little enthusiasm for entering into contact with them and *a fortiori* for promoting the company through behaviour towards encouraging commercial openings. They even have a tendency to "disappear" as soon as the situation becomes complicated, after an incident, a delay, a disturbance – leaving customers to look after themselves and thus provoking a climate of irritation which has often been highlighted by the press.

Of course, the company's management became worried and arranged for these agents, as indeed for other categories of personnel, to take part in huge programmes for "training on service attitudes" in which everybody is seen to explain and demonstrate the need to modify their way of managing relationships with customers in the direction of greater availability. However, these programmes were not a great success and did not have a huge impact on passenger satisfaction, plus they even added to the deterioration in the company's social climate, already marked by repeated social actions among the inspectors. Management interpreted this response as a very negative sign, showing, if proof was really needed, that these categories were closed to any change, and the agents themselves took refuge behind increasingly passive avoidance behaviours, only seeming to take an interest in optimal management of their personal lives – in this case the possibility of going home in the evening as often as possible – and the continual rise in their financial gains, helped in all this by union organizations who were only too pleased to be involved.

So what is the origin of the misunderstanding and failure in this attempt at change? Once again, a wrong apprehension of what an organization really is, reducing it to a set of individual attitudes which have to rely on the good will – or in this case the bad will – of the actors involved. In doing this, we have not taken into consideration this *reality* that we clearly see, as we move forward, is a crucial issue of change and yet at the same time so very difficult to grasp and accept. Here it is the complexity of the surroundings in which the inspector finds himself, his context, which has been neglected.

This complexity can be quick to assert itself in this way, immediately indicating that it corresponds to the *real organization*, the one that needs to be taken into account in the process of change: the inspector is on his own in front of a customer whose needs can only be exacerbated when the situation becomes disturbed. Not only will he express a profound and sometimes aggressive discontent, but in addition he will be hungry for information allowing him to reorganize his time, let his friends know, and so on. However, it is the inspector who is accountable for everything that happens in the company without any possibility of passing on the responsibility for problems to other people, to whom the customer does not have access and about whom he knows nothing. As a humorous illustration here, when the company asks its inspectors to give information to customers, it might have just the same results by reversing the situation. One side has no more information than the other, especially when customers nowadays can use their mobile phones to obtain information that is fuller and more reliable than that available – with great difficulty and with no particular guarantee of reliability – to the inspector.

In fact, this inspector, rather like his colleagues in reception, is living in a compartmentalized organization, where each party takes decisions without worrying about their effects on other parties or even on the whole set-up.[31] Each of these decisions can be justified, legitimated, dictated by the desire to satisfy the customer, and yet its final result may be catastrophic. The same can be said of the choice between punctuality and connections that every transport company knows so well: when a train or airplane is late, must the others be made to wait so that those who are the victims of this lateness can catch their next means of transport? Or, on the contrary, is it important to privilege the network's overall punctuality, so as not to lay lateness upon lateness? Each of such choices can be justified. But however that may be, in the company being used as an example here, not only is the inspector not informed, but he also does not know on what criteria the decision will be based. And when such criteria have been drawn up in common, which is sometimes the case, it is unusual for them to be applied, as those who are in charge prefer to keep their autonomy, their uncertainty, and therefore their power. An inspector who wants to keep travellers informed thus runs the risk of being overruled by a decision contradicting what he thought he could announce and justify.

The same can also be said for station masters who are assessed on the punctuality of departures from their station. So when an incident occurs during a journey and the inspector asks the manager of the next station to call in the forces of order, there is little chance that his request will be heard and executed. Promises will be made to him but not kept, reinforcing his sentiment of isolation and abandonment. It is evident that the problems confronting these inspectors are a long way from those that a strategy for change, anchored on service attitudes, or even attitudes alone, would be likely to handle successfully.

What is revealed here, more fundamentally, is a non-listening mechanism which results from the priority given to the rule on reality, or confusion between the two. Some think that by producing "good" rules, they are doing their work and they devote all their energy and intelligence to this; others feel confusedly that things shouldn't be this way, but find it difficult to assess the situation: firstly, they do not have enough distance for that; and, secondly, if they had this distance, it could sometimes be dangerous to make reference to it. For in all bureaucratic environments, the universalist and egalitarian rhetoric condemns all sense of identity, and therefore adaptation of the rule, even if this is, on a daily basis, the condition for the organization's survival. Doing something is good. Saying something is to expose oneself to reproach in the case of a problem. One cannot expect actors placed in this situation to always live it positively. This explains a few explosions – less easy for unions to control when they themselves are far from the reality.

In the case under discussion, an incorrect interpretation of what an organization really is, the hasty and protective simplification, the more general refusal of complexity, are going to produce perverse effects: results which not only do not correspond to officially designated objectives, but which also aggravate the wrongs that they are supposed to remedy. In the situation we are looking at, one could call this the "vicious circle of discontentment". The less the inspectors are taken into account in certain decisions, for the reason that they do not directly concern them – confusion between appearance and reality, ignorance of the systemic aspect – the more they are persuaded that their company is rejecting them, which is no doubt false in human terms, and yet true in organizational terms. However, it is that and only that which counts for actors who always have more of a feeling for what is real than those who manage them. This results for them in behaviours of withdrawal, of non-investment in work – for which in addition they are severely criticized, with the backing of surveys on real time of work. In such a context, when their "attitudes" are called on to palliate the organization's inadequacies, they come to the conclusion that they are being made fools of, and use their situation of strength to always ask for more, particularly in terms of organizing their personal lives, their working hours and time off. In brief, they play on protest as compensation for organizational ignorance, supported vigorously by union organizations who are only too ready to capitalize on such mechanisms.

This is how conservatism and opposition to progress flourish and prosper in these organizations, where everybody complains that it is impossible to get them to move forward, but where everybody passes the buck. On one side, management departments throw back the failure of attempts at change any old how onto agents who are themselves particularly attached to their privileges and onto their union organizations which feed on this in the proper sense of the term;[32] on the other, the personnel concerned are made extremely suspicious by the fundamental lack of knowledge of the reality shown by those who are inviting them to change. There is often only one way out of this sort of situation – a crisis with all that that entails in the way of drama, financial cost and above all human cost.

We will have the opportunity to return to this case in more detail, in particular when evoking the possibilities of changing the way the cards are dealt. But for the moment if offers us a different vision of what an organization is, of what must be the focus of all attention when things are to be changed.

Part II
The Change Process

6
Review of Pure Reasoning: The Frame of Reference

Let us begin with the following proposition that has already been formulated several times: it is all the more difficult to change an organization when the actors in the organization – leaders as well as employees – have a poor understanding of how it functions. For the leaders, as is often observed, this puts a damper on their ability to make decisions over which they feel, however confusedly, that they have no control. This is what managerial rhetoric calls prudence. Similarly, this leads them to various protection strategies (bluntly called the "cover your ass syndrome" in America) which determined sociologists have been studying for some time now.[1]

For the members of the organization, this lack of knowledge leads them to behave with mistrust and resistance, heightened by the fact that they do not understand what the problem is that is being dealt with, and that what they are told does not seem to them to correspond to reality – their reality – so that, this being the case, change is for them accompanied by guilt: their former practices are seen to be under fire for no good reason. Consequently, access to knowledge of what we called in Part I the real organization, is the result neither of scientific aestheticism nor of some humanistic or philosophical bias. It is a key factor in getting people to both accept and implement change. Moreover, in the preceding chapter, it was pointed out that this is in fact a fundamental point on which authors agree – authors of different cultural backgrounds and of sometimes contradictory points of view. We won't be going back over that.

The problem facing us then is that of carefully working out this knowledge – making a diagnosis – inasmuch as the actors perceive it, even if their perception is of course fragmentary, compartmentalized, disconnected and partisan. What matters is the systemic dimension,[2] that is to say the link between the different parts and between these parts and the whole. It is this added value which is lacking in spontaneous knowledge, in the "quick glance", however well founded it might be on actual experience. The following examples demonstrate this clearly and explain why the actors in an organization, faced with the results of a sociological diagnosis, can be surprised by the facts presented to them, and yet can accept them provided that a coherent – systemic – presentation of the facts gives them the real feeling of having been listened to. It comes both as a revelation and as a release mechanism with respect to the usual practice of dividing reality, cutting it up, classifying it, a practice which for its part produces problematic side-effects which wind up, with use, locking the system up: the behaviour of each individual, taken alone, is *de facto* linked only to the actor who exhibits it. Behaviour appears as the problem when most often it is only a symptom,[3] and attempts to modify it usually focus on the actor alone. An appeal is made to his or her goodwill, convictions or at best personal interests, meant here in the most basic, mechanistic sense of "motivation".

We encountered this kind of organization earlier on, which, overcome by an urgent need to be "customer-orientated", tries to do so by blaming the attitude of employees who work directly with customers. In so doing, they point a bold finger at the guilty ones – those who must change – and obscure the systemic dimension of their behaviour. No doubt this is the more comfortable, simple solution, but as indicated earlier, in the end, changing employee attitudes only becomes all the more difficult, since they now feel with good reason that no one has even listened to them, that is, that no one has understood the real world in which they work and within which their actions have meaning. We will see later on, in a particularly striking case study, that some actors support a bureaucratic way of thinking "by default", since they have no other models, since they believe that tried and true bureaucracy alone can protect them; when they are presented with something else in the name of "good management", or out of sheer theoretical or ideological criticism of bureaucracy, they rebel, fearing the effects that change might have on themselves and upon the reality which they have worked out for themselves, but which no one has taken the time to understand.

The systemic knowledge proposed here requires a frame of reference, which might also be called a mode of reasoning. Developed on the basis of Herbert Simon's early work on bounded rationality,[4] it has since given rise to heated debate and to an impressive body of literature, which is not the concern of this book.[5] It will be presented quite simply, beginning with the author's own work in seminars, developed slowly but surely in the hope of making this mode of reasoning available to the actors themselves. Beginning with a seemingly ordinary example, which is in fact extremely rich, we will attempt to answer the burning question at the very heart of the work of both social scientists and managers wishing to undertake change: why, within organizations, do people do what they do, and consequently why do they not do what they are asked to do? Once this mode of reasoning has been explained, it will be made real through the use of "tools" which are only its physical interpretation – such as the strategic analysis grid, presented in this chapter, and the sociogram, developed in the next chapter.

The dilemma of the shampoo girl

Pure chance led the author to the following case study. It is hoped that the professionals involved will excuse the way I have presented the facts here, intentionally simplified and adapted for pedagogical reasons.[6] A particular company, a world leader in the cosmetics industry, was faced a few years ago with the following question: just like its competitors, the company sold its retail hair products through various distribution networks: supermarkets, specialized shops, drugstores, and so on. Traditionally, the hairdressing salon was not used for direct customer sales. In the salon, the company had only offered so-called "technical" products, available exclusively to hairstylists who could use the products on customers in the shop. Quite naturally, there arose the question of developing specific product lines for hairdressing salon customers. The company took a major step forward and decided to invest in this new sales initiative.

This was, first of all, a sizeable strategic gamble, insofar as the company had first to create new brand names which would then be offered in competition with existing brands, some of which already bore the company name. But it was a major business opportunity, given the number of potential sales outlets: in France alone there are more than 40,000 active hairdressing salons, that is to say, individual shops. There was also financial risk, requiring new personnel, display shelves, publicity campaigns, and so on.

Once the decision had been made, the company began implementing the plan with its usual efficiency and know-how. Marketing studies were carried out, the products developed and tested, a sales strategy carefully thought out, sales staff recruited and trained, and even though salon owners seemed a little reluctant, in some countries at least, the company's influence and its relationship with the profession allowed it to attract those whom it considered to be at the heart of the business.

Then, a long way into this great business venture, a particular question arose which on the surface seemed rather unimportant: in the hairdressing salons, who was going to offer the products to customers? The old theory of how individuals are motivated financially whispered the answer, and, in fact, freed the company from having to take a closer look at the real situation: someone who is paid relatively little wishes to make more (a mechanistic vision of human behaviour within organizations).[7] Certain salon employees fit this description: if, as "motivation", they are given material, financial or other stimuli, they will begin selling the products, no doubt taking full advantage of the enticements offered them. These actors – the "shampoo girls" – are generally young, low-paid apprentices who, as such, should see in the new project a good opportunity to increase their monthly earnings.

Let us take a moment to understand in simple terms what mechanistic reasoning is, as opposed to systemic reasoning. The first takes into consideration only two actors, in appearance the only ones directly involved in the problem: the shampooer and the customer, independent of the context in which their relationship takes place. Direct action on one of these actors (the stimulus offered to the shampooer) should thus affect his or her behaviour vis-à-vis the other (the shampooer will offer products to customers). This approach assumes that the behaviour of these actors is predictable – especially that of the employee, based on a universal model (motivation) – which does away with the need for more careful "listening" to the salon as an organization.

By extension, it can moreover be observed that the use of models – behavioural, organizational, and so on – supplants more difficult awareness of reality. Their use is reassuring since it promises solutions, although they are never based on real knowledge of the problem but on *a priori* hypotheses, on simplistic postulates, or on statements which, after several repetitions, begin to be misconstrued as universal law. This simplistic approach, so typical of the "substantial" theories of management as they are currently taught in many business schools, is a return to Taylorian unique rationality – if indeed we ever really got away from it. Once the main characteristic of an actor has been identified, how he or she will react in the future is "known", regardless of the setting – the organization – in which this actor is employed. In so doing, human intelligence, the actor's adaptive ability, and the strategic dimension of his or her behaviour have all been reduced to nothing, but which, as we are about to see through the example of the shampooer, are absolutely essential.

Let us return to the example. A few months after the new sales plan had been implemented, the company conducted its first in-depth analysis which turned out to be rather disappointing: the results were not there, especially in France, and a quick look at the situation reveals why: despite the benefits granted them, the shampooers were very reluctant to offer products to customers. The company redoubled its efforts, offering new forms of enticement as well as increased pressure on sales representatives, and through them on to the shampooers, but these were just as unsuccessful. The reluctance to sell products was just as great, which led the company to conclude, although with a little overstatement here, that the intellectual limitations of the shampoo staff combined with their lack of enthusiasm prevented them from taking advantage of this opportunity.

And yet why should the "intelligence" of an actor be questioned? In fact, to do so reveals that the solution is inadequate, that company decision makers have not succeeded in understanding the problem, the real problem, since understanding presupposes a different mode of reasoning, not the application of an abstract, theoretical model.

What mode of reasoning? Let us begin with a simple postulate which we will develop later on: in organizations, as in collective life in general, actors do what they do not because they are dumb, stupid or ill-intentioned, but because they are intelligent. In other words, the problems which we find in organizations are the result not of human stupidity, but of human intelligence. Intelligence is not to be understood here as the ability of an elite group forced to understand everything, to control everything, to master and eventually reformulate everything in some kind of perfect formal logic. Rather, it should be understood as the modest ability of the actors, within the specific context in which they work, in the here and now, to find a solution which is, at least as far as they are concerned, the least bad or first acceptable of all possible solutions, however one prefers to say it. This is indeed what Simon called "bounded rationality", which he contrasts with sole rationality, which applies to the models mentioned above; financial motivation in the case of the shampooers. "An example is the difference between searching a haystack to find the sharpest needle in it, and searching the haystack to find a needle sharp enough to sew with", write James March and Herbert Simon,[8] decisively establishing with this simple metaphor the difference between sole rationality and bounded rationality.

Let us take a more careful look at March and Simon's proposition: say, one morning, as you are putting on your last clean shirt you notice that a button is missing. In order to sew it back on, you need a needle; and yet you have very little time if you want to make an important meeting. You have at least two possible solutions.

The first, the result of a careful and scientifically flawless analysis, leads you to look for the sharpest possible needle, the one best suited to repairing the button without damaging the shirt. You will then go about looking for the sharpest needle in the haystack – the sewing kit – since this is the scientific solution … and as a result, you will miss your meeting.

The second solution leads you to consider the different constraints: I cannot leave home with a button missing, I have to be on time for my meeting, finding an appropriate needle in a disorderly sewing kit is not easy, and so on. At this point, you will not select the best solution (sole rationality), that is, the best in technical terms; rather, you will select the one which will help you solve then and there the contradictory problems of the moment. Perhaps the needle is not the most acceptable, but you did not spend 15 minutes digging for it either, and the button can be reattached in time for you to make your meeting: this is bounded rationality. This is not the abstract "best technical solution", but the least bad, the first acceptable one. In sociological language, you have unconsciously adopted a rational strategy, which does not mean that you made a correct choice, nor that we must approve of your solution, but which demonstrates the real meaning of "intelligence" mentioned above.

It is thus understandable why speaking of the actor's rationality or, to say it differently and rather more brutally, affirming that irrationality does not exist in organizations[9] (unless in the shape of pathologies that are very individual and do not form a management problem) does not make any value judgement in advance on the merits or otherwise of taking action. This is a framework of reasoning that helps one to understand (but not necessarily approve) all human behaviour. To take an extreme example, it was an Israeli expert, Ariel Merari, who stated that terrorists are not crazy, that they follow their own rationality, but they are not irrational.[10]

And so, to help the company make some progress in its hair-product sales initiative in salons, the line of reasoning must be turned around, and we must try to understand how – for the shampooer who is intelligent, like other people – the fact of not offering products to her customers can be rational behaviour (strategic dimension) in a world that is much more complicated than the simple one-on-one scenario of vendor/consumer (systemic dimension). To do this, we have to take the time to piece together the world of the hairdressing salon in all its complexity, beyond its apparent simplicity, and modestly observe what is happening, letting ourselves be surprised.

Early on in Chapter 3, we observed the Taylorization of this small world, in the fact that as part of the classic production process of the salon, what is moved about is not the worker but the product to be transformed, in this instance the customer's head (movement from the sink to the seat). Let us add that in this compartmentalized world, there are "rules of the game", as in any organization, that is to say a set of codes of proper behaviour, unwritten of course, which each person must respect in order to survive, or more concretely, to avoid being rejected by the other actors. In a more sophisticated form, this is what we would call "culture": the set of formal and informal rules which evolve over time, encoding the rights and duties of each person vis-à-vis all others. The understanding and acceptance of this "culture" are both a condition for the sustainability of the organization and a mark of integration. In the hairdressing salon, the rule which provides the most structure is the one by which someone belonging to an "inferior" category in terms of qualifications has no right to discuss with the customer what someone belonging to a "superior" category does or will do. Put more directly, this means that the shampooers must not discuss with customers the technical aspects of the stylists' or technicians' jobs. If they do, they will face a situation of conflict, which, if it is prolonged, will cause those employees to be fired by the owner who knows it is easier to hire a shampooer than a good technician.

Now we have begun to use systemic reasoning. To understand the relationship between the two actors (the shampooer and the customer), and the strategy of one of them (the shampooer's refusal to offer products to the customer), we have had to bring in other members of the organization, who at first glance do not seem directly involved (the technicians and the owner of the salon). Here "systemic" means that each of these actors develops a strategy – a strategy to preserve autonomy in the case of the technicians – and that these strategies are interconnected, and can only be understood as a whole, not in isolation.

Let us go a little further into the hairdressing salon, and observe that there are no old shampooers. The reason is obvious: as young apprentices, they have the simple goal of becoming technicians themselves. Either they attain that goal and continue along the path, or they fail and go on to something else so as not to have to continue shampooing and sweeping the floor the rest of their lives. As we continue developing our frame of reference we will say that they have a "problem to solve" which is to become a technician. Here "problem to solve" does not mean to confront a momentary difficulty, but to try to obtain something, and in this pursuit – we have come full circle – the actor develops some rational strategy. This concept is very different from that of "motivation", the one first used by the company to get its new plan under way.

The idea – "from outside" we might say – that low-paid actors want to make more money is neither true nor false. It is simply useless insofar as these actors have not been heard out in an attempt to understand, beyond general abstract models, what they themselves want concretely when they do what they do in the context in which they find themselves.

Note that, for shampooers – to become technicians, that is – the solution to their problem is to be promoted. But this profession is just like every other. Promotion requires a minimum level of stability, a certain time in one place, so that employees can demonstrate their professional competency and ability to be integrated into this human world, which is an equally important factor of success. As we said earlier, each conflict between technicians and shampooers will turn against the latter, possibly ending in their departure in search of a new salon, where they will have to start again as apprentices.

Let us now bring in, say, customer Jane Doe, and suppose that, as she makes her way over to the "sink" area, the shampoo girl offers the line of haircare products. Through careful observation of this interaction we learn that the customer responds to this offer by two highly risky questions insofar as the young shampoo girl is concerned. The first is whether the technician – supposedly the knowledgeable one in the matter – uses these products herself, which of course would make the offer all that more credible. But what can the shampoo girl say if the technician uses a different product, one which she developed herself, for example, in the course of her profession, but which has nothing to do with the one being offered? In fact, to sell a product to the customer forces the technician into a corner, face to face with the *fait accompli*, making it almost obligatory that she too uses the product line. And yet as we saw, the technician tries to preserve her own autonomy, for her own differentiation. Whatever "backs her into a corner" is going to annoy her, resulting in conflict, and we already saw what the result of that would be.

The second question which the customer might ask after being presented with the line of products concerns the possible effects of the product on her perm or hair colour … on whatever work the technician may do. In selling the product, this implies that the shampoo girl will have to field questions with respect to what is going to happen, with respect to what other actors are going to do legitimately, as part of their job, the very ones who deny her that right. Again there is conflict, again the risk of a lost job, which goes against the resolution of the "problem to solve" which we identified: being promoted. In light of this context, knowing that she is intelligent, the rational strategy developed by the shampoo girl is understandable: do not offer products to customers; this is her strategy regardless of her desire to make more money. This is the bounded rationality of the actors; this is what must be understood, "listened to" as we have said, if we want to have some chance of glimpsing the reality behind organizations, and therefore to change their functioning.

It should also be added that even though we have analysed a rather simple setting – the hairdressing salon – with what we might call a sophisticated concept – bounded rationality – not at all new in the sciences, this concept stands largely misunderstood, victim of the dream of a "best solution" which the actors could find if only they were provided with adequate information. This is the illusion which Alan Ehrenhalt exposes when he writes:

> Modern economists probably know more than astronomers in the Middle Ages, but they are themselves prisoners of a simple idea which dominates their thinking: most people in daily life are rational people who carefully calculate what is in their own best interest. They are, in economic jargon, "maximizers of utility". If they are given sufficient information, they succeed every time in coming to a logically correct decision.[11]

The idea of maximization of profit is not the problem. This was explained in clear terms by authors such as Albert Hirschman, Raymond Boudon and even, surprisingly, by Alexis de Tocqueville.[12] There is a logical flaw in the idea of a "logically correct decision" which goes back again to the old notion of "one best way", of "the sharpest needle", and so on. From this standpoint, it would be possible to make the actors predictable – which is the fantasy of every manager who wishes to implement change – simply by giving them the information which would allow them to be "reasonable". "What I have just said could be understood by schoolchildren", said the president of a large French company undergoing some hard times, having lost almost all hope in the face of fierce opposition to his rescue plan on the part of unions and even salaried employees. In fact, he saw that even when provided with frank, honest, accurate information, actors were still unreasonable, at least from his point of view.

To put it another way, one of the most surprising consequences of this intelligence in actors involved in the implementation of change is that, in organizations, *the common-sense aspect is not necessarily considered entirely sensible by the actors themselves*. Most of the time, "common sense" is the conclusion that imposes itself when one has pushed a given logic to its limit – but nothing more than a single logic, that of economic efficiency or social justice, no matter which. However, as soon as such a logic is confronted with the actor's reality, with his or her own ability to find a more or less suitable solution to the context, then it loses its authenticity and apparent universality. That is why, quite simply, one can never convince anybody in organizations of what each of us has actually experienced. If actors do what they do because they are intelligent, there is not much point in trying to convince them to do things differently. Maybe it would be more useful, and above all more effective, to try and *place them in a context in which it is to their advantage to act differently*. Further on in this book, we will call this "using leverage".

In parallel, we are beginning to anticipate that *sharing knowledge* does not mean convincing others that we are right but rather helping them to grasp the real and systemic nature of problems. Afterwards, but only then, will come the time for negotiation of solutions.

Bounded rationality therefore does not imply that the actors are right, nor that they should be told they are right. It is not about giving permission. It expresses the calculations (in the sense of choices) which people make so as to solve one or several problems, the most urgent ones, based on an evaluation of their resources and their constraints. Even if this short definition seems to rule out the perfect predictability of an actor's behaviour – at the most, we might be able to say something about how consistent an actor's behaviour may be – we will see later on that it nonetheless opens some interesting pathways in dealing with the management of change.

How to identify the relevant actors

Let us now turn to a pedagogical exercise which consists of going back to the different concepts used to analyse the so-called case of the "shampoo girl", explaining them one by one. By explaining we do not mean just coming up with "tricks" or techniques – we will still be relatively powerless before the two-dimensional paradox of human behaviour: unpredictable and yet intelligent. Rather, it means shedding light, step by step, on a mode of reasoning which makes a little more cognizable the organizational complexity which this book has emphasized over and over again. How this is done will be presented with a grid (see Figure 6.1), a tool which should help readers actually put into practice this new way of reasoning, applicable to any human system for which one can put together enough relevant information.

There is nothing mathematical about this tool. There is no recipe which guarantees that such a grid can be filled in without error. There

Actors	Problems to solve	Resources	Constraints	Strategies

Figure 6.1

is no scientific proof for a correct solution. But a discussion of these five basic concepts – to which we will later add two more, power and uncertainty – will enable us to reason in terms of the entire collective unit, and to construct a methodology for conducting change.

Every attempt at understanding organizational reality – whether concerning the relationship between actors, or the strategy developed by one of them – assumes that all relevant actors can be identified, that is, those who must be taken into account if we want a reliable interpretation of the phenomena in question. Of course, here "actor" is not the same thing as "individual". An actor frequently has a collective dimension (flight attendants, customers, and so on). Furthermore, relevancy does not mean one's direct and visible involvement in the problem. We saw this in the case of the hairdressing salon, where our attempts to understand why refusing to offer products to customers was a rational strategy for shampooers led to the discovery of actors above and beyond the two directly involved (the apprentice and the customer): namely, the owner of the salon and the technicians, who are part of the relevant context of the relationship.

Note once again that the concept of an actor, once it is well understood, facilitates the use of systemic reasoning beyond a linear, causal or structural vision. More specifically, the actor concept allows us to see that problems are more concrete than structures: to analyse the functioning of a structure usually gives a rather poor result. Actors within a structure are not necessarily connected, and in daily life are typically not concerned with the same questions. On the other hand, to start with the problem (in this case the symptom) one can identify rather quickly which actors are directly or indirectly involved, regardless of the official structure of which they are a part.

A quick illustration of this: a beverage company with a high sales volume complains of trouble in the purchasing department and embarks on an investigation to help it make some crucial decisions. The study involves conducting interviews which, understandably, the company suggests should take place within the purchasing department, in particular with the department manager, the product managers and the purchasers. Here the relevancy of the actors is likened – reduced, one might say – to the structure of which they are a part, the one which is thought to be the cause of the problem. Supposing now that we ask those in charge to express in concrete terms what they see as the principal problem. They explain in no uncertain terms that they are not able to convince their purchasers to avoid overstocking packaging materials, in other words, to limit their purchases to the immediate needs of production.

Let us say, then, that there is one main problem, the purchasing of packaging materials, and that around this problem a certain number of actors interact, regardless of the particular structure of which they are part: the purchasers of course, but also the production manager who is the one most bothered by the problem of surplus inventory. These two actors are part of the company, but work in different departments. Furthermore, how could we understand what is going on if we do not take into account the suppliers, who, moreover, are non-members of the company, and *a fortiori* of the purchasing department? They are, by definition, key actors. In short, around the problem in question there is a network of actors whose connections form what is called a system, provided that these connections are more or less stable. Obviously, if purchasers' job performance is evaluated on the unit price of the item purchased, their shared interests with outside suppliers will be stronger than with the production managers in their own company.

Two conclusions can be drawn from this simple example: the first is that in such a context, without any doubt the purchase of huge quantities of bottles is for the buyers a rational strategy, in the sense that this expression was given earlier in this chapter; the second is that once again in understanding organizations, the concept of a system is much more useful than the knowledge of structures which, like everything related to rules and procedures, is relatively abstract with respect to the real behaviour of the actors.

Finally, note that in an attempt to cast some light on organizational reality, identifying the relevant actors does not necessarily happen in one fell swoop. It is the result of careful reflection. This was illustrated in the analysis of the public system of ground transport carriers in France[13] – the appearance, at the end of work, of the insurance company as a key actor in the system, permitting the externalization of costs on to all motorists.

This shows us that talking of "problems to solve" for an actor does not mean that this he or she "has problems" in the normal sense of this term, nor that something negative is happening. It simply implies that this actor is seeking to achieve something and that therefore, hypothetically one might say, all actors have problems to be solved, even if this only means staying quietly in their corner. One might object by saying that it would be better to choose a less ambiguous description such as "objective", but all such descriptions have a different connotation in management jargon. The important thing here is not the vocabulary, but an understanding of what the concept contains.

Let us now take a brief look at why this concept is so crucial to this reasoning: actors are rational not with respect to a general, abstract, scientific or ethical model, but with respect to what they have set concretely as their own goals. As was said earlier, one can only modify an actor's behaviour – or at least control this attempt at modification – once one has grasped the rationality of such behaviour (and thus the problem that it seeks to resolve). Why? No doubt because the "problem to solve" is the key concept, as well as the most difficult one. Once again, there is no recipe to come up with the "right" answer; no "strings" which guarantee a correct interpretation; only the necessity of listening to the actors in the true sense of the term, and with this listening to develop a hypothesis, continually questioning, continually verifying what they are trying to achieve.

"Listening", a critical and hazardous exercise

There are three reasons why this exercise is particularly tricky and uncertain. In explaining them, we will be able to say a little more about "listening" before taking the concept even further in the following chapter.

The mayor, the jobs and the land

It was stated earlier that a system is a network of interdependencies among actors, related around a single question. The first difficulty lies in the obvious fact that it would be somewhat naive to jump from the idea that these actors are all concerned with the same question, to the idea that they all have the same problems to be solved, which might be, for example, the resolution of the question. A quick example serves to illustrate this point.[14] In the 1970s, a labour conflict arose in France, typical in its day, concerning joint worker–management control. The company in question was called Titan Coder, a truck trailer manufacturer. Government officials in charge of business matters of the day, absorbed in eliminating "lame ducks", decided that there was no way a French trailer manufacturer could make money in a tight market, and tried to interest foreign investors (primarily Americans) to take over the struggling company. The conflict which ensued quickly became an issue of national concern, and employees took over the three manufacturing plants (Maubeuge, Marseilles, and Chalon-sur-Saône), deciding to produce and sell trailers themselves. Everyone got involved, just as had happened around the closure of the famous French watchmaker Lip: the prefects, the sub-prefects, local and national elected officials, chambers of commerce, unions and employers' associations, government ministries, and so on, to such an extent that when we used this case study in the classroom, students would come up with at least 20 relevant actors.

Students were invariably astonished by the actions taken by the mayor of Marseilles of the day, going so far as to call him stupid, saying that the mayor was incessantly suggesting a replacement solution which would allow saving 300 jobs at risk, even though they would be sent to another town. Asked why they felt this strategy to be somehow "irrational",[15] the students would point out that a mayor always tries to save jobs in the area for which he or she is responsible. Yes of course, no doubt, in most cases: but that is an *a priori* model, and just like every model, it dismisses anything incongruous or incomprehensible which cannot be made to fit.

Here the error lies in identifying the problem to be solved: upon closer inspection, it becomes pretty clear that the mayor in question wanted to recover some well situated pieces of land in his own district currently occupied by the manufacturer. This being the case, he was not really worried about the possible loss of jobs; it was not the main issue, even if, like everyone else, he made quite a fuss about it. It was a resource, an opportunity. Getting ahead of ourselves a little bit here, we could say that in this case the mayor's problem to be solved is the recovery of the land, his resource the threat over jobs, his constraint that he cannot by himself evict the manufacturer, and that his strategy is to suggest that it go somewhere else: no value judgement, no ethical or ideological considerations here. We have done a simple "reading" of reality, which, once again, is subject to error. Let us add that this mayor acts no differently from those around him. To put it bluntly, we could say that saving 300 jobs is the problem to be solved only by the 300 people whose jobs are at risk.

All the other actors, beyond the question which concerns them all and which everyone is making a fuss about, are dealing with their own particular problems, for this is how human organizations work – there's no point in taking offence. Moreover, this shows that the key problem of management is not obtaining some abstract consensus on the general values which people adhere to, especially if these values do not interfere too much with their daily lives. Rather, it is understanding the whole set of strategies, and then finding the levers by which they can be made to move in the direction which leaders intend, since this is their job as leaders. We will return to this point later on.

Frequency of meetings

A second difficulty has to do with the fact that identifying actors' problems does not mean that they are themselves conscious of those problems. It is a simple truth that you do not have to know what you want in order to want it, and that even without knowing it, you can still obtain it. This assertion brings us back to the problem of listening mentioned above. To "listen to" the actors is not to ask them what they want and then to act receptive and listen to what they have to say. Typically, the actors do not know what they want, and the very question will only give them a guilt complex about it. To illustrate this point, whenever a leader says to a subordinate "You do not know what you want", the latter could very well respond by saying that it is the leaders' job to know what their subordinates want. That is listening, and once again, its interpretive nature must be emphasized. To sum up, listening takes what one individual has to say about reality, and compares it to what others have to say about the same reality, so as to form a hypothesis on what the actor – once again, an individual or group of individuals – is trying to solve.

Let us take as an illustration the following classic experiment which anyone might try. Take two individuals, A and B, within any organization, knowing that A is the hierarchical superior of B, and ask them a simple, clear, precise question. In theory, we should not question the answers to this question, once we have made the mistake of believing that the actors "should" tell the truth. We will see that they do not tell the truth, but not because they are lying – as soon as we start thinking in terms of truth or lie, good or evil, we are no longer "listening" to anyone – but because there is no truth, or at least, its existence is far removed and abstract with respect to everyday life. Actors, when interviewed or simply spoken with, do not tell the truth, they express their way of seeing reality, or the perception which they think they should communicate to their environment.

The question we are going to ask two particular actors is how frequently they meet in the context of their job. Say that Mr A states unhesitatingly that he meets with Mr B four times a month, and that Mr B with no more hesitation reckons that they meet five times a week. Must we conclude that one of the two is lying? Of course not. Instead, we should use this discrepancy in their perception of the same reality to help us see that for Mr B, their relationship is more important than it is for

Mr A. The question is then: what problem does Mr B seek to solve since he has such a high, or perhaps overly high opinion of his relationship with his boss? Let us consider one response taken from a hundred possible situations, and suppose that this example takes place in one of the classic bureaucracies which is the very subject of this book. B is himself a mid-level executive who is in charge of a certain number of subordinates (call them C, D, E, F, and so on). These employees cannot deal directly with boss A, insofar as they have to follow the overall hierarchy of the organization. On the other hand, in a bureaucracy where everything is governed by rules and procedures, B has very little control over his own employees. He does not grade them, review them, promote them, decide when they can take their vacation, and so on. The only way he can get something from them is to assert each morning that he just met with the boss, and that he learned something important for everyone, without ever saying what it is about. To introduce a concept which will be elaborated later on, he creates uncertainty.

What simple truths have we learned? That Mr B's problem to be solved is controlling his subordinates. Does he know this? It is of no consequence. And the strategy which he uses to secure control is at once to monopolize on access to the boss, and to underscore or even exaggerate how often they meet. How is this kind of analysis useful, even in such a simple case, in everyday life? Say that a new Mr A is appointed, who has no advance knowledge about the organization he is joining, but is equipped with solid principles – models – which he learned in the very best business schools. When in charge of an organization, leaders must, he has been taught, open their door to everyone. Once involved in his new job, he does not ponder the problem, but applies solutions, which are going to prove his worth. Summoning C, D, E and F into his office, he tells them how he hopes to have a direct relationship with them and that his door will always be open if they would like to talk. The employees, who see no harm in the situation, begin to speak openly with their boss with whom previously they had no contact. A little while later, what do we observe? Mr B is withdrawn, he ceases to involve himself in his work, no longer participating in the group as a whole. And Mr A will be able to say that his excellent education allowed him to diagnose the situation of his new organization in less than two weeks: mid-level executives (Mr B here) have no motivation!

Of course this conclusion misses the mark. Mr A has not really understood anything, and because he applied a model *a priori*, without investing in knowledge, he has not learned to control the effects of his decisions, which, even on the micro-social scale of this case study, produced the wrong results.

Let us go back to the beginning, using the proposed grid: Mr B, "low-level leader" of a bureaucracy, seeks to control his handful of subordinates. This is his problem to be solved. He has a powerful resource which is his monopoly on access to the "high-level leader", and his principal constraint is his lack of real power over the members of the organization. His strategy, as we said, is to preserve his monopoly. From the outside, one might be led to say that he is "not very open", that he "keeps tight control", and so on. In fact, he has a rational strategy which consists in preserving and using his main resource. When the new Mr A decides to establish a more direct relationship with his employees, he is applying an abstract principle, and the only concrete result on the existing system is to eliminate Mr B's only way of staying in the game, say his only resource. And what is the rational strategy of an actor who is out of resources? It is to withdraw from the game because the actor is intelligent, and not as a consequence of some theoretical lack of motivation. Here again, real discussion of the problems which actors have to be solved opens new doors to managing change.

The coordinator and the delay

The third difficulty which we mentioned deserves a rather lengthy digression, for it allows us to tackle the problem of uncertainty and power in organizations.[16] Whether the actors are or are not aware of their own problems to be solved, it is rarely in their interest to say so, to put it in full view, unless they can be absolutely sure that it will not lock them into a situation of dependence.

And indeed, in any human system, as soon as actors know what is important for one of their group – what that particular actor seeks to do – they can assess in what ways they control that actor – the uncertainties – and thus the power which they derive from them, that is to say, in short, their ability to negotiate with this actor from a position of strength.

To illustrate this crucial point, which will take us back to the conditions for cooperation mentioned in Part I, we will use an example from the air transportation industry, which for reasons of clarity we will modify somewhat. One need not be a specialist in the business to know that, on one hand, the less time planes spend on the ground and how on time they are on the other, are two conditions for the profitability of any airline. In particular, the so-called "hub" system makes it especially important to minimize late arrivals, otherwise passengers will miss their connections, and the company will have to absorb any associated costs. Let us consider a large European company, a key carrier on the continent – let us call it X Air – which has established its hub at the principal airport in the country of origin. For X Air, as for the others, and especially given the climate of stiff competition which exists throughout the industry, on-time flights are a crucial factor around which the company tries to get all actors to work. And yet it is not easy to get a flight off on time, since preparing the aircraft, especially for long-distance flights, requires a whole set of complex operations. Even if we oversimplify, there are at least eleven important tasks to be accomplished, eleven specialized trade associations working simultaneously around the aircraft, so that it can take off at the scheduled moment.

Indeed, integrating these different activities is the key. On-time departure depends upon it, but such integration is very hard to achieve since the way X Air divides up its specialists means that each team working on the plane belongs to a different department or division, each under a different leader. The maintenance crew has little in common with the freight crew, and even less with the food-service crew. In the traditional organization of the company, one actor has been set up to ensure the coordination of all of these activities – we discussed the term earlier on – the coordinator. We have all had the chance to see a coordinator of this kind in operation, the last person to rush into the flight cabin, papers in hand, confirming that all is ready and that it is now up to the pilot to decide when to get under way. In the past, everyone agreed that X Air's coordinators did their job well, getting all of the different parts to work together well, which put the company among the top ten airlines for on-time flight statistics! Concerning this harmony, many had emotional, even mythical interpretations: it is aviation, it is about reaching for one's dreams – manners were sometimes rough, but they were to the point, and in everyone's best interest.

Several years ago, in the face of growing difficulties, X Air reorganized in the traditional sense of the term, that is, it changed structures and tried to adopt the classic organization of a profitable modern airline. Suddenly, following the reorganization, activity around the aircraft deteriorated, fewer and fewer flights were on time, and cooperation gave way to conflict and complaints. When questioned, the consultants who were in charge of setting up the new organizational chart emphasize that they did nothing to change the situation. In particular, they note, with good reason, that previously coordinators had no hierarchical power to get the different teams to cooperate; the current situation is no different. They add that the current situation is probably either more

tense, goodwill more difficult to find, or perhaps the coordinators themselves are younger and less hardened against people who are not easy to
handle. In short, their interpretation of the concrete and radical
changes which took place speaks about personnel and individuals, but
not systems, and would clearly leave any person in charge both confused
and powerless. This is why the question must be asked in a different
way, in more concrete and practical terms. What was there in the
previous situation that made cooperation with the coordinator a
rational strategy for the members of the different teams working around
the aircraft? Or in other words, using the concepts which were just
introduced: what kinds of uncertainty did the coordinators previously
wield over these teams to get them to cooperate?

This way of asking the question leads to another form of investigation, of pursuing the facts. It avoids concentrating on structures,
definitions of functions, and so on, and focuses attention on contextual
elements, perhaps commonplace and unimportant in appearance, but
which can turn out to be the very ones around which the system is
structured. In short, it leads us to curiosity, to listening, in a situation
that is unclear, that is, without turning to interpretive models which do
not belong to the specific reality which we are trying to understand.

Here let us add straightaway that coordinators, in addition to their
integrational task, are responsible for assigning, when the aircraft is
ready to go, what is called the "late code". This means that if, after all,
the plane does not leave on schedule, it is the coordinator's job to determine and indicate who is responsible. This is all we need to know to see
that they control uncertainty which is all the greater since there are so
many complex, interwoven causes that can make a plane late, among
which coordinators, in the end, can choose as they please.

The analysis does not end there, however: uncertainty controlled by
an actor only gives that actor power if it is relevant, that is, important
in respect to a problem which one or several other actors, or the
organization itself is trying to solve. The notion of relevancy helps
us understand why it is hardly in the actors' best interest to reveal
themselves: "Tell me what you want, and I'll know if I've got you under
my control!" In this instance, the assignment of the late code is a relevant uncertainty not only because the remuneration of the different
crews can depend partly upon it, but because their autonomy depends
upon it. Remember that the quest for autonomy is often a crucial problem to be solved within organizations. A single example of this is that
so long as the maintenance crew is not responsible for late departures,
their boss will leave them relatively free to do their work as they see

fit, to choose their own teams, to schedule their own breaks, and so on. As soon as their team bears the responsibility for late planes, bosses are forced to "intervene" to prevent a bad situation from getting any worse.

The power of the coordinator therefore has nothing to do with the official hierarchy. It can often be even stronger than what has been described here. If, for instance, there is a late departure, but all members still seem to have done their job, the coordinator is the only person who can negotiate on their behalf so that no penalty is assigned. The last ones to enter the cockpit, coordinators can always ask pilots to accept the late code, since they are never penalized on account of their absolute freedom to decide whether or not the plane is ready to take off.

What happened then during the "reorganization" which might explain the abrupt change in the behaviour of employees and the sudden increase in late departures? As is often the case, it was the result of good intentions based on principle, but without knowledge of reality. The organizers believed that, given the important role of the coordinators with respect to on-time departures, it was useless, even absurd, to ask them also to carry out bureaucratic tasks, such as the assignment of the late code. This was therefore taken away from their job responsibilities so as to leave them more time to devote to work "on the job". But in terms of concrete consequences, this was to take away the only real power they had, and for this reason made it much less rational for the different teams to cooperate with them.

What consequences might this have for the development of a frame of reference, as well as for managing change? Organization is not structure. I said it early on in this book and confirm it here, seeing at the same time that power is not hierarchy. But if both statements are true, changing an organization is not changing structure – as we saw – nor "positioning" certain actors within the hierarchy so that they have more power. Much more profoundly, it is changing the real distribution of this power, giving to the pivotal actors real, practical levers which they can use, which have a bearing on the reality of the problems which the actors we want to see cooperate are themselves trying to solve. Cooperation, once again, is not about goodwill or common sense. It is or is not a rational strategy for the members of the organization. It cannot be decreed; it is built up. A few examples of this are provided in Chapter 7.

The leverages for change

From this point on, understanding the concepts of resources and constraints is easy. A resource is what an actor can put to use in the resolution of a problem; a constraint is what must be confronted. The result is that for actors, resources or constraints are never abstract: they exist only in relation to what they (the actors) wish to obtain. Here again there is no ready-made model; emphasis is on the unknown, and thus on listening: one aspect of the picture which, at a given moment, is a resource, can become a constraint, and vice versa. It all depends on the problems which the different actors are trying to solve, and around which relationships are built. Note that this ability to change constraints into resources is precisely what is called, in a traditional approach to business, opportunity management.

There is a classic example of this used to explain the notion to young students: let us say there is an organization in which a rule states that work begins at 8:00 am. To ask whether for employee Y this rule is a resource or a constraint is abstract, so long as one has not yet identified the problem which Y or Y's boss – for simplicity's sake – wishes to solve. If on Monday morning Y would prefer to come in at 11:00 am because of some personal matter, then the rule in question is a constraint. It will require Y to negotiate with the boss's goodwill. But if on Tuesday, the boss asks Y to come in on Wednesday at 6:00 am to deal with an emergency situation, then this same rule can be a resource.

This example is not trivial, for it takes us back to two of the main themes: on one hand, the nature of rules and procedures within an organization; on the other, the nature of change. As for the first theme, we see that rules and procedures do not define what the actors do. They use them both as resources and constraints, make them their own, and in a sociological sense, play with them.

This is nothing new:[17] formal structures, written or customary rules – culture, one might say – form the context of the actors, to which they adjust with the intelligence which we believe them to have. But we can go further here: the intelligent adjustment which actors make, suggested here, not only affects their strategy (the context having been changed, I adapt my strategy) but also the problem to be solved, which in the end opens up many new possibilities for managing change. The order in which this argument has been presented here – actors, problem to be solved, resources, constraints and strategy, was chosen for the demonstration. It does not necessarily reflect the line of thinking of actors whose intelligence leads them naturally to give top priority to means rather than ends. More bluntly, they focus on possible goals, those which they think they can achieve in the context in which they find themselves. The result is that one modification of this context can lead these actors to change priorities, to focus on new problems, and afterwards, and only afterwards, to adapt their strategy to them.

A simple example: participants from all over the United States have come to attend a week-long seminar on the Bloomington campus of Indiana University. Having come by plane and then by limousine, they are left with no personal means of transportation. For their first evening off, this "constraint" will lead them, as the problem to be solved, to focus on spending the best possible evening in Bloomington. Now suppose that a professor announces, near the end of the afternoon session, his intention of going to Indianapolis for dinner or to attend an evening football or basketball game. A participant might now consider this professor to be a resource, and can focus on a new objective – spending the evening in Indianapolis – without even having to have decided what to do there. That can be determined upon arrival. The problem demonstrated by this example clearly opens up a whole new set of possibilities for introducing change into organizations: the fact that intelligent actors in the end select their own goals out of what is possible leads us to view certain contextual elements as levers which can be used in such a way that the actors will modify their priorities and strategies.

Here we see why rules of human resource management, taken in the largest sense – salary, review criteria, promotions, and so on – have tremendous potential concerning the transformation of organizations in general and bureaucracies in particular. Some commercial banks in America have understood this, setting as the number one criterion for employee review the ability to cooperate: rather surprising in a world where numbers are king! The banks measure this ability, for instance, as a function of the volume of business that customer representatives generate on behalf of their co-workers, or the number of customers they work with in conjunction with other members of the organization. In this case, cooperation is no more natural than in any other classic bureaucracy, but it becomes one of the strategies adapted by actors whose problems to be solved have been modified through the use of levers. From the all-important quest for autonomy, they have moved on to the necessity of cooperating so as to satisfy the criteria upon which they are reviewed.

Bringing this clarification of resources and constraints to a close, let it be said that the other actors must be included. Of course, this has nothing to do with our affection for them, even if we have the natural tendency to like our allies and dislike those who are in a position to block our way. But in organizations, alliances and confrontations, just like other contextual elements, are frequently turned upside-down.

There remains the concept of strategy, which has already been developed to some extent. It can be defined, in short, as the rational calculation made by the actors to solve the problem which seems to them either most attainable or most urgent, after an evaluation of their resources and constraints. "Calculation" is not used here in the sense of "mathematical determination". The actors very rarely sit down, head in hands, thinking through what to do. Such methods would cause them to err just as often as a more spontaneous method!

Calculation is used to convey the freedom of the actors, never fully backed into a corner, always able to maintain all or some of their unpredictability, and who are continually making choices which translate into their strategy or strategies. The idea of choice in the day-to-day experience of management is always hard to accept because it implies the enormous responsibility of the choice maker, who, of course, would rather claim that a decision is simply the "only possible solution", and that, consequently, anyone would come to that same decision. This is not the case, and this is why it is so difficult to run an organization, perhaps even in the end impossible, if we understand the expression in the voluntarist sense which it is often given. Organizations do not respond to a set of clear guidelines which actors would be willing to follow because they are fair, logical or reasonable. Organizations are the whole set of rational strategies which develop over time, one strategy in respect to another, and upon which each contextual modification has an influence, in a way which most often seems unpredictable or random, because we do not first bother investing in the knowledge of human systems. We do not have the time, and because we do not have the time we lose even more.

To those who wish to use the frame of reference which has just been presented, a final word of advice. Since reality is of such great complexity, I have suggested a grid with boxes to be filled in. It is reassuring to have something other than emptiness staring us in the face. But I have tried to emphasize that what is important is not the grid, which must not be reified as a tool which can always be trusted or which leaves little room for error. What is important, once more, is the line of reasoning. If this has been grasped, we might as well abandon the grid now; in using it, let us keep in mind these three principles:

1. It is perfectly legitimate to leave "gaps" in the grid. These might indicate a lack of resources or few constraints on a given group or individual – the question mark alone is revealing. Gaps might also reveal our own lack of information or understanding.

2. The grid cannot be filled out "bureaucratically" by starting with actor A, actor A's problem to solve, resources, and so on – then actor B, and so on. It works like a puzzle, piece by piece, by trial and error: it cannot be filled out all at once.

3. Above all, it is not an end, but a means: a means to understand the problem or problems at hand. In the example of the public system of ground transport carriers in France, the grid would have allowed us to see that fraud is a rational strategy for the helpless truck drivers, just as subcontracting out the most complex contracts is a rational strategy for those who are much less helpless. But the job does not end there. The problem is that these strategies arise because their cost is externalized on to the public as a whole through insurance companies. To move from the grid to the problem or problems: there is the process of listening.

7
The Process: From Symptom to Problem

The following scene takes place during a factory visit to an automobile equipment manufacturer in the American Midwest. The unit is mainly involved in the manufacture of various models of radiators on two production lines, one of which, the factory's pride and joy, has just been completely restructured. Our guide is a young engineer, brilliant, enthusiastic, volubly and accurately explaining the whole production system, the reasons for the almost clinical cleanliness of the workshops, the way in which staff meetings are held at the end of each shift to report progress, the absence of intermediate stock – which he considers to be his best success, even earning him a mention in the company's newsletter. In brief, an idyllic picture which confirms the first overall view glimpsed by visitors.

Intermediate stock as symptom

The production process itself appears simple, which again the young engineer reckons to be a success. Huge metal rollers are in situ at the head of the line and unwind at a regular pace. The sheets are pulled along by the belt, passing under successive chambers where processing is carried out. The finished product is immediately removed at the end of the line, as the factory follows a pull production system. A relatively low number of operatives watch over operations in an atmosphere redolent of calm, conscientiousness and concentration. One might just happen to notice that the line has an "elbow" bend, that is, a 90° angle three-quarters of the way along its length – because of the size of the workshop, according to our guide, who does not seem to attach much importance to it.

And yet if one stays to watch alongside this "elbow", one of the operatives can be seen standing inside the right angle, his back turned to the incoming flow ... and nonchalantly leaning on a pile of twenty or so half-finished radiators. This is pointed out to the young engineer, asking if this is not one of those famous build-ups of intermediate stocks which, as industrial history has shown, have the extraordinary ability to reappear just where they are least expected, and no matter how sophisticated the control equipment is that is used.

Beyond the first moment of surprise and, one might say, embarrassment faced with this visual observation in contradiction of the theoretical plan, the unit foreman's reaction is to rush over towards the operative, and hurriedly ask him to account for what has just been discovered, thanks to our presence. The operative does not seem unduly bothered by what is said (he must be about twenty years older than his manager), and calmly explains that this is in fact a buffer stock, but this really doesn't matter because, officially, in the data which are carefully collected at the end of the line, these radiators do not actually exist. He has, he says, taken them over time, without the operation being accounted for. Honour is therefore saved, appearances respected and there is no need to make a fuss about something of so little importance.

Human intelligence as problem

This response produces a completely different effect on the young engineer from the one expected by the operative – he once again starts to re-explain the whole theory of pull production, the justification for zero stocks, and so on, to the workman who listens with half an ear. While watching the scene, we observe that the operative's position, worked out down to the last detail and from which he cannot in any circumstances deviate, does not allow him to see what is going on behind him. Some questions directed at the engineer enable us to understand that each person working on the line has the possibility and even the duty to stop it if there is a problem, generally a defect on a part going by on the belt, or an interruption in the supply of parts. But interrupting a line, especially in pull production, is a serious action which will subsequently require explanation. Before making such a decision, the operative will want to be certain that the incident really exists, will talk to the workman before him on the line, actions requiring a minimum of time ... and which are therefore only possible with the existence of a buffer stock.

Certainly, this workman is intelligent, and there is no way of convincing him to act otherwise for as long as his surroundings are arranged as they are. But our young engineer has leapt onto the solution – explaining to the operative why he is wrong and what he must do.

In his haste, he has confused the *symptom* – there is an intermediate stock – with the *problem* – how to protect oneself in a context which sees the conjunction of pull production, of drastic quality management on the chain and the physical positioning of the operative isolated in his "elbow" corner. It is in fact a rational strategy for the operative to protect himself in such a context. But the confusion between the two dimensions (symptoms and problems) paralyses any action, renders dialogue impossible and, without our involvement, would no doubt rapidly have led to a conflict situation.

So here we are again with the question of convincing people discussed in the previous chapter. Because he only has one line of thought in mind, which to him seems indisputable and therefore universal, our young engineer is trying to get endorsement for it from all the other actors involved. What is at issue here, as in the case of the shampoo girl, is the worker's ability to understand this logic. Unfortunately for him in a way, this worker is intelligent and, above all, capable of absorbing a number of different lines and areas of information – such as the need to be forearmed, the ergonomics of his job, the desire not to be seen departing from the rules in force. The solution he has found deals with almost all the constraints. In fact, all things being equal, it will be relatively difficult to convince or even force him to act differently.

At the end of the day, in wanting quick action, in hoping to find immediate solutions that will avoid us seeming to be "slow", "intellectual", not very dynamic, in being too quick to jump to conclusions or, in other words, to believe anecdotes rather than facts, we are deceiving ourselves. And, especially in terms of change, the mistake is costly. It generates a whole series of perverse effects that are often difficult to control, which are the price that organizations make us pay for *ignorance*. And, in parallel, it paralyses in advance the action of those in charge, who intuitively hesitate to take risks when faced with a situation which they feel that they do not control. It is therefore never the right moment for change, and one then finds oneself confronted with the syndrome of crisis.

What is a step in the process of change?

One must therefore accept the need to lead change in steps, the first of these being, as we have seen, to dissociate symptoms from problems. And yet this idea of steps is itself open to debate, especially as, to start with, it reminds one of the conventional action plans, in which the phases succeed each other in accordance with a carefully pre-established order and tempo. This type of action adheres to ritualism, and it is always the most conservative organisations which are most likely to use and abuse it.

Placing himself at another level, Edgard Schein, a great specialist in the therapy applied to organizations, writes: "*[T]his notion that I must first collect data in order to plan a subsequent intervention is, I now understand, one of the most senseless ideas in the field of consultancy.*"[1] While the idea that diagnosis and intervention must be conducted simultaneously and not sequentially is certainly attractive and pertinent when this is a therapeutic approach, it does however need to be adjusted once this involves managing a process of change, which one does not necessarily wish to result in a destruction phase prior to reconstruction.

And even if one must avoid falling into the *process* of change, the best way of producing immobility, there are *moments* which stand out more or less distinctly from each other and which avoid the "precipitation" which has become such a sign of our times, as noted by James March. "*Unfortunately,*" he writes, "*we are engulfed by the contemporary enthusiasm for an immediate solution … our enthusiasm has become excessive.*"[2] It is therefore important to keep a place for what he calls "research knowledge", as already demonstrated by Chris Argyris to be the very condition for action, provided such knowledge is not just useful, but also usable.[3] This general acceptance of knowledge being a prerequisite for any action, or at least in the worlds of universities and consultancies – since it is still under debate by current managerial rhetoric, as well as by companies that make it a point of honour to ask their managers not to think – is what we call here the transition from symptoms to problems.

Why this talk of "symptoms"?

This medical metaphor is not used by chance, since we only take an interest in change when something comes to our attention.[4] In the same article, Schein writes:

> [W]e need to start with symptoms, with irritating data, with programmes gone up in smoke. There can be a variety of metaphors, but it is self-evident that true change only occurs once the organisation experiences a true threat or real pain. Such pain can be felt in the form of culpability, when one recognises that certain values or ideals have not been achieved. The goal can then be a real improvement, even though it is still based on a tension between what is desired, and what is perceived as being the present reality.[5]

Even so, the pain must fairly severe and, as highlighted by this same author, *"the anxiety to survive"* must be greater than *"the anxiety to learn"* for, as we have continually repeated since the start of this book, reality is frightening and knowledge is disturbing. And no doubt the solution is not found in a dramatization of the symptoms, in an attempt to cause alarm when faced with the seriousness of the problem, but rather in a reduction of anxiety when faced with learning. This is far more widespread among management than among their subordinates, as the acceptance of learning is primarily a "posture" signifying the acknowledgement that one does not know everything, or that one did not know. But is one a true manager when one doesn't know? This brings to mind a senior manager saying to his executive board in introduction to the restitution of the results of a diagnosis that we were going to present: *"If one of you says* 'I already knew', *I shall consider that as serious professional misconduct."* There is therefore a need to demonstrate that the knowledge of problems is not agonizing but in fact quite the opposite, since it allows one firstly to talk to others and secondly to control the results of what one is undertaking to do. Again according to Schein, this is one of the conditions for "intellectual security".

In order to really understand the distinction that is proposed between symptoms and problems, one can reinsert this in all the debates around *knowledge management*, in other words, the capacity that organizations have to build themselves up from knowledge and to pass it on. Knowledge that is unrefined, spontaneous, intuitive, however important it may be, does not form a corpus that can be transmitted as it is. There is a need for work to be done on processing it, analysing it and interpreting it, to ensure that what is communicated has added value in terms of the initial sentiment of actors. This also makes it possible to capitalize on practices, systems in operation, and not just on anecdotes. These must be separated from the facts which lead to an in-depth understanding. To summarize, the symptom can be considered as an *item of information* and the problem as an *item of knowledge*, bringing one to the conclusion that the problem is an *item of information understood.*[6]

The understanding of problems as a listening mechanism

This has major consequences in terms of change, and in the first place on what listening really means. Taken in its first meaning, listening simply means asking actors their opinion on such and such a question, or their hopes and expectations. This can be applied to a company's employees as well as its customers, and the methods used will then be those of a survey, attitude studies or "corporate barometers". The implicit postulate is that what actors have to say on reality, including their own reality, is a true reflection of this reality in all its complexity. Replies which are then made will be "linear", that is, they will correspond point by point with remarks made by actors, customers or employees.

Experience shows that such an approach can lead to catastrophic results, completely the opposite of those looked for. What actors expect, when they talk to those who are there to listen to them, is that they will help them to understand what is going on, why they do not feel at ease or why things are not as they would like them to be. Of course, everybody has explanations that are more or less well founded, supportive and compartmentalized, and seeks to promote them. But if one comes back towards the actors, merely returning to them what they have said in a more or less ordered fashion, they will have the feeling that they have not been listened to, even that one is trying to use their words as a pretext. To summarize this into a formula, *listening is not asking people what they want, it's telling them.*

There is, of course, nothing manipulative in this way of saying things. It simply takes account of the fact that actors have an initial perception of reality, which is not enough to take into account the complexity of the situation, which is not an item of information that is understood. In the transport company mentioned earlier in this volume, we caused a surprise reaction from one of the managers in the following circumstances: when questioning him at length on the inspectors, he used an insulting term to speak of them, emphasizing just how much he considered this category of staff to be unreliable, even dishonest in their behaviour towards the company. We queried the harsh severity of his judgement and he then explained how unfair it seemed to him for these people to use any pretext whatsoever in order to always ask for more... and to always be prepared to go back on strike once these additional advantages had been granted to them. We pointed out that such behaviour was in fact, to the contrary, a very clear sign and, when he showed his extreme surprise, we suggested that obtaining additional material advantages was no doubt not the problem, but much more a symptom. In a way, these officers had done their work by going on strike, and it was now up to him to do his work in understanding why. The true need is there and this is why knowledge is frightening to start with.

Symptoms, these *misunderstood pieces of information*, show themselves in various ways. They are the organization's *events*. Sometimes they are technical and involve breakdowns, delays or a sudden increase in the costs of non-quality; at other times they may be financial and show themselves in a drop in profits, a fall in turnover or a loss of market share; in human terms, they may take the form of high absenteeism, repeated strikes, or employee claims that are never satisfied. And the one-off or sequential response has little chance of sorting things out – in fact, quite the opposite.

For actors have a partisan interpretation, in the strategic rather than polemic sense of the term, of the symptoms which show themselves. It is for this reason too that the absence of in-depth work, in transforming information into knowledge, brings pointless conflict into the search for solutions.

Two examples are given below, with the interesting point that although situated in two completely different spheres of activity, they both lead to the same conclusion.

The first example is that of a French business, which has the intention and no doubt the vocation of becoming a world leader in its market and which is faced with the necessity, if it wants to achieve this aim, of successfully carrying out acquisitions allowing it to diversify – not only geographically but also in terms of complementary activities. It therefore sought to invest – particularly in the Anglo-Saxon world (United States and United Kingdom) – but was rapidly confronted with a latent revolt from its new acquisitions, in particular senior managers, who reproached it for according only marginal importance to economic performance and its measurement. Debate was therefore engaged between them, major benchmarking efforts were initiated, a "project" extending over several years and involving a high number of actors was launched, intended to reach completion with a vast convention during which drastic decisions were expected to be announced that would be likely to profoundly change this company's "culture".

At the same time, while we were working on the organizational diagnosis requested by this company's CEO, one of the French managers pointed out to us, with no little surprise, that it was precisely those countries that were most vehement in demanding that performance should be taken into account almost exclusively for appraising people and units which performed the least well.

That so very pertinent remark alerted the observer – this contradiction, like all the others, is probably only an appearance. It is more than likely that such a focus on performance is merely a *symptom*, which, we must point out, does not mean that it is any less legitimate. But the *real problem*, as one might say, must be something else.

Diagnosis will reveal this: for many years, the company has had a lot of difficulty consolidating its acquisitions although, as we have said, this is one of its key strategies for success. This produces cycles of "investment/disinvestment" which lead some people to think that such transactions follow a logic of "dancers around the CEO" rather than a real strategy. In everyday life, this difficulty in absorbing new units is marked by the almost exclusive presence in the higher echelons of the hierarchy, that is, in the best jobs, of French people belonging to the company's predominant "business" or at least having been noticed there, and representing a very specific sociological profile in terms of socio-cultural origins and training.

The selection mechanisms used for this are therefore *de facto* mechanisms. They do not result from any stated intention, nor from any decisive policy – in fact they give rise to questioning and sometimes gloom from managers who are not far distant from envisaging "quota" systems in order to face up to the situation. What is actually involved is not the conscious and intentional action of individuals, but the informal mechanisms that nobody can control which, at the end of the day, produce the elitist result that we have already shown. When the "careers committee" meets to review the best applicants for promotion to a better job, it "notes" the uniformity of profiles, but that's the way things are.

Seen from the outside, such mechanisms are as frustrating as they are implicit, difficult to identify and therefore impossible to describe accurately – something that, in a world of engineers, becomes prohibitive. Everybody understands that, in order to succeed in this organization, one must, in the broadest of lines, have been born somewhere, have been raised in a certain way and have attended certain specific schools. These are things that are built while you are young and if you are "not part of this system" then you will accumulate handicaps that are difficult to make up for. This explains why this system seems so terribly unfair to "outsiders" who feel that they are the main victims. They criticize it for favouring social performance (the good fortune of belonging to networks and the ability to move around in them comfortably) to the detriment of economic performance. Hence the trenchant judgements bitterly emphasizing that, in this business, there is little hesitation in promoting mediocre people – people who have not shown any particular ability in terms of business results.

Consequently, enthusiastically seeking the measurement of economic performance means seeking justice and fairness, which are indeed the essential conditions for a good consolidation of acquisitions ... The loop has come full circle! By agreeing to focus the debate on this issue – that of economic performance – the company has, in a way, mistaken the *problem*. It is in fact not the smallest of paradoxes to note that its attention may have been drawn by the fact that it is, indeed, a company that performs well, or at least if one compares it with its competitors. That does not mean that it hasn't got a long way to go on the matter, although the torrent of figures, the fascination for what is seen and can be easily described, the assimilation – at the first level and without analysis – of what actors are saying, have probably made it even more difficult to distinguish between symptoms and therefore, at the end of the day, relatively unacceptable. Finally, from having heard too much of the actors, nobody was listening to them.

The second example takes place in a completely different business milieu: during a survey carried out a few years ago on establishments taking in mentally or physically handicapped children, researchers were moved and impressed by the devotion of all the people working in such establishments, in emotionally difficult conditions, bearing in mind the serious handicaps that were being dealt with. At the same time, a persistent problem marked the life of such institutions, generated by the virtual impossibility of personnel to develop a collective "establishment project". And yet they were all in agreement: the interests of the children, especially those who were handicapped, must not be affected by political in-fighting and should be the subject of an easily obtainable consensus. When looking closely, however, it seemed that each person realized all at once that the children's needs were not always sufficiently taken into account (the symptom), and gave, to the defence of the interests of these young inmates, a definition which, if it had been applied, would have ensured the pre-eminence of their profession over the others within the establishment. The doctors gave priority to treatment, the educators to teaching, the psychologists to individual monitoring, and so on. Their good intentions were never at cause, it was simply that they only had access to partial and biased information, which did not help them to reach agreement on the true nature of the problem to be dealt with, that is, the extreme complexity of the situation of these children, which would have required from them a very constrictive cooperation compared with the segmentation and specialization of their jobs, to which they had become accustomed and for which they had been trained.

The tools for listening

There is therefore a need for investigation and, without entering into too much detail on tools which have been presented elsewhere, we are now going to discuss and illustrate some practical applications, with a view to highlighting some of the problems.

The first point looks into the transition from the *occasional* to the *complex*. Generally, indeed, a symptom is one-dimensional. It highlights one part of the organization, the behaviour of one category of actors, it points the finger and the projector on what is seen. In fact, it allows appearance to be apparent. But a simple reformulation in the following terms, "When such and such an event takes place, which actors must be taken into account in order to try and grasp the true nature?", makes it possible to go beyond the initial simplicity. Here, this involves tracing the *sociogram*, that is, *the representation of the relationships between actors, such as experienced by the actors themselves*. This makes it possible both to effect a first illustration of the *system* which forms itself around the identified symptom, and to look at the positive, negative or neutral aspects played by the actors in this system. We will then move on from these relationships to the issues and strategies which underlie them. By remaining at the level of the symptom, we were focusing on the *apparent* actors; by moving on to the sociogram, we will be focusing on what we have referred to above as the *relevant* actors. Here is a practical application, which again takes place in the transport company and allows us to go further into an analysis of this case study.

You will remember that the main symptom attracting the company's attention is the behaviour of generalized avoidance practised by the categories of personnel who are in contact with customers, mainly the inspectors, in a difficult situation. It is to face up to this commercially punitive situation that the company has launched its training programmes on "service attitudes", aiming to change the attitudes of employees in front of customers.

The implicit assumption is that, in this case, only two actors are involved in the relationship, those who are visible – the inspector and the passenger. These are what we call the *apparent actors*. When these same actors are asked to describe their working universe and to evaluate the relationships that they have with the "rest of the world", they give a view which is far more complex and which would become even more complex if all parties concerned were asked to express themselves. Schematically, this universe can be represented as shown in Figure 7.1.

Understanding and controlling complexity

The inspector lives in a universe of which the complexity goes well beyond the simple face to face with the customer, with whom he has,

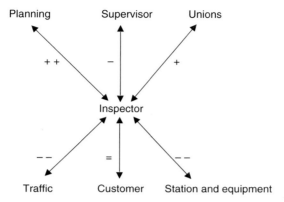

Figure 7.1[7]

in effect, a relatively neutral relationship – particularly in a normal situation when such a relationship boils down to checking travel documents, carried out as quickly as possible. With his boss, the supervisor, relations are stretched: the inspector considers that his line management is of no help to him in his daily life, and even less so in awkward situations. He is alone to face his surroundings, with a distant boss who cannot give him the necessary information, nor help him to resolve his immediate problems, which above all have a bearing on his relationships with other actors. In addition, he bitterly reproaches his bosses, themselves former inspectors, for having "forgotten everything", and for having taken refuge in a passive application of the rules, a long way away from the reality of work, and which mean for example that he will be appraised on his appearance, general presentation, and so on.

"Traffic" is a key actor, which will help us to understand the systemic complexity. In appearance, its relationship with the inspectors should be distant, even non-existent: they belong to two quite distinct company departments. Traffic deals with regulating traffic flow, ensuring safety and continuity and above all, as needed, it makes crucial arbitrations between punctuality and connections, based on criteria which, as we have already noted, were vague, if not non-existent. Inspectors blame them for this lack of transparency and, when they occasionally need to contact them in dealing with an urgent situation, they emphasize the very dubious reliability of the information obtained. When questioned in depth, the traffic officers, for their part, seem to be unaware of the very existence of inspectors, who are not part of their working environment. They have a technical perception of their work, marked by an obsession with security, which means that the customer, in the materiality of his daily problems of punctuality, is not a concrete preoccupation for them.

Under the general designation of "station and equipment", we find, on the one hand, all the actors contributing to preparing the means of transport (cleanness, lighting, heating, arrival at the station on time) and, on the other, all those involved in receiving, directing, informing customers in the station, including the sale of tickets. Here again, the inspectors emphasize just how little care such actors show in their work through a multitude of anecdotes, certain of them being well known to the company which carefully files them under the heading "return of experience", which seems to signify that there has been a problem and that, for once, it was known. This concerns technical infractions, involving the way in which things were done but not taking into account the reports, apparently many and varied, sent in by the inspectors. The officers in charge of equipment, if one only listens to them, defend themselves by saying they do not read the reports, of which they even deny the existence. As for those allocated to selling tickets, they carry out their work under pressure from customers who are always in a hurry and consequently not concerned with asking too many complicated questions. As a result of this, there are discrepancies between the tickets sold and the journeys made, which might lead to a conflict situation in the relationship between customers and inspectors, if the latter did not prefer to refrain from checking tickets in such circumstances, even if this means that the company loses money.

As its name indicates, the planning department is in charge of fixing how inspectors are allocated, in accordance with extremely complicated rules which have given rise to the development of an impressive set of regulations, intended to ensure everybody's equality in terms of workload and working constraints. One can fully understand the importance of this function for an itinerant population, often concerned to carry out the shortest possible shifts – those making it possible to go home in the evening. Here it is not the rule which makes this possible, but the *accommodation with the rule*, which is negotiated directly with planning officers without the need to go through any sort of official procedure. One can understand why inspectors find their colleagues in the planning department to be friendly and obliging. One will see, in passing, that this *power* which conditions the life of such staff is not held by line management, and this gives us an idea of the extent of the confusion, within the company, between organization and structure. On one side we have rules which are supposed to plan for and organize every situation but which are endlessly broken in order to allow life to follow its course, and on the other we have bosses who have no real hold over this life and who therefore hide behind formality and ritualism.

There are many union organizations and they are even more active when in competition for this population which is a key actor across the whole company, since legally transport cannot take place without the presence of inspectors on board. The result of this is continual bargaining, continually renewed negotiations, which sometimes lead to a surprising feeling of absurdity: in this way, it has been necessary to reach agreement on the average number of steps that an officer takes per minute, in order to determine whether the fact of going into a hostel at the end of a journey was part of the working day or not! When questioned on the subject, the inspectors express doubts on the real knowledge that unions have of their daily lives although, with nothing better available, they nonetheless appreciate obtaining additional advantages through their intervention. As for the unionists, truly a state within a state, they have the monopoly on access to top managers, who only communicate through the unions in accordance with mechanisms and rites that nobody ever puts in question. In addition, the human resource department has a good number of former militants among its ranks.

If one now wanted to get this sociogram to "speak", although one should bear in mind that it is only a tool, one would note first of all the extreme complexity and diversity of the *relevant* universe in which the inspector exists, and which has little to do with the official structure to which the organization chart links him. Even better – for him, his boss is not an important part of this structure.

One can then see that the actors with whom he has the most strained relationship are those who affect his professional life, whether upstream or downstream of his work – those who plan the journeys, sell the tickets, make important choices. However, these actors themselves act outside of any anticipation of the consequences of their acts and their decisions on the face-to-face contact between the customer and the inspector. At best, they are not bothered; at worst, they think of him as a nuisance, and are not far from sharing their doubts with management on his true involvement in work. Even if they wanted to take things differently, the company's official organization would make this difficult. The absolute and sought-after segmentation does not push towards this, and does not make it possible finally to leave the narrow confines of one's own action, which leads all those involved towards a sort of resigned fatalism faced with the observation that what is happening is neither wanted nor decided by anybody whatsoever, it is simply *there*.

On the other hand, the inspector has a very positive relationship with the actors who participate in the organization of his private life, who allow him to choose his way of life, like those who negotiate his benefits for him. It would not even be necessary to push the analysis any further in order to understand, at least in general terms that do not enter into the detail of the mechanisms, that the less interest the company, *in its real method of functioning* and not in its statements or its intentions, is able to take in the professional life of its officers, the more they take refuge in their private lives, to which they pay almost exclusive attention. Starting from a symptom, that inspectors do not stay with customers in a difficult situation and reduce such relations to a minimum in a normal situation, we are not far from having understood the problem, simply by looking at the *relevant universe in which they evolve* and which is a long way from their theoretical and hierarchical context of action.

From organizational complexity to systemic complexity

Even in a case like this one, complexity is reduced by the fact that all the actors are evolving in the same structure, which makes their identification easier. But sometimes it is necessary to face systems that are more complex, that are not bordered by any visible frontier and yet which are, paradoxically from the point of view of action, far more "concrete" than structures and organization charts. Let us take a detailed example of this, all the more interesting in that the rules governing it produce effects to the opposite of those expected. This is the system of public inland transport of goods in France, such as it existed a few years ago.[8]

Hidden behind this off-putting statement we in fact find an analysis of the transport of goods by road, when the consignor – who has a load for shipping – does not itself ship its own goods, but instead hands them over to a specialized firm.

Traditionally, public authorities – in this case civil servants in the Land Transport department of the French Ministry of Transport – develop what we have called linear vision. As they see it, the main problem for this sector is that of fraud by carriers – whether independents or employees.[9] It is easy to understand them. When the railway system was nationalized in France (1936), road transport was subjected to a very close and finicky control, covering or having covered all areas of the activity – from the very fact of being allowed to carry goods (long-haul transport licences), through to "welfare" conditions of transport (driving hours, rest periods, and so on), not forgetting the fixing of prices (for a long time there was a compulsory pricing system for road transport in France that set a top and bottom price for every product carried). Lastly, we find European legislation on top of domestic legislation.

Continuing their reasoning, the civil servants in charge add that statistics show that fraud leads to accidents (falling asleep at the wheel or driving an overloaded vehicle), and that reducing it is therefore a measure of public safety. By this means, they manage to convince the Minister to take action. This is in fact a sensitive sector which demonstrates regularly (1992, 1997) and everywhere (for example, Chile) its ability to paralyse economic activity. The Minister takes a pragmatic view of this and only attempts to tackle the problem if he thinks there is a visible benefit to voters – for example, a significant reduction in road traffic accidents.

But where does one start with this problem? This is where linear reasoning comes into play – refusing to acknowledge complexity. If truck drivers are evading the law, slipping through the net, that means the net is too slack. So all one has to do is tighten it – in other words reinforce the legislation directly controlling the activity of drivers (penalty points system in 1992) and multiply the checks without which legislation can have no effect on actors who *a priori* take hardly any notice, for reasons that civil servants can only understand in terms of morality. Although this presentation is caricaturized, it helps to understand how, in the eyes of the state's representative, the "transport" that we are about to analyse as a complex system is reduced to a single activity – conveyance by vehicle – and a single actor – the lorry driver (but only until he breaks the law). And yet you only have to read the actual results of this strategy with its proliferation of rules and inspections to be gripped by despair – fraud is rampant, requiring ever more rules, until the whole system explodes when the vicious circle has become so tight that it has to be broken.

Is there an alternative to this vision which seems both oversimplified and inefficient? Yes, but with two conditions – accepting complexity (which here means not reducing the problem of fraud simply to the truck driver's behaviour) and agreeing to stand back from the actual situation and stop monitoring it too closely, that is, stop trying to understand "how it works". In illustration of this: if there are goods in a lorry, this is because someone (the consignor) has products that need moving. This consignor can directly approach a carrier, generally a "big carrier"– we will be returning to this definition – or a middleman, known in the trade as a freight coordinator-consolidator-contractor-forwarder who is really specialized in the regulations (knows all the ins and outs) as well as able to match supply and demand, making it possible to complete a load or avoid an empty return.

In this business, subcontracting is common practice. The "big carrier" will therefore be able to transfer a contract to a smaller (and therefore less busy?) carrier, in the same way that a coordinator will be able to choose their subcontractor, depending on the type of work required. Let's stop here for a moment: having started from a simple vision with a single actor – the lorry driver – here we are now in the presence of at least four actors – the consignor, the coordinator, the big carrier and the small carrier. And in order to cover every aspect, maybe we should add SNCF (French railways), the country's leading road haulier, the various police forces that carry out checks, and the different administrative authorities – Highway Maintenance, Works, and so on – which draw up rules, distribute documents, and sometimes carry out checks.

Let us now take another step towards complexity thanks to two observations. First of all, pressure on prices. Back when there was the compulsory pricing system, most transactions took place at the bottom price, even, unofficially, below it. Since then, it is still almost the same situation. This gives a clear indication that here it is freight that is scarce but not transport. Whoever is in control of this scarcity – this uncertainty – holds the power. In this case, it can be the consignor, or the coordinator, or the big carrier using subcontractors – all these actors having one thing in common in that they do not drive the lorries and are therefore not directly concerned by regulations.[10] This is a particular paradox of linear reasoning which places the "fault" on the least powerful actor in the system, simply because this actor is "visible" and, at the end of the day, does not know who holds the real power. The "real falsehood" is this – the confusion between appearance and reality.

The second observation is a question – in a country that has always made the middleman liable for its misfortunes, one might have expected that the consignor would organize its own transport; however, it makes use of a shipping company. Why? To understand this, one has to look at the consignor's logic – it has to manage a constraint upstream at the same time as downstream. Upstream, it is pressurized by a production environment that is increasingly oriented towards a pull production system ("just in time"), which leads to "responding" to demand and delivering at the last moment. Downstream, it is faced with its customer who, here again, wants to avoid stocks and to only have the goods at the moment of putting them on the shelves. If, to this twofold constraint, one adds those resulting from transport regulations, it is rapidly going to become impossible for the same actor to reconcile all aspects. Quite naturally, the consignor is going to focus on its own particular problem – the relationship with its customer – and outsource what is involved in this activity to the specialist – the carrier or the coordinator. Crudely speaking, it will be asking for flexibility, that is, fraud, or the boss of the shipping company will be asking for it from "its employee", which boils down to the same thing. Does this mean that everything is just fraud? No, of course not, but if the consignor only calls for this "flexibility" in 1 per cent of cases, the customer's loyalty will, at that moment, depend upon the positive reply from the carrier – in an environment in which we should remember that what is scarce is the freight.

Let us continue the voyage in "real life". Suppose that the consignor's requirement is particularly difficult to satisfy, involving a high level of non-compliance with the rules and, at the same time, a low level of remuneration. The big carrier on which the requirement falls has the possibility of accepting – we have seen why – without running the risk of actually doing it itself. It will in turn subcontract to someone further down the ladder, to the "small carrier" for which we are now in a position to understand the characteristics – which have nothing to do with the number of lorries owned by the business. The small carrier is the one who drives his own lorry – or one of his lorries – and, because of this, has no availability for sales or marketing, depending entirely on others to find freight. This will be given to him straight from the coordinator or subcontracted from the big carrier – who does not do any driving, doesn't really "have his backside in the driving seat" (as they say in the business). What he is given, it is understood, is fraud, and the less free he is, the more likely he is to accept, including when this is accompanied by a remuneration from which everyone has already taken their tithe.

What can we say? That, seen from the system, fraud is not a problem but a solution, and therefore a symptom. It is what marketing specialists call a "differential advantage" in a world in which one must above all get hold of the freight. In such a context, increasing the regulations on the least powerful actors only restricts a little more their room for manoeuvre, and therefore their real possibility of choice. In July 1992, the weakest of these – drivers or craftsmen – brought the country to a standstill in order to denounce such constraints by simply announcing that they were unable to drive less fast.[11]

Let us add another point. If one wants to understand the concept of "transport system" – Crozier and Friedberg's concrete action system – as opposed to the simplistic vision of conveyance by vehicle, one has to look at the question of cost. Everything revolves around cheating the system (also regulating it, according to the sociologist) but at a cost – that of an accident. What next? We are now in the presence of a new actor, whose existence and importance have not as yet been mentioned by anyone – the insurance company which does not pick out, in its own accounts, a specific risk for heavy goods vehicles. It becomes the instrument through which the extra cost generated by fraud – as a method of regulating the system of land transport – is externalized onto the whole automobile system.

As a result, change might be reasoned in a systemic rather than linear fashion. For example, when an accident involving the responsibility of a heavy goods vehicle leads to material consequences, why not involve the whole instructing party chain, instead of just the lorry driver? This is what happens now as a result of the action in 1992. Why not spread the heavy goods vehicle risk, as in the English model, that is, reinternalize the cost of its own operation into the system, thereby allowing it to function differently, at a lower cost, therefore less fraudulently? As a paradox of complexity, the formal logic might find itself turned upside down to the profit of a reasoning that may well be less "simple" in its formulation, but oh so very much more concrete in its perception of reality – instead of the false common sense that tells us "Since fraud produces the accident, let us reduce fraud and we will thus reduce the accident", one can substitute the following approach: "It is by making the cost of the accident insupportable to the whole land transport system that one can succeed in reducing fraud, which is of course the cause of this additional cost." In brief, once reality has been understood, let us reduce the accident in order to reduce fraud!

The need to switch from the symptom to the problem has therefore taken us a long way from consideration of the complexity of organizations and human systems. It has allowed us to take a look at what is meant by *concrete* since it is the problem that is concrete even where it is the symptom that sounds the alarm. We have therefore been led to reassess even concepts that are accepted by the great majority of people, because these make it possible to avoid facing up to such complexity – the concept, for example, of the organization and its environment, what is "inside" it and what is "around" it. However, the very idea of the system is contradictory to this approach, because it starts from the actors, listens to them, in the sense that we keep giving to this term – the reconstitution of their reality and not just the simple consideration of the theoretical environment in which the organization chart places them. We have finally understood that the organization chart is, to the system, what the symptom is to the problem – the appearance but not the true reality. This is what we call methodological realism in order to emphasize that, in the everyday procedures of organizations in general and with regard to change in particular, it is indeed this realism which is so sadly lacking.

We are going to add a final case study to this chapter which will act as a practical application of this approach, this distinction between symptoms and problems, while at the same time excavating some of the methodological aspects covered in the preceding chapter by means of the strategic analysis grid.

The principal resource of the most powerful actor

The company in this case study produces a mass-consumption product and is on the point of being privatized, having been a public enterprise since its inception, benefiting on its national territory from a monopoly in manufacturing and distribution.[12] Even though the number of factories has been reduced over the years, the general organization has remained the same: a head office which everybody considers hypertrophied located in the capital, and factories all operating in accordance with the same model, because applying to the letter an impressive package of standards, rules and procedures drawn up scrupulously by the industrial division with regard to production methods, and the human resource division for everything to do with the management of individuals. In each of the factories, production is carried out in workshops comprised of three categories of personnel – on which we are going to focus our attention, leaving to one side the management team.

The shop foremen, with little in the way of qualifications, arriving there on criteria which have nothing much to do with their technical competences but much more to do with the tradition of providing them with a second job after they have taken retirement, simply watch over the application of rules upon which they are very dependent. They are in fact production accounters who do not invest themselves very much in work. They are paid a fixed salary with little likelihood of progress, which they seem to adapt to without any great difficulty. The production workers either drive the machines or handle the raw materials and finished goods, switching between these two functions every fortnight. Their wages vary and depend, to a significant degree, on the level of production that they achieve. In the event of an incident on their machine, they lose a proportion of their "bonus", even if they are in no way responsible for the breakdown. Finally, the maintenance workers, highly or even overqualified in relation to the requirements of their task, carry out the calibration and maintenance of machines, especially each time there are minor breakdowns. If these become too serious, the repair work is entrusted to an outside company. In addition, they control the union organizations in which they find themselves alongside their production colleagues.

The thing that worries senior managers on the point of facing up to competition, is that they are seeing a breakdown rate that is substantially higher than that seen at competitors, as well as average call-out times on machines for small incidents that are again higher than average in the business. Training programmes have been set up with the intention of making all categories of personnel aware of the problem and strengthening the already impressive competences of maintenance staff. The results have been very disappointing and no significant improvement has been seen. The company has therefore decided to have a diagnostic review carried out by a specialized outside consultancy.

The presentation which has just been made makes it possible to anticipate the principal results: the maintenance staff are the dominant actors of the "workshop systems", since they control what is a decisive factor in the reality of power – they control a relevant uncertainty, as orthodox sociology might say – that is, machine breakdowns, on which the production workers depend for their wages. This observation is not banal, as it allows one to understand the *organizational aspect of a symptom which appears as a technical aspect*. One might say that in such a case, the breakdown is not simply a machine that stops – at the end of the day, a very impoverished vision of reality – *it is the principal resource of the most powerful actor*.

The difference is not slight in terms of action. In the first case – the technical vision – the solution consists of repairing the machines and giving ever more training to those whose task it is. In the second case – organizational vision – wanting to reduce the rate of breakdowns in order to adapt to competition, this means reducing the power of the dominant actor, which is quite another matter and far more difficult to manage.

This is the reason why, even when remaining very cautious faced with any over-hasty generalization, we will see that, as soon as one has identified the principal resource of the most powerful actor, one has a good chance of putting one's finger on the key point of the system being studied. This is both an interesting open door for action (and it must be remembered when reasoning on priorities) as well as a datum to be handled with extreme caution, since one can be sure that an actor does not willingly give up something that allows him to dominate a system. Opportunity and difficulty offered by what others would call the *regulation of the system*: we have just glimpsed the heart of our subject.

The search for autonomy as the most universally widespread problem

Nonetheless, the thread must be pulled tight until we have a complete understanding of the symptoms. The shop foremen are not very "motivated" and keep out of the day-to-day running, which management notes regretfully and impotently. But by reviewing the concepts which have been proposed, it can be seen that these actors, who are supposed to be in a hierarchical situation, in fact have no resources but, to the contrary, a number of not insignificant constraints; in particular the abundance of procedures which deprive them of any possibility of decision and the fact that the maintenance staff do not report to them but to an engineer outside the workshop.

Like all intelligent actors, they adapt their problem that needs solving to the context in which they find themselves – *in which they have been placed* – and simply try to live in peace. In doing this, they *transform one of their constraints into a resource* – which, in the sometimes comical managerial language of business schools, is known as "managing an opportunity" – and hide behind regulations in order to avoid being forced to take action. One can understand that they have a strategy of withdrawal, in the same way that production workers seek to have the best possible relationship with *their* maintenance workers, at the same time as denouncing their arbitrariness in general. The latter, as is the case for all actors possessing a major resource, content themselves with using this with a view to preserving their *autonomy* which, as we will note in passing, in experience *is the most widespread problem that needs resolving in organizations*. They therefore play on the repair times of the machines – second symptom – in order to protect themselves against untimely requests for their intervention which might disturb their work, over the pace of which they intend to maintain control. As one of them says: "No journey without a destination."

And so we learn that, in this small system, which was neither wanted nor created by anybody in particular but has developed over time into its current existence, the breakdown is the major resource of the dominant actor who, because he is intelligent, uses it and thus inflates the length of time that he is involved on the machines. We have moved on from the symptoms to the problems, using a method of reasoning which, for reasons of practicality and transmissibility, we have formulated in the shape of tools that are easy to use. But at the same time, the reasoning which was used, and the results that were obtained in this way, make it possible to revisit the problematic of change, by once again focusing on realism. For the technical perception, which legitimizes the reduction in breakdowns, is finally that, *aesthetically*, non-breakdown is better than breakdown. As a young MBA student said to us one day, particularly shocked after reading this case study, "This organisation has got to be changed because it cannot please as it is."

That may be true, but it goes without saying that, for as long as the company is in a monopoly situation, there is no real reason for touching anything at all, to the extent that the *extra cost* of *regulation* by breakdown is *externalized* onto a third party, that is, the customer. On the other hand, adaptation to the new context, which forms the transition to a market economy, cannot take place through a simple change in structures or attitudes. It will presuppose – it has presupposed – a completely new deal of cards, that is, the fundamental transformation of the methods of functioning. And the analysis which was made helps to gain a better understanding of the issues. It is the *strategy* of the different actors which must be changed, putting them into another context which they will probably find not easy to accept, at least with regard to the maintenance staff.

This will presuppose that one does not try to plan everything or confront everything all at the same time. It is going to be necessary to fix priorities, and what has gone before makes it possible to glimpse how to conduct the reasoning which is going to fix them. At the same time, it is evident that changing strategies presupposes a different context, that is, an emphasis on the resources and constraints of the different actors involved. These are the leverage effects. Here we will see that the methodological framework, which we have just reviewed and summarized, is only very slightly contingent on the context which it allows us to study. It is a method of reasoning which focuses on the why of action, which emphasizes the importance of the context, no matter what its nature. The same can be said for the levers, with one important shade of difference – that the *nature* of the levers used, their actual content, is itself contingent.

8

The Process: From Problem to Priorities

Knowing whether it is necessary to fix priorities, or instead to decide on what is most appropriate to try in order to cover the overall problems identified, is currently being debated among the specialists on change. We have already noted that Schein considers that, from the moment of collecting information, one has already started on the process itself and that therefore there is no such thing as *phases*, except at a very superficial level, in which the action plan takes the place of real action. Similarly, there are many who criticize the idea of a succession of sites, in the name of the required simultaneity of action, which must help to prevent the creation, between different parts of the organization, of variances which would later be relatively difficult bring back together.[1] No doubt they are right, if only because of the systemic dimension of organizations.

Intuitively, the majority of managers who have responsibility for major changes have adopted this viewpoint, and have always tried to have all events under control by building programmes that are intended to forecast right down to the smallest detail in terms of what might happen and what aspects must be dealt with in close-up or from a distance. This tendency makes itself particularly felt during merger processes which witness the creation of a multitude of "steering committees", each one in charge of a specific area concerned more or less directly with the merger. Such an approach is understandable in this case since there are only a few of the different parts of an organization which are not concerned, and above all because, in such circumstances, we see the appearance of legitimate anxieties on people's future prospects and employment, which need to be dealt with without too much delay.

Can one deal with everything at once?

And yet everybody can see that the programme is quickly transforming itself into a number of sites where the natural tendency is to live more or less autonomously, without those who have been put in charge of their *coordination* – a term which clearly indicates that naturally the sites are separate from each other – being able to make the link between all the suggestions and initiatives, sometimes in contradiction to each other. Because of this, in the bank which was introduced earlier in the book, it was necessary to call in an outside consultancy in order to compile an inventory of the different projects that had been initiated, assess their compatibility, and make proposals on withdrawing certain of them, modifying others, and so on. In brief, the management of sites opened for the merger has become a more worrying problem than the merger itself, and has progressively monopolized a high proportion of energy, until it was realized that the actors on the spot were forced to find practical solutions which were in fact far more interesting and useful than what was decided on in *ad hoc* committees.

Similarly, in the transport company, even though it is not in the process of merger nor visibly undergoing a major crisis, but in which the directors are supposed to carry out a true cultural revolution, the "priority action programmes" have multiplied in trying to cover all aspects of the "project", which gives the overall orientation and vision. The result is identical: the life and death of such programmes depends above all on those who are in charge and results in meetings, committees, memorandums of which nobody tries to have a precise understanding. As far as their real impact is concerned, in real life they produce the same effect as an overabundance of procedures in any organization: they make those in charge of applying them free to choose those that suit them best, which they use, producing the effect which has already been seen elsewhere – too much integration kills integration.

It is no doubt for this reason that, for years, the transport company has tried everything. No stone in terms of management methods has remained unturned. The culture of its managers and internal consultants is, in this respect, seamless. They have read everything there was to read, taken part in every colloquium, been part of every adventure. And yet, despairingly, nothing has changed, and the conclusion that the directors have drawn from this does not focus on the way in which change was managed, any more than on their real intention to make things evolve. It points a finger at who is to blame, that is, the consultants who have made money out of the company. And yet managing these consultants was part of the management team's responsibility – in general and more particularly in the case of change.

Systemic change does not imply overall action

Such failures arise from the confusion between the systemic nature of organizations, leading one to consider that each part, even if identifiable, is linked to the whole, and the consequence which is hastily drawn from this that one cannot focus action one a single part without taking responsibility for the whole. In fact, *there is no contradiction between systemic reasoning and the idea of priority*. The first implies that the most effective means of action to change a part is not necessarily to carry out a linear-type action, while the second suggests that if one wants to *enter* into a process of change one needs to find the right door. The priority is to find the door, systemic reasoning is what helps you to open it.

And in fact, if changing organizations means changing the strategy of actors, then one can understand that it is difficult and no doubt unnecessary to want to change all these strategies in one fell swoop. Such an attempt might bring Orwell to mind, and in point of fact the very idea of the intelligence of actors which is at the heart of our approach is in contradiction with Orwell's world, even if the end justifies the means. It is therefore necessary to find another logic, different from absolute planning, far from abstract and universal action plans, and accept a random element which at the end of the day is irreducible, since it concerns human freedom, which once more shows itself as a major difficulty in abstract and standardized approaches to management.

This random element which is so terrifying but inherent to every process of change is impossible to predict and measure. Once the door has been opened, and even more important before it is opened, it is really difficult to know what we will find behind it, and to control those who will be rushing through it. This has a major consequence when one is seriously striving for a successful action – *the final result of the action must not be evaluated solely or principally with respect to the initial goals.* Proceeding in this way means "cornering" those who are in charge of the process; it means artificially limiting their capacity to profit from new situations that arise; it means making the overall organization blind, deaf, incapable of learning.

As in negotiation, the action of change structures new opportunities because, based on the priority which has been fixed and which it is believed will substantially modify the game, the actors have adapted themselves, have found new solutions, certain of which will need correction, but which to a great extent constitute the *spontaneous way in which change spreads*. We will therefore arrive at an extremely accurate steering path, which will be based on the actors themselves, rather than an attempt at the absolute control of the whole process which is in any case bound to fail. Here what we call priority is not the most important nor even the most urgent problem. It is the part of the system on which one thinks one has the most possibility of acting (strategy of the possible) and where modification has the best chance of changing the functioning of this system, and therefore of launching and enabling the whole process. In most cases, this is what makes it possible to demonstrate to actors that nothing is permanently written and that it is possible to do things differently.

Nonetheless, the definition of one or more priorities comes up against a difficulty called "the billiard ball effect". One of the features of a system is the coherence of its component parts with each other, and researchers are well aware of this – sometimes falling back in admiration once they have understood the overall logic of their subject of study. They have the feeling that they have reconstituted a puzzle … and of course they don't want anybody to come along and move a single piece.

This is the "fascination of the Cobra" exercised on us by this systemic harmony, which means that its sometimes catastrophic final result runs the risk of being forgotten. In this case, as in front of the snake, one only seeks to remain motionless. The principle of reality, however, recalls us to action, but the difficulty remains in finding the angle for attack which will make it possible to lift the constituent contradiction of any action which takes place in this problematic: how to reconcile what is *desirable* (acting on what would be the identified priority) with what is *possible* (there is a reasonable chance that the phenomena of resistance will not scupper the attempt).

Once again, this question is made even harder, in that what we are trying to change are neither structures nor superficial attitudes, but the strategies of the actors. Of course, reflecting on *implementation* will also open up paths for us, but we will see that there is no ready-made answer to the question asked. Either, as has been suggested, the priority is found around the principal resource of the most powerful actor and one is going to come up against serious difficulties, or else the action is going to pinpoint on the edge of the system and its effects are not guaranteed. It is therefore each situation, in its specificity, which will make it possible to weigh the elements in play, for we have never been so far away from possible recipes, from "devices", which would help us to avoid making mistakes. Nonetheless, through the two examples that follow, I am going to try to illustrate the two situations most frequently encountered – it is up to everybody to take them as examples and not as models.

The case of the European Development Bank

The first of these examples is in the context of a big financial institution in Southern Europe.[2] At the time when the survey was carried out – towards the end of the 1990s – this bank, in its "retail banking" part, shows three *symptoms* which are worrying top management and which justify calling in an outside expert. The private and professional banking network is beginning *to lose money*, and even if low profitability is acceptable in this country bearing in mind the extremely sharp competition, the situation is showing signs of deteriorating beyond the business's limits. At the same time, one can see a *draining away of customers*, not in the form of a massive haemorrhage, but in a slow and regular movement mainly affecting the most profitable customers. This disaffection, which appears clearly in the statistics, is, however, minimized and even denied by those in charge of the network, especially the account executives, persuaded of the loyalty of "their" customers, whom they manage exclusively, monopolistically, in a logic which, on observation, appears closer to that of independent workers than to that of account managers for a bank of this type; and yet, surprisingly, despite these first two negative indicators, everybody in the network *achieves their objectives without any great difficulty*, which shows that the anxiety manifested by general management is far from being universally shared by line personnel.

These three symptoms therefore give rise to much debate within the bank and interestingly one can observe that it is not the figures which help the actors to come to agreement. Despite their apparent objectivity, they raise very divergent doubts, arguments and interpretations, thus reinforcing the bad atmosphere which reigns in the bank: everybody suspects everybody else of manipulating these figures and using them to their advantage. Above all, discussion rapidly becomes heated, so much are the actors concerned absolutely convinced that they are doing everything they can, without counting what they give in terms of their time and energy. There is nothing surprising in this: this is what actually happens in circumstances where the actors, focusing on the symptoms, cannot come to agreement on the problems.

What does analysis show, when one focuses on the four principal actors in this situation: the customers, the commercial advisor, the branch managers, and the network management? In terms of the *relationships* between these actors, one is first of all surprised by the almost friendly closeness between the commercial advisors and *their* customers. With only rare exceptions – such as the few customers who indicate their doubts on the extent to which the products offered to them actually meet their real needs – everybody is happy with each other.

The account executives watch jealously over their portfolios which they share with nobody, not with the branch manager who in any case has no customers to manage, nor even with their colleagues. When one of them is in need, which is a rare occurrence, the others help him – not by handing over customers but by transferring part of their results, even if this means manipulating the figures.[3]

As for the customers themselves, they are delighted if, by playing on the bank's poor image as echoed in the press, they manage to obtain, from their contacts, ever more discounts, rebates, services not charged. It is evident that account managers are assessed on turnover and not on profitability.

In contrast, one is struck by the absence of relationship between customers and branch managers. When one interviews the former, they never mention the latter although, on the other hand, they express very negative opinions on how badly the bank is managed, for which they hold network management responsible. An account holder never misses an opportunity to emphasize how happy he is to have opposite him a contact who is capable of offsetting the deficiencies of an organization that is heavy, bureaucratic and probably corrupt. But in so doing, they are referring to the account executives and not the branch managers.

Between the latter and those who are, in spite of everything, their subordinates, relations are ambiguous. Managers complain bitterly of the high level of autonomy enjoyed by commercial advisors, an autonomy which they feel little able to counterbalance, and emphasize to what extent they have no information on customers, the market and its potentialities and, more generally, on business within their branch.

The reporting system is sparse, quantitative and does not take real situations into account. It is not on such a system that the manager can rely in order to exercise any sort of control, nor indeed on his hierarchical authority to the extent that, since promotions within the bank have been blocked for an undetermined time, any judgements he may make on employees are without real effect. As for the account executives, they find managers to be relatively conciliatory and appreciate the fact that they do not hesitate to fight with financial management in order to obtain better physical conditions.

In its judgements, network management is strict with everybody. To the sales staff, it reproaches their practices aiming to favour the customers at no matter what price; it insists on their fanatical individualism which leads them to "hide the copy" from the rest of the organization, thus depriving it of the visibility needed for its own action. It has often organized meetings with the advisors, but these have proved to be unfruitful, strained, even aggressive. In addition, it deplores not being able to rely on its branch managers, whom it perceives as overscrupulous, always ready to say yes to everything, without anything ever happening. In particular, it does not succeed in obtaining from them any more information than it obtains from the sales staff. The assumption of complicity between these two actors is clearly evoked. To finish, management emphasizes that this situation is all the more prejudicial in that it makes its own work, continually launching new products some of which are the best on the market, defining new priorities every day, which are immediately transformed into new action plans. In brief, everybody bustles about busily for a disappointing result but with nobody perceiving the fundamental causes.

Such is the situation, described as seen by the actors. Analysing it allows one to brush out what is overall a conventional portrait of this organization. It will have escaped nobody's attention that, in this bank, the person who has *the reality of power* in his hands is the commercial advisor. For this, he has a particularly important *resource* through his monopoly of access to the customer. With very little in the way of *constraints*, one can therefore understand the two *strategies* that he develops, that is, firstly, the provision to his customers of ever more advantageous conditions in order to keep them captive and, secondly, the retention of information,[4] which, as we have seen, even extends to his own colleagues and which helps him to preserve his autonomy, which is no doubt *the problem he needs to solve*, in the sense that we have used it.

Responsible but not guilty

Stopping a moment on this first observation, two points merit highlighting, which are going to have all their impact on the form and content of a process of change. In terms of form, the method of analysis used avoids casting any direct or indirect blame on actors. Reasoning in terms of *rational strategies*, it is good to anticipate that it is these strategies which need changing, but it also means affirming that they constitute *an intelligent response from the actor to the context in which he has been placed*. Because of this, there is no apportionment of "responsibility" in the sense of bad intention, and it therefore serves no purpose to argue at length on the crafty intentions of one person or another.

Better even – if one wanted to go into the details of this case, one would quickly see that, if customers have a relatively negative perception of the bank, it's not just because of the image given to it by the media, but also because the sales staff criticize their own organization in front of the customers, they distance themselves from it, its heavy and bureaucratic "back office", its incapable directors – and only think of their careers. In brief, in their commercial relationships, they sell themselves and not the bank, they manage the contact on an individual basis and not a collective one. In addition, this is not peculiar to them as it is well known that the more one affirms living in a restricting and rigid universe the more one seems flexible and adaptable in relation to one's contacts. Unforgivable, the moralist will say. Certainly, but here what is at stake is the intelligent logic that the actor pushes through to its conclusion. And it is not contradictory with the feeling that he has of doing everything he can and holding the bank's survival in his hands. At this stage, moralizing criticism will only exacerbate the conflict, just where the strategic approach makes it possible to insist on the devotion of each person *even while* noting the final result which requires a profound change.

Turning now to the content of the change process, we have just identified the principal resource of the most powerful actor. There is again no doubt that here we have the key point of our organization, which will in principle appear to us as the priority we are looking for, the one which, if we succeed in dealing with it in a strategic manner as opposed to in a technical or authoritarian fashion, will enable us to unbalance this system which nonetheless seems so very hermetic. However, even if this intuition has a good chance of proving itself well founded, it is not enough on its own to build the strategy of change. The analysis must be pushed to its conclusion, partly in order to find and identify other priorities that may exist, but also and above all in order to draw up the reasoning on the levers to be used in order to change the strategy of the actors, including that of the most powerful of these.

So this brings us to the branch managers, who appear to be singularly destitute in this system. Not only do they have no control over the essential source of power in this organization – access to the customers – but also they have no real means of action on the commercial advisors since they do not influence either promotions, reduced to little if anything, or pay which follows rules which have nothing to do with them. In counterpoint to this absence of resources, they suffer from the same lack of information as the rest of the bank. In such a situation, wisdom – intelligence – consists of protecting oneself, of not going out of one's way to seek conflict with the sales staff who are more powerful than them, and even of participating in the general opacity which characterizes this organization.

In fact, it is a situation of inverse dependency that is observed, frequent in bureaucracies of this type. The head depends more on the subordinates than the subordinates on the head, and this gap between formal power and real power is far from being inconsequential. It leads the custodian of officialdom to "compensate" for his lack of organizational resources by always asking for more financial resources. We have already observed the phenomenon, we now find it here. But it must be remembered that there are something like 800 branch managers who, to a greater or lesser degree, adopt the same strategy of "always more", leading to the notorious vicious circle of inflation and bureaucracy that these organizations know so well.

What can the network management do faced with these impenetrable local units which maintain it in profound ignorance of the living reality of the market, contenting themselves with ritualistically filling out forms with information without really knowing what this corresponds to? One can understand that protecting their careers becomes an essential preoccupation, which is not too obvious in this universe where ignorance of the real can always lead to taking the wrong decision or not seizing a good opportunity. This leads the team to a strategy than one can only qualify as extremist: in order to cover themselves, they always need to start more projects, more priorities, more action plans. It is movement which takes the place of action and, as always in such cases, the multiplication of activities is an exact translation of the obscurity in which each of the leaders finds himself. In this respect, one might speak of military or ballistic strategy. The less one knows where the target is, the greater the temptation to sprinkle widely in the hope that luck will help us to hit something. But in doing this, those who are in charge of implementation – the commercial advisors on this occasion – only have more freedom to choose what they want and decide what *their* priorities are within this heap of decisions that are not particularly integrated and in fact are often contradictory.

From the symptom to the problem

There is no need to go any further in the analysis to return to the initial *symptoms*. It is indeed this that makes up the step that we have called the transition from information to knowledge, and which is made accessible by what has just been said. It is also important to avoid falling into the frequent trap which consists, after an excellent analysis, of proposing an interpretation of the symptoms which has little to do with the analysis and which, most of the time, leads towards technical explanations.

- Why is the bank losing money? Two reasons have appeared during the analytical process. Firstly, we have observed that *in the context in which they find themselves*, it is a rational strategy for sales staff to offer always more advantageous conditions to their customers, so as to ensure their loyalty to them and not the bank; and, secondly, we have understood that the less organizational resources branch managers have, the more financial resources they ask for – even to the extent of cheating on the truth of information used to obtain them.
- But then why do customers, and particularly the more profitable among them, tend to leave a bank in which they have been able to obtain pretty much everything they wanted? We have noticed that, in order to preserve their autonomy, the account executives do not share their information, nor therefore their customers, with anybody, not even with their colleagues. They prefer, rather like the brokers we sometimes find working in stock market trading offices, "passing" the customer over to a competitor rather than allowing one of their own to benefit, at the risk of putting a spanner in the works for ending the monopolistic management of customers. As has been said, they manage the relationship on an individual basis and not on an organizational basis. However, this strategy does have a limit – it quite naturally leads to sales staff offering their customers *the products that they know and only those*. Contrary to appearances, this is not a lack of qualification – nobody can know all the bank's products – it is more an absence of strategic advantage in sharing one's customers. Of course, everything works for the best in an ideal world, provided the products that the salesperson knows are the products that the customer needs. As soon as a gap appears, then the good individual relationship is not enough to compensate for a weak offer, and the dissatisfied customer goes away, even if, in other areas, the personal relationship with their contact remains excellent. This situation tends to be more frequent where the customer is more sophisticated, with complex requirements, and where their profitability would have good chances of improving if the bank managed to satisfy their requirements, which the system, as it is now, does not allow.
- And yet everybody achieves their objectives without difficulty? In fact, there is a double process of budgeting in this bank. The first is official.

As soon as it is time to draw up the budget, the network's management decides on the main lines and then distributes them over the rest of the organization. The reality is quite different. Placed in a situation of non-information, as described above, which we must remember is linked to the strategy of the sales staff, management seeks to obtain some reliable forecasts from the next level down – in this case, the area managers. Those who don't know better turn towards the branch managers who themselves turn to their own advisors. In brief, these are the ones who fix their own objectives, and one can see why they should have so little difficulty in achieving them, since it is easy, outside of any control, to underestimate them in the name of genuine caution.

The choice of strategic priority

As can be seen, all the problems that have been identified behind the symptoms refer to a main cause which is certainly not unique – the strategy of retaining information by the account executives. One can understand that, for them, communicating on the reality of what they do on a daily basis with their contact and which might, for the bank, be a crucial source of living knowledge, really means giving up their principal resource, and therefore their autonomy, which one knows to be priceless for the actors, especially in a context like this one where the possibilities of promotion are reduced to virtually nothing. By keeping the information they have for their own protection, they produce the "chain reaction" which has been identified, and based on which it was possible to explain the initial symptoms. It is for this reason that *opening up the game of the sales staff can be defined as the priority*. It is not simply that this is the most important question – others such as the information system are just as important from a practical point of view – but it is from that point that the deal can be changed and that other actions will become possible. This is how a priority is defined as opposed to a comprehensive but "flat" approach to all the problems that need to be handled.

At the same time, this strategic vision of priorities feels far less safe for managers than the one that consists of decreeing, from above and in a "set way", all the actions to be conducted. The priority here is going to be the "trigger factor", the one that will make it possible to pull the thread of change. For change, at the end of the day, is far more a thread that is pulled than a final plan that is put into operation. Action on a clearly identified priority after careful analysis leading to a secure understanding of the problems is going to open up the field of what is possible and reveal opportunities that the construction of an overly rigid plan will be forced to clear away. For it cannot be repeated enough that, from the first step they take, intelligent actors are going to find news solutions, different and often unpredictable arrangements. They are going to negotiate their acceptance, structure a new game, all those things than even the best-informed planner has no chance at all of anticipating, since the scope of human freedom is wide and forces them to accept an ever-increasing proportion of random events.

But at the same time, this is what makes it possible to go further. From this point of view, the action of change can be considered as the creation of positive chaos. The leader's role is not to reduce such chaos in the name of consistency of control or predictability. It is to render it acceptable to everybody, to give it a meaning, to reassure.

In addition, this approach through the strategic priority avoids focusing on the technical solutions which are so reassuring and controllable. In the bank's case, it is tempting to immediately reappraise the information system, that is, finally to favour the channels rather than what runs through them. The temptation towards technical solutions in organizations is as powerful as that which attracts towards the structures. But it comes up against a major obstacle which, as has already been said, lies at the heart of the problematic of change: despite all the attempts to finish with this obstacle, people are, and will always be, stronger than the technology that is put against them. More or less quickly, they have every opportunity to oppose a new system of measurement, or counting, of control. They know how to turn procedures, to find solutions that are always renewed in order to conserve an autonomy that others are trying to take away from them without anything in exchange.

In fact, changing the technology, like changing the rules and procedures in a linear and not a systemic vision, does not generally produce durable change.[5] Both are costly (especially technical changes) at the same time as producing results that are cosmetic rather than concrete. However, by defining an organization as a set of actor strategies, by insisting on the fact that changing means above all changing these strategies, we have largely orientated the search for priorities. These can *only* be strategic. The remainder fall within the definition of resources or, which is not negligible, of levers, that is, of what one will be using to change what the actors are doing.

The systemic aspect of priorities

If we return for a moment to the bank case, a twofold priority, *of a systemic nature*, is proposed. Not only is it necessary to act on the commercial advisors, but also to modify the simultaneously withdrawn and inflationist behaviour of the branch managers. And if one wants to anticipate briefly what will be said of the levers, both can be conducted in the context of the same action, again based on a systemic reasoning which might be stated as follows: is it possible at the same time to make it more rational for the sales staff to share the information that they have on customers *and* for the branch managers to become for them a resource providing something other than always more financial resources?

One can think of different solutions – here is the one that was adopted by the bank: it based itself on what conventional management terms "the management of opportunities", that is, the possibility of transforming resources into constraints. In this particular case, it was pointless to continue appraising sales staff on the turnover that they were earning, to the extent that they themselves fixed the amount that was achievable. It was therefore decided, taking inspiration from a current practice in American business banks, that over a period of three years considered as experimental, the advisors would be appraised on their "capacity to cooperate", and their pay, with higher variability, would depend on this capacity. Of course, the problem of measuring this then arose, for which two criteria were chosen with all the safeguards thought necessary by those in charge: firstly, the amount of business that each advisor would pass on to his colleagues, compared with what he would deal with himself; and, secondly, the proportion of customers on which he would work jointly with other colleagues, with regard to those that he would manage on his own. Because of this, he would find himself saddled with new constraints and forced to arbitrate between his autonomy and his pay. As always in such cases, the actor tries to maximize both gains, but there is no doubt that his strategy shifts in the direction of greater transparency – a condition necessary for satisfying the new criteria of appraisal.

But at the same time, while it was becoming more advantageous for account executives to share their customers and therefore their information, they still needed to be orientated towards the competences that they might need in order to satisfy the complex of customers. In addition, there was nothing to show that such competences were available within their branch. Everybody will have understood that it was to the branch managers that this responsibility for orientation was entrusted, thus transforming them into resources for the sales staff, to whom they now had something to contribute that was directly in relation with their concrete working problems. What was given to these branch managers was not *authority* in the hierarchical and Taylorist sense of the term, it was something for them to control which was important for those whom they had to lead. It is called *power*.

In passing, this leads us to observe that one has, through this, brought the actors to play together just where, in the previous situation, they were only interested in retaining information, or even direct opposition. It is this idea, that finally in any social group, one does not win against the others but with them, that they tried to introduce into this universe by creating solidarities between actors that the earlier system was pushing towards withdrawal and isolation. The game has stopped being a no-score draw.

9

The Process: From Priorities to Levers

As soon as the priorities have been identified, the question arises as to how to modify the strategy of intelligent actors, how to bring them to make other choices, to find solutions that are acceptable to them. This question is at the heart of the problematic of change, and all those who have had to manage the real and fundamental transformation of an organization have had to confront it. Technical, administrative or even financial problems always find solutions. It is rare for them to represent major obstacles. But those that are commonly known as "human problems" in everyday language, and which are in fact problems of organization, are far more difficult to overcome.

Three trends for a mediocre result

The expression itself is interesting. In organizations, the human is a problem, in the sense that he does not submit easily either to the overall rules, procedures and codes which are supposed to make him predictable,[1] or to the wishes of his bosses, however powerful they may be. Curiously enough, these bosses work hard at maintaining the illusion of their power, of their ability to steer the course of things, through their charisma or their leadership style. But it is not enough to explain to people what should be done for them to do it, nor to appeal to their reason for them to become reasonable. Unlike an accepted idea, the reasonable is eminently contextual, that is, subject to a partisan interpretation from the actor. In other words, what some people conceive as common sense is not necessarily seen as common sense by those at the receiving end of it. This is probably what explains the three main trends that have been observable, especially since the end of the 1980s, in people's conceptions of action and change: these can be incantatory, coercive or linear, thereby interpreting the extreme difficulty in confronting such human intelligence, which we endlessly make into the core of the problem. These trends illustrate attempts to avoid taking it into account, to go round it, often in the name of general interest, of authority, of management, or of apparent common sense.

The limits of belief

Not only is incantation already the most universally widespread practice in organizations, but it is also continuing to grow. It is even so extensively acknowledged and accepted as a tool for guidance that companies do not hesitate to give a semi-religious tone to staff or management meetings when explaining their "vision" and what needs to be done. More basically, the incantatory tendency now becoming rife in organizations is resulting in a subtle shift of semantics: when they talk of their "strategy", by this they mean what they *hope to do* and not what they do. "Our strategy is to be number one in our main markets" they say. In fact, this is an objective, a project, while strategy consists of the actions that one takes to achieve this.[2] This shift expresses the huge gulf which separates an intention from the concrete way of realizing it. And so we saw, in the 1980s, a multiplication of "company projects" or "departmental projects" ... which, as their name indicates, were only projects and in fact, in many cases, never got beyond this stage. More than ten years later, the tendency is the same – the promotion of the "fundamental values",[3] the *core values* which overall are praiseworthy and positive principles, although for the most part somewhat remote from the effective practices of actors, including top management. The few businesses that realize this mostly come to a single conclusion – that one needs to be modest in one's assertions of values. This is a first step towards realism.

The torments of project management

To illustrate this point, we can use a version of incantation which has caused, and which continues to cause, many problems for companies – project management. This consists, particularly in organizations structured by businesses, such as car manufacturers or their suppliers, of designing and producing products or parts of products cross-functionally, by temporarily associating with the project actors from the "trades", that is, the traditional vertical structures as inherited from the Taylorist system of thought. At the head of such cross-functional units, which are formed and unformed as dictated by circumstances, as is their vocation, we have the *project managers*, in charge of getting everybody to cooperate with a view to achieving the best possible result.

Plenty of difficulties appear as soon as these project managers are asked to become "leaders of men", capable "of commanding their troops" – all formulas relating to incantation far more than to action, which might produce the neologism of "incantaction", in which many people would be able to recognize themselves. And, in fact, as the obvious advantage for those who have been allocated to the project is to continue privileging the logic of their own trade – since this is where they are appraised and where their budgetary resources come from – they are going to stick closely to this and the project will continually see ever more delays, ever more defects, and everybody will be able to reproach everybody else for their incompetence, their unwillingness. Calling for cross-functionality as an absolute necessity in order to offer the customer quality at the lowest possible cost will never be enough to change the strategy of the actors. This is the harsh law of human intelligence.[4]

In this case, the question raised is not that of the project manager's "charisma" or of his devotion until exhaustion in order to accomplish his task. It is a question of his power, that is, of how he effectively controls those who have been allocated to his project and which will mean that they are going to have an interest in cooperating with him: it is not enough to know that he is the boss, but it is necessary to realize that this is a project. More generally, one issue, on which incantation has no bearing, is the observation that, in organizations, one has more to gain by cooperation than by opposition. So, for example, it would be naive to think that cyclists in the Tour de France throw themselves into a fierce fight to carry off the top prize. If this was the case, only a ridiculously low number of them would finish the race. In fact, they share out the rewards, under the vigilant eye of the man they themselves call the "squad leader" who makes sure that everybody wins something. For if the strongest won everything, without discernment, the whole system would put itself at risk. In order to survive, it needs the cooperation of all. But once the squad leader is no longer capable of imposing his law, is no longer in a position to "control" the race, it becomes a free-for-all.

The ineffectiveness of coercion

There is then a great temptation to fall back on coercion, and plenty of companies have not been able to resist this for long when the context has allowed it: because actors do not want to do what they are asked to do, let's try to use authority in order to make them – rather like the traffic policeman confronting an offending motorist. Of course, in such extreme cases which are fortunately not part of everyday management, coercion can give results. And yet these will always be limited. It would not occur to anybody today to assert that prison eradicates or even reduces delinquency. Some even say that it increases it, through an effect of the system which might well be analysed with the tools suggested here. In the year 2000, one in 174 Americans was "living" in prison, and this proportion is continually increasing...

In organizations, coercion is expressed on a daily basis by threatening internal memos, increasingly strict and numerous rules and procedures, which all propose to drastically reduce the freedom of actors and to enclose their slightest deeds and acts in a clear, defined and non-amendable context. From this point of view, and despite the sometimes mollifying words that accompany them, the various and varied ISO standards provide an excellent example of this reasoning and these practices, as has already been pointed out.

In doing this, what one is seeking to curtail, to control, even to reduce in the military sense of the term, is the actors' freedom, that is, their capacity to make choices which do not correspond to those stated by the organization. This, in particular, is what happens when actors are asked to adopt a behaviour that is in contradiction with the context created for them. Instead of trying to adapt the second to the first, one steps up the pressure, the regulations, the repression, in the hope that these will steer those concerned to an unlikely acceptance. It is, for example, surprising to see the contemporary fad for "cooperation" on the part of companies and managers who nonetheless continue to assess everybody on an individual basis. The result is simply catastrophic and some, in a reflection of the French tax authorities, even reach the point of drawing up "cooperation protocols", as if this difficult behaviour, so constrictive and unnatural, could be regulated in a protocol!

Coercion is an impossible means of action which only produces effects in the very short term, and generally when the work situation has deteriorated, thus depriving actors of alternatives. But their freedom and their intelligence (it can be seen that we do not have one without the other) are pretty well irreducible. Organizations are swarming with examples that show the extraordinary capacity of actors not to do what they have been ordered to do, if they do not perceive the interest of this. From this point of view, the administrative environments are a goldmine. On the one hand, they reason only by coercion, whether this is for their contacts or their members; on the other, tolerance of non-performance is extreme. On the one hand, the arsenal of regulations and procedures is impressive – for its quantity – in its intention to leave nothing to chance and especially not to arbitrariness; on the other, the diversity of solutions and practices is remarkable. In parallel, it is almost impossible to change anything at all in these organizations – so inextricable does the tangle of issues created in this way appear at the end of the day.[5]

Linear reasoning and systemic reasoning

The linear vision of change, while of a different nature, still follows the same logic. This consists, after having identified a problem, which is in fact confused with the symptom, and located the actor who is carrying it and therefore the "culprit", of focusing the action directly and exclusively on this actor. The key word for this type of action is *"since"*. Since A produces B and not C as he is asked, let us act on A to make him produce C. This is what we saw in the last example discussed in the previous chapter: *since* fraud produces accidents and *since* fraud is mainly perpetrated by small carriers who have no concern for the general good, let us focus on them an action which is both massive and coercive through the intermediary of new regulations defining how they must work and not by creating a context in which they will benefit from working differently.

This approach, that might be qualified as simplistic, refutes the systemic dimension of organizations. Not that it is not sometimes necessary to act directly on an actor in order to make him change – we will be looking at an example of this – but in most cases, it is not by directly targeting the offending action, excessive speed for example, that the desired result will be achieved. Most frequently, in fact, it is in the environment around this "problem", often among the other actors, that one will find the leverage for action. In other words, in the linear vision, one demands, by force if necessary, that an actor does something with the hope that this will resolve the whole of the problem or problems, while in the systemic vision *one puts him in the situation of benefiting from doing something*, at the same time as looking at the overall resulting effects which will not fail to show themselves.

Action by leverage or recognition of the actor's intelligence

From this point, what will be suggested is, first of all, to play on the *levers*. By this, we mean the component parts of the context of actors, which, correctly altered, are likely to bring progress to their problems that need solving, and thereby to their strategies. The physical metaphor of the lever is not without interest: it does indeed consist of applying weight somewhere in order to obtain a movement somewhere else, as opposed to what has just been said for the linear approach. Acting through the effect of leverage, this consists of changing the resources and the constraints that both sides have in the system so that they "align" their behaviour accordingly by wagering on their strategic intelligence and not by seeking to reduce it.

This does not in any way imply the idea that these same actors are going to accept the new rules of play easily and without discussion … thinking that would mean having misunderstood the concept of intelligence. The levers used, as we will see, can be very restrictive and the term "intelligence" does not refer to the fact of finally accepting a change because the necessity for it has been demonstrated to you. It is in fact the capacity to adapt to a new context. The question of resistance or acceptance must be dealt with at the time of drawing up the method of *implementation*, that is, the definition of conditions which make new solutions playable by those involved, often disturbing compared with previous situations.

This is particularly true when one gives new constraints to actors, who will inevitably, at least to start with, reduce the margins of freedom and autonomy that they have formed for themselves, before finding new arrangements. If this line of reasoning is continued, we will understand the importance of this point: we have already pointed out that the identification of the most powerful actor's principal resource generally *but not universally* makes it possible to reach the core of the organization and of the symptoms which set off the alarm. In such a case, the control of a powerful resource pushes the actor towards a radical strategy, without apportionment, turned towards the exclusive and non-negotiated defence of its own interests, to the detriment of the interests of others or of the organization as a whole. In this situation, the lever will consist of creating constraints for him in order to get him out of his one-dimensional logic and force him to negotiate, if only with himself, on contradictory imperatives, which will lead him towards finding new solutions – no doubt better balanced ones.

When cooperating is not rational

An example will help to illustrate this remark: a European airline has been undergoing a major crisis since the beginning of the 1990s. Not only is it facing very hard-line labour disputes, but also its results are deteriorating to the point that it is beginning to lose money on a scale rarely seen before in the business and which will lead it to immediate bankruptcy without vigorous financial intervention from the public authorities. Many studies were then conducted in order to identify the causes of such losses (the problems), and among all those brought to light, there was one that particularly drew attention: in order to carry out the maintenance check, also known as "interim maintenance" and consisting of immobilizing an aircraft for some ten days, twice a year, this company puts another three days on average more than its main competitor. Calculations based on the number of airplanes in the company, the average number of passengers per flight and the average daily frequency of turnaround, show that these three days finally result in a loss equivalent to 540,000 passengers per year.

The question then arises as to where these three days come from, how "performance is constructed" in a way. After investigation, one finds oneself faced with a classic problem of organization: for understandable reasons of safety, the maintenance department is structured in divisions (we should remember that organizations often have the vocabulary of their practices), which divide up the different parts of the airplane that is undergoing maintenance. There is thus an engines division, an onboard computers division, a cabin division, and so on. When one observes how these units function, it is clearly apparent that time is lost due to very poor management of interfaces, a systematic lack of co-operation between the different divisions, which are more likely to oppose than to find mutual solutions. They are not even located in the same premises and none of them appears particularly bothered by this.

The first reaction from managers, shocked by this realization, is to appeal to the good sense of all concerned, forcefully emphasizing the collective interest of survival, and vigorously denouncing the fact that the company is being endangered by those of its members who refuse to cooperate. Numerous seminars and "team building" exercises are organized so as to bring people closer together and teach them to know each other better, all of which seems an elementary condition for working better together. This is the incantatory phase which does not give outstanding results. Questioned individually, most of the actors declare themselves ready to cooperate with their peers, but remark that these do not seem to be similarly inclined. In a word, everybody would like to but nobody does.

It is therefore necessary to get away from this psychological and guilt-inducing approach and reformulate the question in strategic terms, following the framework which has been suggested. The symptom is clear, it is the three days "on top" needed to carry out the interim maintenance. But the query on the problem is as follows: why, in the system as it is, do actors not see the benefit of cooperating? And on what levers could one act in order to bring them to work together, without having to give them a moralizing talk on the superiority of cooperation in relation to distance and non-cooperation? Analysis provides a simple answer and without any great originality. For reasons of safety, as mentioned above, each division is appraised on the number of incidents affecting the part of the plane for which they are responsible (rate of computer breakdowns for the computer division, for example). Each division therefore finds itself focused on its own work, which it devises independently of the others, to which it pays little heed. As a result, the total maintenance time for the airplane is not the problem that anybody is expected to solve, it is seen as remote and theoretical and, in any case, not as a concrete constraint that is really felt by the individuals. Once again, they adapt themselves to the context, not the words. The one-dimensional and vertical nature of the criterion for appraisal leads to the one-dimensional and vertical nature of the action by actors.

Bringing actors to acknowledge the complexity of reality

It then appears necessary to give them one or more constraints which bring them to acknowledge other elements of reality. The problem is not so much to get them to move from one vision to another as to get them to assimilate several and bring them to arbitrate by finding new solutions. Of course, the result for them will be a less comfortable universe, precisely because this involves arbitration, choices and, more concretely, new ways of working with others. It would be up to the actors themselves to discover these new cooperations, thanks to the "constraint of constraints". In the precise case that we are looking at, two criteria for assessment have been crossed: the one in force previously, still for the reasons of safety already mentioned, to which has been added, for all divisions, *the total maintenance time for the aircraft*, whatever the incidents that may arise during the check.

If we now take a step backwards, we see that the usage of levers has changed over time, no doubt under the impact of the growing complexity of situations that managers are asked to manage. To start with, it was simply a question of getting an actor to move from strategy

A to strategy B. Playing on a simple element of the context – pay, for example – can successfully produce this effect.

But today, what is increasingly expected of those who are in a position of responsibility is that they acknowledge the plural, contradictory and conflictual nature of action by integrating not one but several logics. This puts them in an uncomfortable situation, which is difficult to live with, and which is part of the development of working conditions already mentioned. To obtain this result, we therefore use several levers – combinations of quantitative and qualitative criteria for appraisal – which will bring the actor towards finding an optimum between two or more logics and not the exclusive triumph of one over the others.

In a football team, when forwards are assessed only on the number of goals they score and are put in competition on this criterion, their advantage is certainly to score, but also not to favour the effectiveness of their partners. If one takes the "assist pass" into account, it then becomes advantageous to be not just the scorer but also the one who makes it possible to score. And what can we say about the American basketball teams and their "triple double" which leads to recognizing, for each player, the number of points scored, the rebounds captured and the assists made? In this case, the levers bring the actors to the maximum degree of collective action.

These more restrictive conditions under which they are placed raise protests from the actors concerned. In the case of the airline, they emphasized the injustice which consisted of making the fate of one side dependent upon the goodwill of the other side and of appraising, and therefore remunerating or promoting people on something which, at least in appearance, did not depend on them. But management held good, basing its decision on a campaign of in-depth information which showed actors the harmful effects of the previous situation, without, however, holding them individually to blame. Little by little, the maintenance staffs adapted themselves and, at the end of the day, presented their supervisors with proposals for organization making compatible the criteria for appraisal which had been imposed on them and which they had until then seen as incompatible. Not only did they suggest that a certain number of operations on the different parts of the airplane could be carried out in the same place, but they also showed that they could take place at the same time.

To summarize, the lever used allowed them to move *under their own volition* from the sequential compartmentalization characterizing the traditional technical bureaucracies, to the simultaneous cooperation which, in all areas of production, is the principal factor for reducing costs and improving quality. This, in fact, is what happened in this case, and one might note in passing that this fundamental transformation of the organization, resulting in substantially improved results and having encouraged the actors to considerably change their working methods, was carried out *without touching the structures*, and without requiring changes in attitudes. Structural adaptations were carried out *at a later point* when they were simply a confirmation of a state of being. They did not therefore represent an additional anxiety for actors, having been, in a way, made part of their daily life. With regard to attitudes, without entering once again into complex sociological debates on attitudes and behaviours, the example shows that these are a consequence and not a cause and that attacking them in priority is of little benefit, or even the major disadvantage of "theorizing" and pointlessly introducing conflict in the debate on change.

Two lessons to be learned

The above example of levers that have been used advisedly shows two important lessons to be learned.

- Firstly, it emphasizes the huge importance of human resource management systems when conducting change.[6] By human resource management systems, we mean all modalities of appraisal, of promotion, of pay, of career management; in other words everything that affects the well-being and future of individuals at work. It is these systems which conceal the highest number of opportunities with regard to the levers that can be used, simply because the intelligence of actors leads them to adapt themselves to the criteria on which they are assessed, appraised, promoted, remunerated. However, these criteria still need to have *concrete effects*, meaning that their satisfaction, like their non-satisfaction, must involve positive or negative sanctions. If this is not the case, as in the administrative sector, they remain theoretical and have only a slight effect on real behaviours.[7] This poses a question of *coherence* as already mentioned above, which clashes with the traditional segmentation of organizations. Human resource management departments draw up systems without an exact understanding of the reality – problems – or even independently of the results that they are trying to achieve. However, on one side, having a "demand" in relation to the actors and, on the other, creating for them, via the criteria, a context that is not coherent with this demand, does not cause problems so much for the actor who will be able to accommodate himself and play around with them, as for the organization which will never be able to control – in the sense of master – the effects of systems that it has put in place.

- Secondly, it reminds us that one of the main changes affecting organizations today is the transition from one-dimensional universes to multi-dimensional universes. Such a development can realign the distinction made by Peter Drucker between manual workers and "knowledge workers".[8] This transition is seen in the fact that there are few actors who remain in contexts of "mono-constraints", who can continue to have a narrow and segmented vision of action, excluding both cooperation with others and acknowledgement of the final result achieved. In the same way that the structures of organizations become increasingly fuzzy and complex, despite repeated calls for simplicity, so do the environments in which the actors evolve become ever more diversified and contradictory.

Calling for more simplicity, more clarity, is appealing and reassuring although, finally, rhetorical, unrealistic, once again incantatory, to the extent that the complexity is simply consubstantial with the need for multiple collaborations in modern businesses. But from the point of view that we are looking at now, this complexity must be translated into the levers that are used to modify actors' strategies, without being afraid to put onto their shoulders the constraints which will persuade them to integrate contradictory elements into their action. Experience shows that they do this very well. In other words, existing complexity rehabilitates conflict.

Difficulty in identifying the relevant levers

Nevertheless, the case which has just been presented only gives a partial idea of the difficulties there are, in most situations, in finding and using the right levers. And in fact the intention was merely, by taking into account only the actors concerned, to create a new context for them, without also having to look at their environment. This situation is not the most frequent, even if it is the most tempting, and the levers to be manipulated are mostly situated outside the precise field of the actors themselves. We will therefore be talking of *banding effects*, by reference to the successive shocks of billiard balls which finally cause the last ball to go where the player wants it to go.

The transport case discussed in the previous chapter already introduced an idea which can now be explored more fully. It was shown that, in order to reduce the speed at which drivers were driving, it is relatively ineffective to push an extremely repressive action directly onto them, to the extent that they are dependent and lacking in viable alternatives. In so doing, one only adds new constraints to those that are already leading them to the strategies that one wants to amend. One thus increases their situation of dependency, and therefore their vulnerability with regard to other operators in the system, who therefore find it all the more easy to manipulate them. Using this lever even produces exactly the opposite effect to that wanted: the more that drivers, whether independent or on the payroll, are deprived and restricted, the more likely they are to accept any sort of transport job, and therefore sidestep the rules … which will lead the public authorities to regulate this activity even more severely, and all the conditions will come together for an endless vicious circle. In fact, this is more or less what experience has shown over time.

On the other hand, the systemic analysis which has been carried out, because it has made it possible to understand the problem, and because it has highlighted the "inverted priority", has suggested that it was by acting on other actors that one could modify the strategy of the road hauliers. This banding effect leads one first of all to focus the action on the order givers, the consignors or their agents, the ancillary services, even if their main characteristic is not to carry out the transport themselves and, *a fortiori*, never even to drive a truck! And in fact this is why the competent authorities do not know them – administrative segmentation is a virtually insurmountable handicap for the systemic apprehension of reality and therefore for the apprehension of reality alone. And yet by involving these actors, who find themselves upstream of the transport, in the downstream consequences of decisions that they take officially or unofficially, one can hope to bring them to change the pressures that they apply to the drivers, even if, as should be remembered, their capacity to adapt to the new context created in this way will be high.

Levers, banding effects and reinternalization of costs

In addition, the concept of *externalizing costs* such as already discussed has allowed us to glimpse a more complex phenomenon: reintroducing the cost of the accident within the "transport system", making the reduction of this cost the collective "problem to be solved", particularly for protagonists who until now had not suffered any consequence, this leads to action by the intermediary of an actor whose importance has only appeared at the end of the reasoning process – the insurance company. It is this that, through its methods of functioning and of calculating premiums, allows the whole system to regulate itself around fraud. One can see that by acting on this actor, based on the mutualization of road transport risk or any other form of calculating premiums, the lever will finally put pressure on all those who decide things for which they are not prepared to assume the consequences. And this new and *indirect* constraint will come and relieve their natural propensity to make use of the situation of dependency in which the lowest members of the chain find themselves, in order to preserve their most profitable markets.

We can discuss the feasibility of this solution. In particular, one cannot help but see that reducing fraud to a level that will generate fewer accidents runs the risk of resulting in an increased mortality rate among businesses operating nearest to the edge of legality. So it is not certain that the policy maker will be prepared to conduct such an action, even if, with the same quantity of goods to be shipped, one might assume that the disappearance of a few businesses would not result in short-term frictional unemployment. We will need to return to this issue in Chapter 10.

But the important thing here is that the reasoning employed has distanced us from the linear vision and made it possible to use, *to the profit of change*, all the resources offered by the system's complexity. For this complexity is only a handicap if one does not have the intellectual tools, the methods of reasoning, which help to master it and to draw advantage from it. It is then that complexity becomes frightening and leads to inaction, to non-control of action, or to symbolic action – made up of a mixture of sabre-rattling and ineffective penalties. To the contrary, knowledge and acceptance of complexity open up unsuspected margins of play. These make it possible to glimpse a variety of opportunities and above all avoid focusing exclusively on the visible part of the iceberg, that is, on the symptoms.

This is what we can check again with the transport company that we are using as a "guiding thread" and which was introduced earlier in the book. Thanks to this case study, we will see not only that using levers can consist of giving *resources* to actors and not just constraints, but also that the variety of possibilities offered by complex organizations can prove to be both useful in practical terms and enjoyable in intellectual terms.

Linearity of reasoning and complexity of organizations

We can remember the major symptom worrying the company's managers – agents in direct contact with customers have a recurrent tendency to flee from them, as soon as they find themselves in an awkward situation, although their mission is precisely to provide information and even solutions to travellers in difficulty, and to reassure them if necessary. Higher management gives individual and psychologizing explanations to this behaviour of flight: the great majority of agents are assumed to be lazy, unmotivated, interested only in their personal lives to the detriment of any professional investment, even at a low level. The action of change should consequently focus directly on them, and should aim to change their "attitudes", as if, like we have already said, the relations that they have with customers were taking place outside of all context, in an empty universe, which would leave them totally free to adopt whatever attitude they choose.

Management therefore acts by incantation, since coercion is revealed to be impossible bearing in mind the power held by the unions which, by definition, would immediately oppose it. Now, since general management is itself appraised by the regulatory authorities on the frequency of labour disputes, as all the other actors have known for a long time, it is totally imprisoned by powerful and determined unions, with whom it "plays" in priority, whom it thinks of as its exclusive contacts, for the reason that they are decision makers in the event of labour troubles. Paradoxically, this implicit alliance excludes all other actors, in particular the agents themselves, thus producing the remarkable vicious circle which so characterizes this company: the more management is afraid of the "social" context, that is, the unions, the more ready it is to satisfy claims made by these organizations, and the less capable it is of listening to the real working problems of the agents who, because of this, become ever more frustrated and demanding, thus encouraging union activism. In-depth analysis of this situation has made it possible to highlight two points which will be useful when reasoning on the introduction of real changes in this business.

The weakness of middle management

In the company, middle management is almost totally stripped of power in the face of the agents that it is supposed to manage. With the notable exception of what is happening on the ticket sales platforms on departure, where managers represent a real resource for the sellers, to the extent that they are capable of both opening extra counters in the case of too much pressure from customers and, even more important, of repairing an issuing machine in the case of breakdown, something that is crucial at peak times, other supervisors or managers control nothing and contribute nothing. They are not in the transport vehicles with the inspectors in the case of incidents and they are able neither to provide them with the information they need nor even to influence decisions which will be taken in terms of choice between punctuality and connection, which as we have seen are essential in the face-to-face management between inspectors and travellers.

The ravages of verticalization

More generally, in this business, the agents at the end of the chain have no organizational resource to accomplish the mission which is officially assigned to them in the management of customer relations and where they are reminded, day after day, of the decisive importance of this for a business which is developing in an increasingly competitive world. Because of the extreme segmentation that is rife in the company, nobody makes the link between a decision made in one "pipeline" and its consequences for actors located elsewhere, and therefore not directly concerned: we have already seen that the verticalization of organizations renders any systemic vision virtually impossible. The consequence of this method of functioning is that actors have the strong feeling of being laughed at, in the most literal sense of the term, meaning that they are asked to do something difficult without ever being concerned about feasibility and therefore reality.

The systemic effect resulting from this is that, for these agents, the only resource available to them is comprised of the union organizations that they follow, not because they are more aware of their situation, but in some sort of a way by default, using better material advantages to compensate for the actual disinterestedness in their professional lives demonstrated by their managers. The three strategies that they develop are therefore very rational: escape, as soon as the situation gets complicated and contains risks of conflict with customers; union demands that are always met and yet continually renewed for material advantages of all kinds; strike action at the slightest opportunity, the expression, not understood by line management, of a request to be really integrated into company life and the decisions that are made there. It is wrong to say that in this company the union organizations take up too much space or space that does not belong to them. They occupy the space that has been given to them, and indeed this is immense.

Micro-decisions and definition of priorities

Such analysis of an organization, with its appearance of enormous complexity, at least makes it possible to use simple terms in formulating what would be a true change – simply for the agents to accept that they must remain with the customers in the event of a difficult situation. This ambition is far from being modest, for there is no doubt that it is more difficult to implement it than to draw up a vast action plan that is never applied, or to overhaul the structures, which does not change a great deal in the behaviour of actors. One can fully understand the *priority* such as it has just been defined: for the agents who have to face the travellers, this does not signify a change in attitudes which would only depend on themselves and on their goodwill; it means that the consequent parties in the system have been modified in such a way that a new behaviour has been made possible.

This is no longer a change, it is a revolution which will induce some sizeable effects, showing in particular that it is possible to act differently, that nothing is permanently fixed or paralysed in this company. The dynamics of involvement across the rest of the company will no doubt subsequently provoke other major changes which, little by little, will lead to a fundamental transformation of the whole, measurable by the reactions of the customers, as well as in the change observed in the strategies of the actors.

Crossed priorities

There is a *second priority* remaining to be defined: on what category must the first efforts be focused? This question is necessary, for if one was trying to get all the agents to change at the same time and at the same speed, one would certainly come up against obstacles such that the overall action would be bound to fail. This also sheds new light on the concept of priority. Not only is it important to identify a key point making it possible to unbalance the system, but it is also necessary to locate the most profitable category, the one where change has the value of symbol, of proof, of demonstration in the eyes of the other actors and in particular the managers, because they are the most difficult to convince of the possibility of getting things moving.

This approach is what we will be calling the search for *crossed priorities*, to the extent that it means combining a field of action with a category. In the case that we are looking at, it is the inspectors who must play this role. They are the ones with by far the greatest visibility in relation to the public, as well as in relation to their peers. They mark the rhythm, they start the movements, they are a barometer for the company, those to whom management lends – in vain – all its attention. Getting them to change behaviours on a subject as delicate as their tense relations with customers is, in a way, to reverse the whole of the company's logic.

Achieving this sends us back to the question of levers. There is no point, as has already been said, in simply trying to convince the actors. In an equivalent context, that is, in the same system of resources and constraints, their strategy of flight would remain the same. And at the same time, the resources that one might wish to give to them, since this is what they lack, are in the hands of other actors who, for organizational rather than personal reasons, have little concern for the situation of the inspectors in front of customers. As a general rule, it is a multitude of little decisions which are made on a daily basis and which have an effect on this situation. Returning to these, changing them or tackling them in a different way is the work of an ant which implies self-effacement and does not involve huge and visible changes in overall structures or regulations. Such action by means of "micro-decisions" is already in itself a considerable change of context for the inspectors.

But more precisely, the first lever used should be applied to the controllers, the ones who decide on traffic flow. This would involve obtaining from them the definition of reliable and effectively applied criteria when the question arises of the final choice between punctuality and transport connections. One might suppose that if such criteria, if they really exist, for the moment remain vague, this is because the controllers carefully look after the areas of autonomy in their work. It will therefore be necessary to offer them something in exchange, or create a constraint for them that will give more clarity. It will then be up to the company to define a framework within which the choice will be made and possibly a system of positive or negative sanctions attached to its implementation. This definition will make it possible to return to the inspectors and set up an agreement with them which could be formulated along the following somewhat colourful lines:

> We, the Management, have listened to you and taken a look at your reality. We have understood that if you leave the transport system in a difficult situation, this is not because of lack of interest or professionalism; it is because our method of functioning does not permit you to stay. If we undertake to obtain from the controllers that they base their decisions on criteria that are reliable and known to you

and if we penalize the non-application of such criteria, if in addition we make it our business to ensure that the machine maintenance service reads and takes account of your reports on incidents, assuming that you effectively write and communicate these, are you prepared to commit yourselves to managing the relationship with customers when a problem occurs?

This formulation helps in understanding that the change is not imposed, that it is not a mechanical effect of the levers used. It is negotiated with the actors, not by speaking to them of moral, general or abstract principles on public service, but by starting out from their own daily reality. In relation to this, it is proposed to give them the resources which will make a change of strategy acceptable – rational – for them. At the same time, we have seen that granting such resources will depend on other actors which will not be any easier to budge. Here again, it will be necessary to use levers, some of which have been mentioned. Nothing is simple, in point of fact.

From close-up control to conducting the orchestra

But whoever says "negotiated agreement" also says "responsibility". The interesting aspect of what is suggested here is not simply changing the strategy of the inspectors, it is also giving them responsibility, making it possible to introduce systems for assessing what they do – something that was impossible to implement while the organization was unable to provide them with the slightest resource.

And one can clearly see the "avalanche effect" of change that is produced by the use of levers: local management finds itself equipped *de facto* with new resources with which to face the inspectors, as guarantors of the effective use of the criteria which have been defined. It will be able, little by little, to reset the stage, to get away from behaviours of withdrawal and return to the place that the previous method of functioning did not allow them to occupy. In counterpoint, action by the union organizations will be changed by this. Not only will they no longer be in the situation of being the only resources and the only interlocutors for the inspectors, but they will also need to make an effort in parallel with management in order to adhere to the professional realities of their principals and steer away from ideological or terrorist statements.

In such a case and due to what we have called *banding effects* which are inseparable from the use of levers, the proposed change is no longer solely a change in the behaviour of the actors; it is a fundamental evolution of the company's dominant practices – the "culture" as management writings might say – which, if it occurs, will open up new possibilities, will reveal opportunities, will make it possible to continue the movement far more effectively than absolute, rigid and long-term planning of the overall process. This will no doubt be less secure in appearance, to the extent that experience shows that it is pointless to try and predict all the consequences induced by the use of levers.

I have overemphasized the extreme intelligence of the actors to think that all their reactions, all the new arrangements that they will not fail to find, are predictable. And it is indeed they who reveal the new *solutions that are acceptable* while the role of management in this scenario is closer to the orchestra conductor than to the finicky controller watching that things progress in accordance with a predetermined plan.

10

Implementation: The Moment of Change

Having access to a good problematic on change and a solid methodology for analysing organizations is one thing. Implementing change is quite another, and far from easy, as all those interested in the question have been able to see, whether observers or practitioners. On all sides, there is great reticence in accepting to "launch" oneself into the process, which no doubt explains the amount of time and energy spent on drawing up plans which are endlessly being written and are never finally applied. In terms of change more than anything else, the best is the enemy of the good and finicky perfectionism is a powerful factor of immobilism. As everybody shares the same fears at the moment of undertaking something, it is often enough to show managers that all is not ready, that the different steps are neither clear nor under control, that one is not guaranteed the agreement and support of such and such a category, for everything to be blocked and transformations to be adjourned *sine die*.

The principal factors of immobilism

In some organizations, this pressure towards conservatism is aggravated by the turnover of managers which means that none of them is interested in taking the slightest risk during their short stay at the head of the company, which is part of a career path which must not be marred by any incident. In such situations, change becomes something which everybody is more ready to talk about than to do anything about. It is the organization which is made use of to the profit of those who manage it and not those who serve it, and change is even more likely to become a dominant rhetoric where it is not actually practised.

This is summarized well by Charles Noble when he writes:

> Implementation is not a very popular topic with many managers. Senior executives often invest in week-long retreats, extensive marketing research, and expensive outside consulting services, trying to develop the strategic plans that will lead their companies to a prosperous future. Too often, though, these plans never come to fruition – the expected results fail to materialize.[1]

To which should be added that what we are talking about here is not so much defining a strategy for the company, but putting organizations in place, that is, methods of functioning, which will lead to their implementation and possibly their success. The difficulty is only the greater, since in reminding us that the methods of functioning are above all what people do, the way they work, decide, collaborate and sometimes protect themselves, we will at the same time have been reminded of the extent of the issue.[2]

This reticence with regard to implementation and its difficulty is understandable, but it generates a paradox just as management likes them. It is understandable to the extent that, for all the reasons given up until now, this constitutes the most delicate and often the most hazardous part of the change process. We have known for a long time that we have few difficulties in drawing up plans and strategies, even if a good number of these stay in desk drawers or simply end up as dead letters: drawing up detailed programmes is a favourite exercise for immobile organizations, as we have already seen. Even decision making, although often dangerous, does not at the end of the day constitute an insurmountable obstacle, if the responsibilities are sufficiently diluted in complex discussions aimed at reaching the famous "consensus", that is, finally taking everybody on board the same boat. But as soon as it involves taking official action, "deploying" it, that is quite another matter. Why?

Calculation of cost-effectiveness

Observation of the mechanisms at work in organizations in general, and in companies in particular, shows that decisions for change are most often taken in accordance with a logic of "good reason", the one appealing to an actor's good sense in order to be understood: bearing in mind the existing situation, there are good reasons for doing this ... But that "good reason", however evident, however legitimate it may appear, can be likened to the good old "one best way" of Taylorism: because it is, or is assumed to be, the only way, a decision made must be imposed on all, without possibility of discussion. Questioning it, criticizing it, even fighting it can only be the result of incomprehension at best, intellectual dishonesty and bad faith at worst, and in this respect is a matter for reprobation to start with and then sanctions to follow. Implementation, from this point of view, is therefore nothing more than a simple problem of routine management not really worthy of much interest.

Reality is quite different, even if plenty of "deciders" pretend to ignore it in the name of a theoretical "general interest": any decision for change has a greater or lesser impact directly on a human system and the strategies of the actors who are in it. We should remember that such strategies represent the intelligent solutions that these actors have found to gain the most advantage from the context in which they have been placed. This is the yardstick they will use to assess, implicitly or explicitly, the decision taken and not its managerial legitimacy. It is a simple "cost-benefit" calculation that will be made and which will determine the acceptance or refusal, by the actors concerned, of decisions which are taken. *And it is against this calculation that implementation will find itself pitched.* So it is understandable that the more this phenomenon can be anticipated – it is investment in knowledge, and listening, so often mentioned already in this book, which permit such anticipation – the more the strategy of implementation can be adapted to this reality.

However, it is precisely the primacy given to the programme, that is, to what it *must* do, as opposed to the knowledge of reality, that is, what it *can possibly* do, that prevents one from anticipating the reactions of the actors. It is here that we find the paradox: since this capacity of any system to refuse what is proposed to it is, at best, underestimated and, more generally, ignored, its implementation is subcontracted by the managers to their subordinates, who are left to define the technical procedures that will give concrete expression to the decisions taken. In fact, the subordinates in question are going to have to face up to difficulties far superior to those that their bosses had to deal with when making the decisions in the first place. They are bound to come up against the strategic interests of those involved, against their capacity to oppose, to bend the rules. They will need to come to terms with the different stakeholders and indeed start again from scratch, sometimes including even the decision process itself, where necessary, this time round, involving actors who have until now been ignored – a situation which will not fail, in return, to have profound effects on the content of such decisions.

It is striking to note, in the multitude of cases of this type that we have had to study, to what extent, once the decision has been taken, the bosses stand well back as if implementation were no concern of theirs. Or rather as if, because they themselves have done their work and done it well since the decision taken is technically sound, any difficulty in its application can only come from the clumsiness of those who are in charge of applying it or from the bad faith of those on whom it is applied. The manager becomes the Pontius Pilate of the process of change and cannot really help it if Jesus ends up on the cross! In other words, at the end of the day he has the easy choice while others have the thankless task of reconciling the desirable with the possible … even if it is always desirable but not always possible to do so.

The example of insurance companies

The effect of this paradox can sometimes be encouraging, as, for example, when we see some junior managers, most often fairly young, thrown into an assignment thought to be of little prestige, and who suddenly find themselves in a situation where they must manage interests which are of course beyond them but which are also beyond their bosses. This is what has happened in a good number of insurance companies: traditionally, insurers have always subcontracted the relationship with their end customers to intermediaries of various kinds, whether agents, brokers or even salaried sales staff who, although members of the companies in question, were quick to gain their independence. As a consequence of this choice, the companies became extremely dependent on such intermediaries, including when this involved launching new products which they believed to be of undisputable interest for the survival of the whole. In the United States, for example, the leader in the domestic market for general insurance had the most awful difficulty in getting its agents, even though exclusive, to enter the life assurance market.

Because competition was becoming increasingly fierce in this sector as in others, it therefore seemed crucial for the companies to restore contact with the end customer so as to have a better command of the impact of their communications and a closer control over the application of their product or pricing policies. To do this, they wanted to use computerized and electronic tools, suggesting the centralization of all information available on customers or the systematic collection of all electronic addresses for such customers. The implementation of this, as one might have guessed, was only expected to produce technical problems which helps to explain why, in most cases, it was entrusted to computer departments!

All – as far as we know, without exception – had enormous difficulties in applying these new orientations and some never succeeded at all. Naively, they explained to their intermediaries that such arrangements would improve and facilitate their own work – so even less reason to oppose them! However, the managers of the computer departments in charge of such projects progressively discovered the amplitude of the problems that they were coming up against and that neither themselves nor those making the decisions had anticipated. To their surprise, they discovered that the monopoly of access to the customer was, for the agents, brokers and other salaried sales staff, a priceless resource which guaranteed to them a certain level of power, autonomy and remuneration. And, all things being equal, agreeing to give this up, no matter how good the reason, amounted for them to professional suicide in the true sense of the term, to the extent that, in the long term, they easily anticipated that some of them were certain to disappear, with the companies reabsorbing part of their current work. Faced with such difficulties, the managers in charge of implementation generally called in outside consultants, who often only reinforced the technical orientation of decisions that had been taken, to the detriment of a strategic understanding of the real issues. The development of a "good information system" has once again taken the place of effectively listening to the actors concerned. The general disorder thus grew bigger, the problem became even more conflictual, until certain managers finally gave up on their project, waiting for better days which did not necessarily arrive.

The inertia of organizations

Organizations therefore naturally manifest a huge inertia which is not specifically linked to their size. In this matter, having to manage a smaller unit is no guarantee that it will be easier to produce movement, rather the contrary. Pressures towards change will only be more reduced and the reproduction of previous practices will become the rule.

In his case studies devoted to two companies – Laura Ashley and Firestone – Donald Sull shows with great relevance how immobilism in organizations is constructed and theorized. After noting that "the problem is not an inability to take action but an inability to take the appropriate action", he analyses what he calls the "active inertia" which runs rife in companies and which is an enlightening demonstration of the abstract nature of managerial vocabulary, as well as its frequent use as a screen for inaction, in a logic identical to the one we have identified around "action plans". Thus, in Sull's opinion, strategic plans lead to blindness, processes are transformed into routines, relationships end up as obstacles and values become dogmas. And he concludes:

> established processes often take on a life of their own. They cease to be a means to an end and become an end in themselves. People follow processes not because they're effective or efficient but because they are well known and comfortable.[3]

The word "comfortable" must not be used lightly, in the simple sense of feeling right somewhere or having characteristics which make life easier. Whatever their objectives and ambitions in relation to customers, markets or the general public, whatever their "project" and the "vision" of their executives which underlie them, organizations have a natural tendency over time to privilege their internal logic over their mission, which constitutes the principal source of inertia and explains why managers feel the need to theorize this unmentionable practice.

The theory, with its accompanying vocabulary, is what will explain, justify or cover over the ever-growing distance between declared intentions and effective behaviours. The more an organization falls into routine, privileges the repetition of well known and well mastered solutions, the more, in reality, it will only function to protect its members to the detriment of any other consideration such as service quality or cost reductions. At the same time, it is going to adopt a modernist or technocratic vocabulary corresponding to current trends, together with superficial practices assumed to represent or symbolize profound changes – use first names in the American style, ostensibly leave one's door open, mix with other job categories in the staff canteen, and so on. But as soon as this puts "comfort" in jeopardy, things become far more difficult and resistances more numerous and more open. They come from all around.

The vicious circle of conservatism

Among managers, there are those for whom it is never the right moment and who endlessly put off until tomorrow what they should be doing today. How often does one hear senior managers delivering, with surprising detachment, a brilliant analysis, usually very relevant, of what is not right in their organization, pointing the finger at all that should be changed, defining with lucidity what the final result should be, at the same time as emphasizing in apology that "Now is not the time" and that "People – the others, of course – are not ready." It is a constant in a lot of organizations to observe this vicious circle of immobilism: on one side, the managers would like to change, at least in appearance, but consider that their troops are not ready to follow them along this road; on the other side, the troops in question do not see why they should make a move when those in charge show such immobilism. Most specialists, however, are in agreement in recognizing that it is at the top that the essentials of the problem are to be found.

In this way, Hammer and Stanton write as follows on the specific case of setting up a process organization:

> Because the changes involved in becoming a process enterprise are so great, companies can expect to encounter considerable organizational resistance. We have found, though, that it's rarely the frontline workers who impede the transformation. Once they see that their jobs will become broader and more interesting, they are generally eager to get on board. Rather, the biggest source of resistance is usually senior functional executives, division heads, and other members of the top management team. These senior executives will often either resent what they see as a loss of autonomy and power or be uncomfortable with the new, collaborative managerial style.[4]

The observation is shrewd and can easily be generalized to cover all situations of change. It also shows that "comfort" and its defence form an obstacle that is evenly distributed across all categories of an organization and are not simply created by "people".

The defence of whose assets?

The intermediary organs of representation – the union organizations – are to a greater or lesser degree in the same situation, the only significant difference being that they are not in charge of the company's management, nor responsible for preparing it to face up to the future. However, the behaviour that they develop is the same since their logic is the same. Involved in the actual functioning, having for the most part adopted the segmented structures of their members along the same lines as the organization in which they are implanted, they perceive any tendency towards change as a threat. When they focus on the "defence of assets", the expression used can be understood at two levels. These are the assets of their principals, certainly, the conquest of which is always amplified and idealized by a warlike vocabulary, but they are also, and maybe above all, their own, their structures, their practices, their jobs, their routines.

This situation leads to many blockages which, as we will see, are all the more difficult to overcome when the "weight of welfare" is heavy in an organization. This is what we have already seen in the transport company case in which the union organizations become the privileged, even exclusive, contacts for a general management that is paralysed by the fear of social organizations. In order to avoid strikes and other demonstrations of discontents by its partners, management satisfies claims that are always more numerous and sometimes far-fetched, but which are in fact those of the union organizations themselves, and so always orientated towards conservatism and reinforcement of the existing order. Of course, as in the case of the management, such conservatism conceals itself under a progressive vocabulary, vaunting service to the customer, the public, the citizen or the student.

It is also probable that such union conservatism is behind the impressive fall in the membership rates which today characterizes all developed countries, with the sole exception of Sweden. In France, the rate of unionization fell between 1985 and 1995 from 14.5 per cent to 9.1 per cent, an absolute record. Over the same period in the United States, it fell from 18.1 per cent to 14.2 per cent. And what about New Zealand where, over the same time, it dropped from 54.1 per cent to 24.3 per cent.[5] Behind this phenomenon there is not just a general disinterest in the common weal. When employees want to defend themselves, they spontaneously find their own forms of organization, as was shown by the irruption of "coordinations" in France. It is the unsuitability of the methods of functioning for taking new problems into account which is at cause. At the start of 2000, France provided a particularly striking example of immobilism linked to the strict defence of established union positions.

For obvious reasons of improving the service to the taxpayer and reducing the cost of this service,[6] the Minister for Economy and Finance in this country was trying to merge or at least bring closer the two main administration services of this Ministry – the General Tax Division and Public Accounting – while the unions were violently opposed to the project. They mobilized employees and local councillors for the motive that this measure was a threat to employment and involved closing down local administrative units, thus complicating the lives of users and local parish councillors. The official denials, even though in good faith and with proof to support them, were of no help. It was necessary to withdraw the reform and the Minister was forced to pitifully present a resignation that was rapidly accepted. And yet most of the observers were in agreement on one point. The real issue of the battle was a re-appraisal of the balance between the two main union organizations in this Ministry. One was particularly established in one administration, the other in the second, and a tacit agreement allowed them to benefit from this situation without seeking to compete against each other. The planned merger, which, in effect, resulted in the absorption of part of one of the administrations concerned by the second, would have had major consequences on the balance between the unions. However well founded the foundation for the decision, it was unacceptable by definition.

And what about the employees?

There is nothing to say, finally, that change is spontaneously more acceptable by the employees themselves. This is a "basist" naivety which must be corrected. The organizational changes which were pro-posed at the dawn of the twenty-first century are indeed those of *work*, the ways of doing it, including relationships that one has with others in the businesses. However, work in contemporary companies has always had two functions: a production function – producing goods and serv-ices to put on the market – and a protection function – protecting those who work not only from the hazards of life by providing them with the means of subsistence, but also from others, such as customers and col-leagues.[7] What we can see today, what is in fact targeted by most organizational changes, is the end of the work protection function. The "duty of cooperation" which is imposed on everybody with all that that implies in the way of negotiation, confrontation, dependency and dis-comfort in work,[8] is one of the most significant aspects of this. Actors anticipate it with too much difficulty, and their intelligence allows them to understand and to catch sight of the concrete consequences of what they are being asked for. They are required to abandon a great deal without necessarily being offered a reasonable alternative.

This situation shows itself to be even more delicate in that the organ-ization concerned is bureaucratic in nature, that is, turned in on itself and its members.[9] In such a case, it is not the legitimacy of change which will pose the problem. All serious investigations show that employees, even those in the most immobile of organizations, under-stand that work can no longer be what it was, which does not prevent them from regretting it; what will be the determining factor here is the implementation, that is, the way in which the problem is shared with them and in which they are associated with the search for solutions.[10]

Change in little steps

The consequence of what has just been said is that change in organizations has two major features: in the majority of cases this is not voluntarist, in the sense that it is not the result of a decision to change made by a responsible actor. It arrives of its own volition, following on from spontaneous developments or small decisions which, when put end to end, lead to something new and often unexpected. Change happens… without people noticing, and the "leader's" role is therefore not so much to be in front, thanks to his "vision", as to follow behind and, if he can, to accompany, and in any case not to hinder. Then one day one realizes with amazement that things are no longer what they were. The external context changes, decisions are taken in a field which profoundly affects another field, thus creating a natural process of which one does not speak simply because one does not see it. This is the way in which the great majority of organizations have succeeded in adapting themselves. It is also the fault of this process that others have died. Spontaneous change is, above all, the reign of the random, of surprises that may be good as well as bad.

But that means that *the change being looked for is a phenomenon that is far more reactive than proactive.* It is a response and not an anticipation, as shown by that sports adage which states that one should not change a winning team. One must wait to lose before reacting, and experiences of change from "cold" situations (that is, non-emergency) – although they do exist – can be counted on one's fingers.

From a certain point of view, there is nothing surprising in that. Changing something that is going well is simply not legitimate in the eyes of the actors concerned. Although one can get them to understand and really grasp the necessity when things go badly, they will nevertheless feel frustration in having to change things that are going well, and will not fail to put those "playing God" on guard. Rarely will you see healthy people sitting in doctors' waiting rooms. In terms of organization, prevention is a cause which still remains to be pleaded. However, finding the "right moment for change" poses the problem of legitimacy for action, that the hierarchical position is even less capable of dealing with when the stakes are high in terms of power or comfort for those concerned. Everybody knows today that it is a crisis situation that confers such legitimacy, sometimes modestly called "learning the lesson from failure". The true lesson should be that one must not wait for the crisis.

Why change when everything is going well?

We have been able to observe a situation of this type: a European business is producing a "commodity" that it distributes either directly to its biggest customers or by means of a network of independent dealers who serve the general public. It is a world leader on its market, very well established in North America, where it is performing remarkably well. Its president, who provides the benchmark in the business, enjoys an excellent image outside and an undeniable charisma with managers and employees inside the company. Management is sound and the stock market price translates the very positive evaluation of the financial markets. The organization is uniform, wherever in the world operations are being run, and has recently been modified to give better satisfaction to customer expectations: regional structures have been put in place, within which teams of technical sales engineers maintain direct and fast-moving relationships with customers, so as to satisfy any new requirements within the shortest possible time. The principle is simple: the requirement of proximity in relation to customers involves the fullest possible decentralization of operations, and freedom for people in the "field" to decide how they want to manage their relations with their environment.

Such reorganization did not pose any problems and the financial results continued to be remarkable. And yet the president expressed a doubt on its real effectiveness, more linked to personal intuition than to the deterioration of any particular indicator. He had a survey carried out in several countries in order to better understand how the company really functioned and the way in which local actors had assimilated the new set-up. Research showed that his intuition was correct and that the decentralization was producing a perverse effect likely to be damaging over time to the relationship with customers who, seizing the opportunity offered to them to address easily contactable local representatives, did not hesitate to transmit to them all their demands, which were of course proving to be far more numerous than anticipated.

Faced with such an influx, the technical sales engineers moved as quickly as they could. They gave priority treatment to the easiest questions, those that were within their field of competence, and put off until later those that required an investment in terms of searching for new solutions. Their being overstretched allowed them to justify the choices they made, without management, itself snowed under with work, having sufficient distance to appreciate the reality of the situation and maybe correct it. The customers did not take long to understand that, if they had a question that was the slightest bit complex in content, requiring innovation, it was better to turn towards a competitor eager to win new market shares from the world leader which, in this way, became the champion of routine, while its competitors, thanks to market demand, went several lengths ahead in terms of technological innovation. The market, however, was buoyant enough for this phenomenon, still only at its beginnings, not to be seen in the financial figures.

Nevertheless, seeing the results of the survey which confirmed his intuitions, the president decided to correct the line of fire and change his organization once again in order to make it more responsive. Among the actions put forward was, in particular, a significant change in the methods of appraisal and remuneration for engineers together with the overall line management chain. This measure was intended to correct the quantitative drift induced by the abundance of requests, and to place everybody in the position of having to arbitrate between replies that were easy and those requiring research and inventiveness.

The change met with failure. Not because the results were not good. It was simply not put in place subsequent to a generalized opposition in particular from upper management which did not see the need for changing something that, despite what the president had to say, ensured the company's success. Everybody found themselves in agreement in emphasizing the risks that would be incurred by stirring up the opposition of the engineers, from whom so much was already required, and managers in the different countries voiced their doubts on the wisdom of changing yet again something that had only just been put in place. It was a true action of lobbying which took place, backed by scarcely veiled threats, until the president cancelled his project – to everybody's great relief.

The windows of opportunity

One might conclude from this that change does not happen when it is necessary, *but when it is possible*. It is the appearance of this *window of opportunity*, to use military parlance, that is known as the *moment of change*. This moment is, by definition, difficult to identify since it does not obey any specific rule which might be theorized by means of a reliable model. It comes from an alchemy which must be felt rather than demonstrated and which doubtless corresponds to the meeting point between a situation which is undeniably deteriorating and therefore known to everybody, and the feeling shared by a majority of actors who cannot and will not continue as before.

It is for this reason that certain crises, even major ones, are not enough to make change possible. If these are only seen in a deterioration of results that do not really put the organization in danger, if they are only expressed by a poorer service rendered to customers who, in any case, do not have much choice, and, lastly, if they concern units whose members enjoy protection such that they would need a lot more to make them aware of the catastrophe, then there is little chance of their triggering any reaction at all.

In such characteristics, one can recognize the French national education system which everybody agrees year after year is totally against any shape of reform, even though the results that it produces are in inverse proportion to the resources that it consumes. This world is so turned in on itself, with advantages of every kind, not the least of which is, for a high proportion of its members, to avoid actually teaching pupils, that any change is, *de facto*, a threat to such advantages. The environment can shift to a point where it becomes inevitable to make a fundamental change in the organization concerning not only the training of teachers and the disciplines that they teach, but also the modalities in accordance with which they are appraised and remunerated, as well as the way in which they perform their jobs; but nothing happens, it is never the right moment. One can see that the pupils are different, more difficult, more demanding, but this is only a matter for regret, not for adaptation.

The defence of advantages that have been acquired by this type of organization tends to make it so blinkered that it puts the whole system – or at least some of its members – in danger, to such an extent that one French union had no hesitation in talking of "mortiferous advantages".[11] The mechanism is easily understood – the world changes but the organization stays as it was. And yet some of its members are in daily and head-on contact with this changing world and their management of this relationship becomes all the more difficult since internal methods of operation disallow any adaptation at all, making front office tasks always more stressful, difficult, thankless. Career management, which in short[12] puts the youngest and least experienced teachers in front of the most difficult pupils, gives no chance to one side (pupils) or the other (teachers). But everyone is so sensitive on this point that any attempt to change something other than simply allocating more resources to this bottomless pit is perceived as an intolerable aggression. One can see how this situation can paralyse all those involved and how anybody wanting to rashly overdo things would be quickly called to order.

The transport company shows almost exactly the same characteristics and helps us to understand how executives can *miss* the moment of change. Faced with a worsening service which leads high contribution customers to turn towards other means of transport as soon as they possibly can, management continues imperturbably with its odd face to face with the union organizations, for reasons already mentioned above. These, as already said, function in accordance with their own special logic, conservative by definition, and in this case immobilist. Both partners are in agreement on the necessity to do nothing that would threaten the delicate balances, thereby increasing the disinvestment of categories who get the feeling that nobody is concerned about them.

But all the surveys that were carried out have shown, on the one hand, worsening work situations, to which actors only accommodate themselves by reducing the constraints, that is, by doing less and less work, and, on the other hand, a certain readiness to try and "do things differently" provided one is capable of discussing with them alternatives which concern their everyday reality and not simply the deformed and biased perception that institutional partners have of them. Paradoxically, as already seen in other companies, it will most probably be through a major crisis *provoked by the agents themselves* that the opportunity will arise for fundamentally changing this organization. From this point of view, the Air France case study, which will be presented in the next chapter, is a classic of its kind. It was necessary for the employees to take action, occupy runways, workshops and offices in order to get something decided, simply because it was no longer possible to carry on doing nothing.

Listening and the moment of change

One can therefore fully understand the necessity for *listening* in order to identify the moment of change. This must be primarily aimed at the actors themselves and not those who represent them, about whom we have already said that they have an apprehension of reality that is distorted by their own interests. This is not a case of short-circuiting or anti-unionism. The unions, like other actors, must be put in a situation in which they will have an *interest* in doing their work. This will occur if, when faced with their assertions and demands presented in the name of their members, a management is capable of putting forward an understanding of reality gained in the field and constructed on a true analysis of working situations. It is this *true reality* which may constitute a real opportunity to do something with the backing of the actors, and not by directly confronting their opposition which is more assumed than real.

Experience shows that listening, which is what we are talking about here, is made easier when an event occurs, whether this is a failure, a major crisis or any other shock striking the organization. In such circumstances, the actors talk, communicate their personal understanding of events, *which is always interpretable from their own situation*. A failure will, in most cases, allow the person speaking to say, not what is not right in general, *but what is not right for him*. The event in question will be quickly forgotten in the conversation to make way for an open discussion on what the actor himself feels as intolerable or needing to be changed.

In other words, the actors will use what is happening as an unexpected resource for expressing something that until then they had only felt in a confused way, or that the ambient conformism virtually prevented them from admitting to themselves. One of the great virtues of crises is to make the inexpressible expressible and allow individuals to realize that they are all thinking alike without ever having dared speak of it to each other.

A failed merger: a formidable means of revealing an organization's underlying problems

This is what happened in a big bank in Northern Europe at the beginning of the year 2000. The presentation of this case will help to highlight some facets of the opportunities which appear when an unexpected event occurs and loosens the tongues of the actors concerned, even if caution suggests, once again, that it should be used only as an example and not as a model.

This financial establishment on the European marketplace has a solid reputation for serious and sound management, built up over time by presidents coming from the civil service. And yet the caution of such management has not prevented it from expanding outside the national territory, particularly with regard to all investment bank activities. To do this, the bank has proceeded with well targeted purchases, mostly in North America, which show it to be an influential operator in world financial markets.

Culturally speaking, the dominant feature in this organization is a high level of conformism, somewhat "stuffy" relations and a rebuttal of interpersonal conflicts, which continually pushes towards a search for consensual solutions, even if this means delaying the decision making process. Traditionally, one waits for things to be "ripe" before launching oneself into action, that is, for them to have been accepted before being officially decided. In appearance, the social climate is excellent, supported by good levels of pay, attractive career possibilities, and not insignificant advantages, acknowledged by the employees.

Like a good number of its sister banks, this bank was sucked into the whirlpool of mergers and acquisitions towards the end of the 1990s. This has pushed it into reviewing its strategy which, until then, had been more inclined to privilege alliances over marriages – jealous as it was of its independence and its specificities. So as not to remain outside the big concentrations, the directors chose to launch a friendly takeover bid for one of the major business banks on the marketplace, known and respected worldwide for more than a century.

The transaction was launched in all transparency and with full agreement between the two executive teams. Task forces were quickly set up, even before the markets had given their verdict. These teams combined managers from both establishments, happy to work together on forming an overall structure with more weight. As always in such circumstances, a few frictions were revealed around some perfectly understandable susceptibilities, although actors were in agreement in saying that here there were real opportunities for discovering new things.

But the story comes to a sudden stop with the arrival of a third establishment, itself a big and generalist rival of the first, which launched a hostile takeover bid for both banks which had already gone a long way in their merger process. After various incidents, causing the whole country to hold its breath through that summer, the affair sorted itself out in a surprising way – the first bank managed to slip out of its predator's clutches, while the investment bank, although not its principal prey, stayed trapped.

The managers and employees followed events on a day-to-day basis, especially those from the investment bank side, primarily concerned by the initial merger project. A defence association was set up and management appealed to the patriotism of its employees, calling on them to refuse to hand over their own shares to the hostile competitor. There were no defections, which helps to explain the president's feeling of huge success with the final outcome – the bank had saved its independence – which he hastened to share with all the head office managers, using an improvised general meeting held in the bank's main lobby to tell them the details of the final negotiation.

Curiously, this presentation was poorly received, generating an unpleasant atmosphere, and a huge gap appeared between top management, who saw the event as a victory, and management staff who appeared disheartened by this end to the adventure. Without actually spelling it out, the service provided by top management was criticized, and they were reproached for having lived the event only from their own point of view and not having "felt" how the employees were living it.

This persistent malaise was to lead the person in charge of the investment bank side, by definition the most affected by this epic, to start up a survey with his managers for "listening" – this is the term used – to them in order to understand how they themselves have experienced this period of time. The method used would help to understand reactions, not from an emotional point of view, but by putting them in relation to the organization's method of functioning. This is what we have already defined as listening, which, we must remember, does not consist solely of asking people what they want or why they are not happy, but also telling them.

The results were surprising: the merger's failure – for this in fact was how managers had seen the events – was, amazingly, to loosen tongues in this usually tight-lipped environment. Senior management was to be brutally and unreservedly exposed to question, almost as if the task force teams set up to prepare the finally abortive merger had formed a sort of external audit revealing all the bank's weaknesses – organizational as well as strategic. Everything took place as though the merger had represented, in the collective unconscious, a non-dramatic and official way of resolving these problems.

All this was clearly understood from a certain number of paradoxes encountered during interview sessions conducted with the managers. In this way, although they showed themselves extremely critical of their organization, which they reproached pell-mell for its lack of strategic vision, a terrible weight of bureaucratic red tape which seemed to grow and flourish, an absence of coherence in decision making, an archaic and relatively unprofessional management, methods of promotion only poorly linked to real performances, and so on ... in parallel, each person individually appeared content with their lot, with their work that was generally thought to be interesting, with their remuneration that was considered generous, or with the many opportunities that were offered to them.

Along the same lines, human resource management was subjected to acerbic criticism with regard to the lack of serious career management for managers, to systems of remuneration that were distant from the reality of work and the business world...although at the same time everybody was more or less satisfied with their lot and with the proposals for development which were actually made to them. Certain reproaches were focused on actual business practices, in particular risk management, a sensitive subject of great bureaucratic complexity as soon as it involved obtaining authorization, while others targeted the excessive centralization and pointless intervention of too many varied and sundry managers... which everybody seemed to put up with in their corner by setting up official networks allowing them, finally without too many problems, to escape from limits and obstacles of all kinds. The organization's capacity to manage its customers, especially the most important ones, was seriously contested, highlighting the extreme compartmentalization that was prevalent in the company, the multiplicity of contacts, the continual short-circuiting...without anybody, however, at any particular time having tried to change anything whatsoever, with each person building up their own customer portfolio, managed as autonomously as possible, and only calling on the rest of the establishment with the utmost caution.

Interpretation of the malaise

Such contradictions – which, like all contradictions, are only apparent – led to a reappraisal of the bank's real method of functioning, and above all to an understanding of the origins of this vague but clearly identifiable malaise, which meant that this universe which was seen by everybody as very stable, if not conservative and immobile, was in fact ready for profound changes. The contradictions only existed if one stayed with the official picture of the organization, seen as homogeneous and integrated, which in reality was not the case.

It appeared that, behind the rhetoric of belonging to a single establishment, the company was made up of very independent small or medium-size units, within which everybody managed to find the necessary arrangements for carrying out their work under satisfactory conditions, with regard to immediately looking after customers, as well as the creation of opportunities to develop business. Hence, consequently, a strong link with one's own unit which, paradoxically, weakened the general organization by making it the target for all criticisms, whether justified or not. In their local universe, each person had the possibility of demonstrating talents recognized by their peers, had the feeling that they were "playing in the first division", and above all had the freedom to build up their own customer portfolio, which increased their value on the job market.

But at the same time, the company confusedly felt the need to control the centrifugal pulls developed by all these little entities, always tempted by greater autonomy, and content with "doing their deals" in the services suggested to them by central departments. For this, it was continually strengthening the structures for steering, for coordination and for control: always more meetings, more resource centres, more support functions, and so on.

The gap, which never stopped widening between these two areas, allowed each side to use the other as a foil and an alibi: the central units considered local brokers to be interested solely in their bonuses and personal futures, while the brokers saw "head office managers" as being totally cut off from business reality, purely concerned with preserving their positions.

This situation thus led to one of those rather unoriginal vicious circles that are frequently encountered in this type of organization: the peripheral units were continually seeking to expand their freedom and margins for manoeuvre, thus creating a powerful centrifugal movement which, in the eyes of the central functions, gave them the appearance of an impenetrable world, requiring always more control and organization. The antagonism between the two sides continued to grow.

The problem was that this method of functioning set limits on global performance in a world in which competition was becoming ever more intense. On the one hand, ambitions with regard to customers, themselves becoming more and more global, were reduced to what each unit was capable of offering through its own competence alone, without ever making use of possible synergies; on the other, uncontrolled risk management, sometimes over-lax, sometimes over-cautious, left the bank dangerously exposed on the market. And even for the managers living in these small units and liking them, career prospects were seen to be very dependent on the size of such units and their possibilities of growth.

And so, ultimately, it was the commercial possibilities for the whole bank that were severely penalized by this method of functioning, in precisely the sector on which it focused in priority. And this "game", quite possible in a stable situation, suddenly found itself threatened by pressure from competitors, reinforced by that from shareholders to whom considerable promises had been made. In brief, everybody was trapped in a zero-sum game where the failure of the merger – which had clearly shown, through the contact with another bank working on the same market niches, that other practices were possible, that considerable developments were in progress at competitors – forced actors to open their eyes. The dissatisfaction that was expressed, the growing frustration and the bitter criticism, sometimes without disguise, of general management could be interpreted as so many signs sent out by the managers who were unanimous in demanding fundamental and rapid changes.

Where nobody had seen anything but conservatism and conformism, there suddenly appeared the *will and the possibility* for a far more far-reaching change than even the most optimistic among them had dared to contemplate.

The alchemy of change

This is the *moment of change*, and this example provides an opportunity to reflect on it. In their initial vision, the senior executives had indeed understood that, at one moment or another, it would be necessary to change the organization's practices. Previous surveys had in particular shown that their local representatives were finding it increasingly difficult to respond to complex customer expectations. However, up until then, and in order to avoid making any fundamental changes to working methods which might have met with conflict from a certain number of actors, their response had been "always more": more central structures, more committees, more coordination functions, which of course led them to wonder about the reasons for the exponential growth of such functions and their cost.

Expecting immobilism from employees, these senior executives saw the merger as a chance to get things moving without having to take the risk themselves of initiating the movement *ex nihilo*.

It was in fact the non-merger which produced this effect and which opened the window of opportunity into which everybody rushed, all reproaching one another for their previous immobilism. This was the *developer* which enabled this moment to be seen.

The word "developer" is used here with its chemical meaning: spread over an apparently blank page, it "developed" everything that was in reality on the page but that nobody could see, since without the developer the page would continue to appear uniformly white to the eyes of those around. But at the same time, the appearance of this developer, of what will play this role, is unpredictable. Firstly, because provoking a crisis oneself in order to change an organization is perhaps possible in theory, but a luxury that nobody can afford to offer themselves. If the crisis arrives, it may be profitable, although the cost in human and financial terms is generally substantial, but it can hardly be provoked knowingly.

The example which has just been discussed suggests something different, once again a long way from being a paralysing form of planning: one can be aware of the need to change, and yet also be anxious when it is time to take action, especially, as we might repeat, if nothing in the situation really justifies it. Even better, we have just seen that everybody can be in agreement on this necessity, and yet nobody will say it out loud, for fear of being isolated or out of step. So those who can, the senior executives, create an event – in this case a merger. But what happens then is difficult to predict and control and there is nothing to indicate that it absolutely must be done. What has been started often provokes unexpected reactions, which must be seen as so many opportunities to be used. In the bank's case, the merit of its senior executives is not in having undertaken a securely hedged process, but rather of having been able to listen, to go beyond the spontaneous discontent and of having used it as a lever. By doing this, *they have turned the constraint into a resource*, which is no doubt the best way of not allowing the moment of change to slip by unnoticed.

And this fundamental unpredictability of the moment of change redefines the role of the manager or "leader" that we have seen shaping itself over the pages. At the end of the day, it is not putting everything that will happen under control – or at least attempting to put it under control. Not only is this impossible, as experience has frequently shown, but, when one tries too hard, one generally seems to produce blockages, associated with the bureaucratic nature of the formal procedures that everybody strives to put in place in order to cover themselves. This role is far more evident in a continual process of listening, not superficial or biased, which makes it possible to glimpse possibilities a step ahead and use them to advantage.

It means, finally, *accompanying* things with the actors themselves, in an atmosphere of trust. The more thorough the listening, the more such trust will be natural and reciprocal. It is managers who *do not know what is going on* who are the principal factors of blockage to change in the organizations of which they are in charge.

Using dissatisfaction as an opportunity

One last point merits our attention: whether speaking of a "window of opportunity" or "legitimacy" of change, one always refers sooner or later to a crisis situation, a malaise, in any case outside of daily routine, which makes it possible and acceptable to get things moving. In doing this, one rediscovers a paradox that specialists have been emphasizing for years – *one does not achieve change with people who are satisfied*. The phenomenon was particularly evident towards the end of the 1970s in banks and insurance companies, when they tried to introduce computers into the management of all their operations and when certain of them tried to reduce the lines of hierarchy. They quickly came up against a lack of enthusiasm or even direct opposition from their most satisfied employees, those who benefited from the previous system, from its opacity with regard to the real content of their work. Certain companies therefore decided to try some experiments, forming groups made up of employees identified as being dissatisfied with their lot, initially perceived as being not very cooperative and not terribly interested in the company's life. The success was immediate. Those involved played the game and discovered new ways of functioning that were more open, more in step with what the company wanted to do, and who were subsequently able to make themselves heard by the whole organization. This was also a way of getting away from those zero-sum games which, as we have seen, can be so very paralysing.[13]

In such a case, it is the *opportunity for change* which should be spoken of, rather than the moment of change. Being on the lookout for all the dissatisfactions which manifest themselves in human populations, *and hence the desire for change*, is once again to give oneself the possibility of transforming what is only perceived as a constraint into a resource. Our habitual stubbornness in considering those who are not content, and who say so, as a threat – because by doing that they are implicitly criticizing us, because they challenge the established order of things and run the risk of spreading like an oil slick, or simply because they do not agree – prevents us from grasping the opportunity that they represent. Nigel Nicholson says much the same when, after having discussed evolutionary psychology, he asserts: "[D]espite the excellent press that change is given, almost everyone resists it – except when they are dissatisfied."[14] It almost goes without saying.

11

Implementation: Playing on Trust

At the end of 1993, Air France, a flag-carrier for many years and the pride of a whole country, marked by a history made up of daily exploits, literally exploded. Not only was the company producing record losses, the like of which, until then, had never been seen in the business, but the fall in unit revenues was picking up speed dramatically.[1] During the month of November, there started to appear the signs of social unrest which, little by little, spread like an oil stain and rapidly transformed themselves into an occupation without concessions of the runways on the capital's two main airports, thus causing a complete paralysis of traffic. One can measure the extent of the malaise through such actions, because attacking the work tool, particularly over a long period, was not in the traditions of this business. At the same time, the conflicts grew more severe to the point where, in places, they led to physical violence between managers and employees. There was great confusion, the unions were sometimes left behind and, after much tergiversation, the public authorities, giving way to all kinds of pressures, decided to get rid of the company's president who had nonetheless fought tooth and nail to try and save what was savable. This departure was supposed to cause a shock and thus unblock the situation.

His replacement was quickly appointed. He was not in any way a specialist of the aviation sector. A former French government prefect who had successfully conducted difficult negotiations in New Caledonia, he had also held the post of president of the Paris City transport authority (RATP), from which he resigned in a blaze of publicity after a disagreement with his supervisory Minister. He had the reputation of being a free mind, capable of sorting out even the most conflictual of situations. He immediately surrounded himself with a team of loyal supporters which, in a way, "doubled up" on the existing team, but was not made up of aviation specialists. It appeared as time went by that this character was in fact somewhat of an advantage since it allowed these senior executives to focus an open and unbiased eye on the company and on events.

A true listening process

The new president immediately attacked the most glaring problems, calling for immediate measures, in such areas as unit revenues or purchasing. Far be it from me to say that his sole preoccupation was to carry out a sociological diagnosis which would then allow him to resolve the overall difficulties. Nevertheless, one of his first decisions was to give himself the means to understand what mechanisms were at work that explained the simultaneous deterioration in results and social climate, since he sensed that these were both linked. Indeed, everybody had been struck by the lack of understanding which had progressively spread between executives and employees: the former, aware of how serious the situation was, appealed to the company patriotism of employees for them not to complicate this even more with social unrest; the latter had agreed to make real efforts, particularly in terms of productivity, which not only did not result in an improved situation, but also did not prevent management from suggesting a freeze or even a reduction in salaries. It was therefore a matter of urgency to get out of this blockage situation, and the president believed that this was only possible by resuming a dialogue based on *real and unbiased knowledge*.

This was why the decision was made to give one month (including Christmas and New Year!) to a team of sociologists specializing in organizations, in order to carry out a series of one-off and extremely targeted business reviews on the company's supposedly sensitive areas. These covered freight, maintenance, Paris stopovers (Orly and Charles de Gaulle), cockpit and cabin personnel. In total, 105 in-depth interviews were simply carried out with a carefully selected sample of people. The fact that the survey was carried out at all is surprising. While advice of caution was given to those conducting the interviews, while everybody expected the worst difficulties, or even the refusal of agents to reply to questions, it was in fact the opposite that occurred. Not a single refusal and a fairly warm welcome, revealing a strong desire to express themselves. It is true that it had been decided to play the game of transparency: from the very start of the investigation, several interviewees posed the question of how much it was costing, since the previous involvement of a firm of consultants had been the subject of much controversy. The interviewers answered the question openly, thus creating an atmosphere of trust which did not waver.

One saw agents arrive for interviews with a piece of paper in their hands on which they had written what they wanted them to ask on their behalf. Intended to last one and a half hours, the interviews, some of which took place at night in the workshops, sometimes lasted as long as three hours,[2] and revealed a wealth of information, expressing much bitterness and a feeling of having been frequently deceived, but also high hopes of seeing things change. This suggests that the next part of the process could and should rely heavily on this goodwill, provided one knows how to use it advisedly.

The factors of a generalized lack of understanding

The presentation of these results to the management committee was a delicate manoeuvre. Despite the precautions taken by the president and by the consultants making this presentation, these results showed, by means of a series of carefully chosen examples, the gap that had formed between the organization's theoretical functioning and its actual functioning, as well as the extent to which the latter had ended up escaping from the control of upper management. One characteristic was particularly noticeable, seen in all the sectors being studied – one was in the presence of a universe that was segmented in accordance with a technical logic, continually enforced and reinforced by the requirements of security. This produced a verticality, or bureaucracy, in the sense of the priority always given by the organization to its own problems, which tended to generate catastrophic vicious circles.

On the one hand, this way of working, without any cooperation between people who were attached to different services and logics, badly affected the quality of service rendered to the customer and led to losses of market share, especially in relation to high contribution customers; on the other, the same mechanisms increased costs, as seen everywhere, without everybody's goodwill and dedication, which really existed, being able to offset the deficiencies of the overall system. So, for example, remarkable gains in physical productivity had been made to freight, in the loading and unloading of aircraft but, because the methods of functioning had remained the same, they resulted in longer time periods and therefore in a less effective service. This was only one case amongst several, but it helped in understanding why the company's performances *and* the social climate deteriorated simultaneously.

On one side, the gains in productivity had been achieved in a mechanical and sometimes brutal manner, without paying attention to conditions which made them possible and effective; on the other, they had resulted in heavy pressure on employees, which had only led to aggravation of the overall and individual situations. Under such conditions, appealing for a new financial effort from the personnel could only lead to all kinds of fantastical interpretations on the identity of those who were appropriating the gains achieved, and the conflicts expressed the message from the organization to its executives, which could be summed up simply as follows: "Do it, but do it differently."

Breaking the traditional relationship between the organization and its employees

Another contradiction was observed, again showing that, although the need for change was clearly evident and although real and in-depth actions had been initiated, the strategy for implementation had been partly neglected. Traditionally, in this business, employees had benefited from good conditions of work and satisfactory wages. Well protected in the more general sense of the term, they had, in return, developed a culture of loyalty and dedication to the company, which was seen on a daily basis in the acceptance of the overlapping of schedules, a particular care in work and a concern for the task to be accomplished under optimal conditions. All this did was express the traditional loyalty–protection link that was encountered in this company, as in plenty of others, and to which agents had long been attached, as evidenced in the operational myth which meant that, whatever the difficulties, an aircraft always left on time.

But under pressure from competition, the need to control and reduce costs became apparent and resulted, here as elsewhere, in this link being broken, since the company was no longer able to offer its employees the same conditions, the same advantages nor even the same protection. When one of the components of this tacit agreement was broken, they responded by breaking the other, which was immediately interpreted by some managers in terms of a loss of motivation, or even as the sign of moving from one generation of employees who were dedicated and competent to a generation of youngsters who only had a moderate involvement in work. Here again, understanding was at its lowest ebb, encouraging biased interpretations, accusations and more radical conflicts.

Such results called for fundamental action on the methods of functioning, but these seemed difficult to undertake in their present state, bearing in mind the degree of distrust which had spread across the company. The president therefore suggested that the results should be presented in strictly identical terms, using the same supporting evidence, to the highest possible number of the company's employees. This was done during a multitude of "restitution" meetings, held over a very short space of time, which made it possible to discuss with agents the principal characteristics of their organization and to share with them, little by little, a similar interpretation of the main problems that the company was facing, expressed in organizational terms and thus never casting doubt on the goodwill, involvement or dedication of a professional category. These presentations gave rise to debates, animated but never aggressive, allowing everybody to express their feelings and also giving the sociologists an opportunity to correct and complete certain of their analyses. The unions were not forgotten and were the subject of a special presentation on which certain of them reported to their principals in terms which expressed, at the very least, a wait-and-see neutrality.[3]

The sharing of knowledge

In order to sanction the massive support given to the main results of the business review, it was decided to send out a questionnaire to 40,000 of the company's employees. This short questionnaire containing 19 questions, two of which were "open", allowed everybody to express themselves on the principal observations and, at the end, to freely put forward suggestions for improvement. Once again, there was great surprise. There, where the prophets of doom and gloom were predicting a poor return, disinterest from personnel, close to 20,000 replies were received, thereby posing the technical problem of how to process them. The open questions were scrutinized in the boardroom by volunteer employees from different parts of the organization and working without time limits on the questionnaires.

The main results were communicated to the rest of the employees through the intermediary of a "journal on the debate" created for this purpose by the new director of human resources, in charge of the operation. They showed, in addition to a massive support of observations, a surprising availability for investing themselves concretely in the search for solutions and, if these appeared justified to them, a great openness faced with the possible sacrifices that might be asked of them. Nothing naive in all that. It was in fact a *quid pro quo* situation – the employees did not intend to limit their involvement to replying to surveys or questionnaires that would justify decisions they would have no option other than to accept. They clearly wanted to go further and to be able to propose their own ideas on a new organization of work, on new practices, or even changes to structures.

It was this package which was proposed in a referendum, fortunately an exceptional procedure in a company and which had the positive results that we all know. This consultation, carried out in a context of transparency, helped to build an agreement between the employees and their executives, focusing at the same time on the process of change and its methodology, and on what, in exchange for this different way of working with them, the employees were prepared to accept. This was not in any way a blank cheque made out to the management team, as shown by subsequent events.

The search for solutions

It was on the basis of this agreement that an impressive number of task forces were set up in the company to take charge of the "processes" that appeared and posing the most problems. Their functioning was particularly innovative. Each process was reviewed from the *customer's point of view*, as revealed by a specialized agency. The idea was simple, even though it still remained barely understood: if one wants actors to work on new methods of functioning, there must be something which gives meaning to such a change, failing which the debate becomes theoretical, abstract and ideological. In an organization such as this one, as well as in most others, it is the customer who provides meaning: first of all because it is the customer which gives the company a living, but mostly because, as soon as one "pulls the thread", one discovers *an ocean of possible different practices* that nobody could even have imagined. To sum up, starting from the customer is starting from the end result since, for the customer, this is the only thing that counts, while segmented areas are only interested in specific results.[4]

In parallel, these task forces were "nurtured". To start with, they were not built in line with any "political" logic, that is, including actors under the motive that it was tactically important for them to be there, but instead their work was fed from the detailed results of business reviews carried out previously. This meant that discussions were continually refocused on the existing reality and on the means of creating a different one. In this phase, the inventiveness of those involved showed itself to be extreme, in the same way that the emergence was seen of personalities who had previously been condemned to stay out of sight by the company's traditional methods of functioning. Categories which until then had ignored or scorned each other now started to talk; not for any reason of comradeship, but because the necessity was apparent, in the name of this new logic anchored on the customer, of bringing together what had until then been kept apart in the name of a logic of formality or technicality. It was these task forces which provided the bulk of the proposals and recommendations which were subsequently implemented.

Forming and coordinating the task forces was, as a general rule, a key factor in the success of this type of procedure. In the very "political" tradition of our companies, the development of such groups was the subject of very particular attention so as to avoid upsetting anybody with the way in which they were made up. But quite naturally, since such groups are formed on a political basis, they do what they were designed to do – that is, politics. This way of doing things must and can be reappraised based on the introduction of the customer logic which brings to light the new collaborations that are necessary. Similarly, the coordination of such groups must leave nothing to chance. What is meant here by "nurture" is the fact of not allowing their work to be boiled down to an exchange of impressions or diffused feelings. It must be orientated and steered around shared observations and established facts, not mere anecdotes. Such methods have always aroused the enthusiasm of those involved, no doubt because of their capacity to take the drama out of debates and thus encourage further work on them.

In the case of Air France, it would be naive to think that everything took place without incident and in an atmosphere of frankness and openness. Nothing removes the effects of taking sides in an organization. Power struggles remain the same and the defence of sectional interests does not just fade away overnight by some miracle. In the same way, not all suggestions were put into application, in fact far from it. But it is this new process itself, far more open and trusting, more risky as well, that made it possible to take decisions which, until now, had been rejected without even looking at them.

What lessons can be drawn from the Air France case?

We therefore need to stand back a little and look at the main characteristics of this approach to change, and see whether they can be generalized in terms of steering an action of this type. There are four major points for discussion.

1. This involves steering by *method* and not by substance or procedures. And it is certainly not by chance that one speaks of "method X" to designate what was done in this company. Here the word must be understood in its true meaning of a way of proceeding, as opposed to a precise and serene knowledge of what must be done to the basis of things. Everybody in the company had an evident awareness that fundamental changes were necessary. This did not necessarily mean that they were possible or even that the *moment of change had arrived*. To reach this stage, it was necessary to change the deal, not just by immediately proposing solutions that nobody would have believed in, nor by drawing up a complete action plan covering all the aspects identified as needing modification. Such an approach would certainly have been doomed to failure through its lack of credibility and firm foundation in reality. What was done here was to think things through differently, starting from a procedure which did not really take into account the sector's specificities – which everybody had always tended to exaggerate – but which proposed *steps*. These focused less on the progress of change itself than on the progressive involvement of all actors in the process. Regaining the trust of employees first of all required that they should be shown trust, which was in fact what happened.

2. The first of these steps was an *investment in knowledge* which, as we will see, does not need to be exhaustive, provided it makes it possible to highlight the key points of the actors' reality, and to understand the problems behind the symptoms. We have seen that the previous situation was, to the contrary, a situation of *ignorance*. This is an endemic disease in companies which often do not see the necessity of knowledge and prefer to devote the best part of their resources and energy to solutions. They invest in collecting data which is attractive by its abundance, they gather "information", "advice" and "opinions", they rarely build a true knowledge base. It should be said that their usual consultants hardly encourage them in this, especially since building up such a knowledge base does not give them much in return, and also they only rarely have the necessary training. Notwithstanding the fact that the solutions so quickly found in this manner are not generally suitable and try to resolve problems that nobody knows about, they produce unpleasant side-effects. They come into conflict with actors who do not know what one is trying to remedy; they make them feel guilty by expecting them to change their practices even when they have the impression that they are already doing their best; they aggravate conflictual situations and phenomena of resistance. In brief, the cure is worse than the disease.

3. The knowledge built up in this way has been *shared*. Such sharing is one of the exercises which arouses the most reluctance from executives. In fact, they cannot imagine that their employees might be ready to accept the reality that a serious survey shows to them. They suspect them of obscurantism and escapism when faced with the facts. This is total nonsense. On the one hand, because experience shows that, as soon as actors have the feeling that what they are being told is not partisan, that not only is it taken from what they themselves have said but also that thorough work has made it possible *to add value* to their own arguments, they discover that they have been listened to, in the deepest sense of the term. They are thus enabled to understand their own vague feelings on things, to tie this in to a vaster whole which gives them a sense of direction and shows that they are not being made to bear an individual responsibility which is not their own. On the other hand, because trying to flee from reality is more the state of the managers themselves, often frightened by realizing that what they are supposed to be managing is in fact to a great extent escaping from their control and, in any case, does not function at all in the manner claimed by official rhetoric.

It is surprising to see, once a survey of this type is proposed, to what extent appeals for caution are multiplied, to what point even the most authoritarian bosses can do little to get their reluctant senior executives to accept this investigation. And yet none of them has any hesitation in communicating and circulating their organization charts! This means that people are quite willing to discuss theory, but rarely practice. Contrary to a preconceived idea, the company is an empire of abstraction as soon as its real method of functioning is involved.[5] But what everybody accommodates themselves to in normal times can become a severe handicap when it is necessary to change things, for this fear when faced with what is real is infantilizing for actors who reject it.

In addition, the sharing of knowledge is the start of trust while most organizations are places of distrust. In the same way that one finds it difficult to accept that everything is not planned in advance, because one fears what the actors are going to do with the margins of freedom allowed to them, one also remains perplexed as to the way in which they will use the knowledge that is given to them. *"Empowerment"* – since that is what this is – is a fascinating subject for seminars, an inexhaustible theme for articles, and a far more painful procedure.

What does this mean, in fact? That one has given the actors the necessary resources and elements for getting away from their partial vision of reality, in order to understand their side of things thanks to a grasp of the whole picture, that one enables them to go beyond the anecdotes and reach the facts. This is the way in which they acquire *more power*, which is indeed the literal translation of the word. And this power, they are going to use it, which rouses all sorts of fears, such as intelligence generally arouses. For orientating this use of their power in a positive direction for the organization is not easy, to the extent that, the more armed the actors are, the less likely they are to accept without argument doing what they are told to do, with the partisan and ideological speeches which usually seem to accompany injunctions. It is essential to reckon *with them* and not without them or against them.

4. It is for this reason that the last part of the strategy of implementation, such as we have been able to observe at Air France, consisted of *associating the highest possible number of actors with the search for solutions*. One can see an interesting paradox. It often happens that executives, who in fact do nothing to hide this, call in top consultancy firms, of world renown, to "legitimize" their decisions. A "recommendation" proposed by X, top expert on the subject, cannot be argued with. And yet it is, without hesitation, as soon as the actors find it unjustified because it generally makes them bear the total cost of change. However, what better and more fundamental legitimization can exist than that provided by the interested parties themselves, when they are asked to find solutions to problems that they understand and share? Certainly they will find more practical and concrete solutions than any outside consultant, provided they are given a little help. In any case, they will open the way to such solutions. Schein writes as follows on this subject:

If you give people knowledge of the way that they are linked to one another and in which their whole system functions, they have the capability of perceiving what must be changed, and they do not need you to suggest to them a model of what is not right and the way in which you are going to change it.[6]

It is this model of trust which is best able to unblock the most strained situations and to make acceptable what one would never have dared imagine.

General trust and individual trust

This in fact involves trust at two levels. The first is general and postulates that one can trust the actors to understand situations provided they are given access to knowledge; starting from that point, they will accept these situations and will help in searching for solutions which are not solely partisan, even if these solutions can sometimes, briefly, be unfavourable to them. One thus creates the conditions for an implicit exchange in which the actors can give their agreement to measures that, at other times, they would have rejected, because, firstly, one has accepted to tell them the why and wherefore of things and has relied on them to find the way out and, secondly, they expect an improvement in the future, which will include salvaging their own situation.

But there is also individual trust, from day to day, the trust involved in the hierarchical relationship, which, when effective, helps to avoid plenty of dramas and makes change possible on a day-to-day basis. Jean-François Manzoni and Jean-Louis Barsoux have tried to define the five conditions for trust in discussions between managers and subordinates. What they point out is not surprising: in their opinion, the boss must first of all create an atmosphere which is favourable to discussion; both sides must reach agreement on the problem's symptoms; they should next arrive at a mutual understanding of what is causing poor performance in certain areas; they should then agree on performance objectives and their intention to continue the relationship; finally, they should consent to communicate more openly in the future.[7] From this point of view, trust is more formalized, more "contractualized" than what we have developed here. But the idea is the same and favours the game of "openness" as opposed to distrust, indifference or suddenness.

The correlation of strategies for change

And yet it is necessary to see that the strategy of change which is proposed here is far from being universally accepted, and that it is no doubt closely linked to the European context in which it has been developed and in which most of the examples given have taken place. It favours participation, the human factor, the search for support from the greatest number. But by standing back slightly from the situation, one can see that the requirements of the modern world, such as the sudden acceleration of economic cycles, which is seen in the appearance and rapid disappearance of many companies and in the growing importance accorded to satisfying the shareholder, are leading to the opposition of two theories and therefore two practices of change.[8]

The first is diametrically opposed to what has just been put forward in this chapter. Specialists call it the "E theory", because it gives absolute priority in action to the economic value. They are in agreement in recognizing that it is "hard" since it considers that the only legitimate measurement of the company's success is the value created for the shareholder. In a process of change, this involves the massive use of financial incentives, resorting drastically and without scruples to layoffs, to downsizing, to restructuring – all of which so marked the end of the twentieth century. This is of course characteristic of the North American world and insistently sends us back to the practices that a certain number of writers have no hesitation in considering as the key factor for the United States' success compared with the result of the developed world.

The "O theory", given this name because it favours organizational capability, is far more widespread in Asia and in Europe. Nobody will be surprised to see that this is close to what was done in the Air France example. The goal that is generally pursued is to develop what is usually called a "company culture" by investing in human capabilities through an individual and organizational learning process. In most cases, companies adopt this when, prior to the appearance of the need to change, there existed an implicit contract of loyalty–protection between them and their employees – this was indeed the case for Air France – and where the abrupt termination of this contract would carry serious risks of the organization finally exploding. Underlying this situation, one can see that what is favoured in this approach is maintaining strong links over time between the company and the people working in it. One might even think that the more such links are woven over a long period of time, by little successive touches, by obtaining ever more advantages, the more resorting to "soft" strategy becomes necessary, even if this does further deteriorate the situation.[9]

And indeed, these two approaches are even more different than they appear at first look on six key points:

1. First of all, the goals which, as we have seen, are, in the first place, to maximize return on short-term investment for the shareholder and, in the second place, to develop organizational capabilities. Here we find a classic distinction on something that we have already highlighted[10] and which, if we put the customer alongside the shareholder, allows us to set the logic of the assignment (E theory) against

the logic of the organization (O theory). One can understand why the more bureaucratic things become – priority given to their own constraints – that is, the more importance is given to protections available to their members, the more they will push towards the second option.

2. Next, leading change which, in the E theory, will be carried out by commands from the top, and which members of the organization will obey without questioning their validity or their consequences. This can be seen every day in the North American world without provoking any more reaction than that. To the contrary, as we have seen above, the O theory will encourage everybody's involvement, in line with the modalities that we have attempted to point out.

3. More fundamentally, in the E theory, priority will be given to what one calls "systems" in the Anglo-Saxon sense of structures, rules and procedures, based on the belief, solidly anchored on strict methods of control, that the actors are indeed doing what such systems enjoin them to do. Curiously, this returns us to the initial dream of a bureaucracy – this time in the conventional sense of the term – as thought of by Max Weber and which would be an organization capable of producing general and impersonal rules as well as applying them: this is only possible with the backing of a severe system of sanctions. The O approach, seen from this point of view, is more pragmatic and corresponds partly to what has been discussed in the first part of this book: what one proposes to change in priority are the *behaviours* of actors rather than their attitudes, by creating new contexts for them. Here the systems are used as levers, in a perspective which is itself *systemic*, but in the sociological sense of the term. One wagers on the playing capabilities of these actors, rather than on their diligence to follow, to the letter, what is laid down in writing.

4. At the same time, the process will be different. In comparison with what was observed in the transport company – which is nevertheless European – this will consist, in the E theory, of drawing up plans and programmes that are as accurate, comprehensive and restrictive as possible, but this time making sure of their effective and rapid implementation. The O vision will favour experimentation, evaluation, comings and goings between the goals to be achieved and the results observed, and then generalization even if this means continually watching that the necessary adaptations are made.

5. The levers used will not be the same, nor will they be used in the same way. The E strategy will focus on monetary incentives, linking them directly to short-term financial results, such that stock market

rates will allow them to be continually evaluated and considered to be incontestable. We have virtually come back to a "Taylorist" vision of the motivation of individuals at work. In the O strategy, the financial rewards are used more to accompany change than to produce it. But above all, it is the overall tools in a human resource management policy – appraisals, promotions, assignments, pay packages – which will be used here as levers for change. Of course, the more the organization tends to rigidify these in an earlier phase, the more their implementation will be delicate and will require negotiation with the interested parties.

6. Finally, in both cases, calling in outside consultants takes on different meanings. In the first case (E theory), it is they who analyse the problems – in fact, focus most of the time on the symptoms – who sketch out solutions and look after the implementation of their own recommendations. All the big consultancy firms have in fact drawn up methodologies on this point which can easily be duplicated. In the second case (O theory), the consultants are a support mechanism and appear as facilitators who help not only management – as Beer and Nohria seem to want – but also, as I have tried to show, all personnel to find their own solutions, which will then be the subject of a formal validation by those in charge. But the – slight – distinction that I have just introduced with regard to those who need to be really supported and helped, closes the loop: it shows that trust, as accorded to all those who are involved in a process of change, is still far from being universally admitted.

12
The Particular Case of Public Organizations[1]

Public organizations present an interesting paradox from the point of view of change. On the one hand, their reform is on the agenda in the principal industrialized countries, for reasons which are easy to understand – they will not be able to escape from the fundamental changes that one is seeing across the world and which concern all organizations, whether public or private; however, on the other hand, nowhere has this reform been carried out very convincingly or, if so, then in the greatest difficulty.

Such changes, that I have already had the opportunity to describe,[2] occur under the impact of globalization which, on a daily basis, is showing itself in a growing pressure from the customer or from the user to bring costs down and improve the quality of goods produced or services sold. The result is a veritable revolution in organizations which does not express itself solely in the notorious reorganizations so loudly applauded by the world's main stock markets. This involves radical changes in the job sector within all developed countries. On one side, the concrete methods of working are very rapidly redefined with regard to hourly, weekly or annual rhythms as well as to relational modes with others; on another side, the link to the organization and to the company in particular is "jeopardized" in some way, and not only with regard to the situation on the job market, completely shelving the celebrated loyalty–protection exchange which has characterized the salary relationship from the beginning of the century until the mid 1980s.[3]

In parallel, the highly differentiated intensity of the desire to change displayed by the different countries expresses the difficulty of this task. This ranges from high and sometimes single-minded commitment, as is the case in the United Kingdom, through to a situation in which the word "caution" is a euphemism (France, for example), not forgetting countries which, in the image of Sweden or Germany, have made the choice in their strategy of privileging experimentation, tests, and then their generalization. Similarly, one sees the appearance of substantial differences between those which put the accent on the managerial dimension of change, thus emphasizing the sometimes astonishing deficiencies in the matter of public bodies, and those which focus on the processes and try to rebuild them into a new logic, at the risk of reproducing the mistake of confusing the rule and its clarity with the real functioning that is obtained.

One can at last see that such choices and strategies with regard to change can sometimes be extremely chaotic – going from the privatization of public services or even administrative segments to their re-nationalization as soon as the perverse effects produced become intolerable. Even where these are not really public organizations as such – even though their running methods may be identical – debates around the future of rail transport, for example, do not appear to be anywhere near being settled. This chaos shows clearly that change in such organizations will take time and, for the reasons that we are about to try and analyse, will also come up against difficulties going far beyond what has been written up until now.

And so, whatever the strategic choices made, none of the countries involved has had an easy task of it, once this has meant implementing real change, even if most of the actors concerned contest neither the urgency of reforms nor the need to profoundly change the methods of functioning of public organizations. Here we see a case in which there is a distancing between what the actors can understand and what they can accept, between what a good strategy makes it possible to predict, negotiate and announce, and the possibility of implementation. Everywhere, we find difficulty, conflicts, then negotiations which stem not from an abstract resistance from changes, but rather from the issues of such changes. If these issues are not properly understood, pushing such organizations towards a very specific problematic and strategy, far from any technocratic or ideological approach, the transformation of public administrations runs the risk of finally showing itself to be more costly than expected in human and financial terms; especially, of course, in countries where it is the subject of the strongest misgivings.

The stumbling block of legal and legalistic visions

A first difficulty is quick to appear: the very strong legalistic or legal cultures which characterize most Western countries, have dramatically boosted the confusion between organization and structure, where we have seen to what extent this handicaps the actual problematic of change. This is easy to understand in the administrative world, marked simultaneously by legalism, a Weberian tradition in terms of how the state is designed and the chronic absence of management culture. The consequence of this has been the usual assimilation of reform with change of structures, and the transformation of policies of change into a more or less skilful and well founded reconstruction of the administrative Meccano.

But the effect was worse here than elsewhere, for these areas are where territorial defence is at its fiercest. This concerns not only senior executives but also union organizations, as was shown in Chapter 5 with the example of the French tax authorities. Doing this reinforces the factors of blockage, sometimes irreversibly, and the actors only become more reluctant to launch themselves into an adventure which they believe to be lost in advance, educated as they are by the trials and tribulations of their predecessors.

Neither structures nor rules

One can only be surprised by the blindness of so many public reformers and their inability to observe that the interest focused on structures was on the decline in other areas, to the profit of that focused on real methods of functioning, such as already defined. This understanding of organizations on a simple mode, as if formed from the way that people work, make decisions, solve their problems, cooperate or not – in brief, like a set of rational strategies from intelligent actors – makes it easier to understand and therefore to anticipate the difficulties encountered. They stem from the particular characteristics of public authorities as organizations, and therefore from the levers on which one can act to make them change, which are more limited and more difficult to manipulate *because, precisely, over time, the members of these organizations and their representatives have fought to protect themselves against their possible use.* There is therefore a need to lay out what characterizes such areas and makes change both so necessary and so perilous.

What defines the functioning of public authorities is neither fundamentally nor principally the corpus of rules which govern them, but their application over time, which in many countries has resulted in a multitude of local, specific, particular agreements. These have always had the fixed objective of increasing the various protections from which the members of such organizations benefit, whether this involves protections in the face of customers or users on whom one has imposed one's rhythm and constraints; in the face of bosses whose real power has been reduced to nothing by the impressive array of rules and procedures, which have gradually taken the place of the hierarchy; or even in the face of others, with one's peers and colleagues, thanks to the segmentation around the succession of tasks which has allowed everybody to protect themselves from the demands and constraints of cooperation. From this point of view, one can say that public organizations are in essence bureaucratic and that this comprises the major difficulty in their real and fundamental change.

Extreme bureaucracies

The word "bureaucracy" is not used here in the polemic sense of an organization which would always produce more paper and would be slow, heavy and not very responsive. This word is meant to emphasize a far more fundamental phenomenon which is at the very heart of difficulties with change for administrative bodies: *a bureaucracy is an organization which is characterized by the fact that all the criteria that it uses are endogenous*. To say this in more simple terms, it is an entity which in all its acts gives priority to its own problems, whether technical or human, as opposed to those in its environment. This form of organization corresponded to a certain time in contemporary history which was characterized by the general scarcity of goods and services that the citizens of developed countries aspired to consume: either material goods to which industrial mass production corresponded, or services amongst which those provided by agencies under state control were not the least important, in order to ensure both social order and state of law. Max Weber in his time, together with Jeremy Rifkin or Robert Reich today, have very clearly described the issues and modalities of this period:[4] For Max Weber, as for Henry Mintzberg, the word "bureaucratic" conjures up a collective order, a legitimate domination founded on a set of rules and procedures, a professional and process organization.

Such a mode of action must also be applied in the same way to those governed by the bureaucracy as to its own members. Virtuous towards its "subjects" because it establishes and ensures the equality of all under law, bureaucracy is also virtuous towards its members whom again it manages on a principle of strict equality – at least in appearance – which little by little excludes differentiation, judgement, evaluation on the basis of results obtained compared with the expectations of those being served; all of these being things which, in modern administrative language, can be summed up by the word "arbitrary". The strongly pejorative connotation of this word in these areas, while in fact it only expresses recourse to free will, shows clearly to what extent human intervention – judgemental, prejudiced – is rejected to the profit of uniformity and identicalness.

The protection function

In fact, looking closely, such principles of action, of which nobody contests the initial legitimacy, have led to a maximization in these organizations of the function of work protection which has been mentioned in earlier chapters. To the three traditional protections – against life, against customers, against peers – has now been added that against hierarchy, against the boss who makes judgements, who grades or appraises. One can understand without much difficulty why changing such organizations poses even more problems than for any others, to the extent that their endogenous natures are developed to an extreme, and that the union organizations have given themselves the task of defending them at any price, often excluding any other consideration of cost, effectiveness and adaptation to world changes.

Nonetheless, over time, doubts arose on the virtues and effectiveness of such methods of functioning. Quite naturally, such doubts came to light at the end of the 1970s, when the resources available to states for feeding the onward progress of such organizations and for amassing the resources that they distributed to society – which conferred upon them their legitimacy and led taxpaying citizens to close their eyes – dried up. If one adds to this the "capillarity effect" – that is, the rapid transformation of organizations acting on the market – and therefore the possibility for the citizen-customer to compare the way in which he is treated by the various organizations, we see the striking appearance of two features of public bureaucracies: they distribute services that are globally of poor quality but at a very high cost. However, this dual observation of the "extra cost of poor service" is closely linked to the endogenous features of the administration services mentioned above. To understand this, let us try to highlight the two constraints to which administrative bodies traditionally give priority when erecting their methods of functioning.

What makes up the extra cost of poor service

The first is strict compliance with the succession and specialization of tasks. In a still widely predominant Taylorist logic, production of the service is broken down into "successive acts" and the organization reproduces, even in its structures, this sequential logic. One can easily anticipate the advantages and disadvantages of this method of functioning. Advantages for members of the organization: *they do not have to cooperate*. They simply pass around *files* once they have, at their speed, dealt with their share of them, thus avoiding any situation of dependency in relation to one another.

Again, it is this protection function in relation to peers, colleagues, others in general which is absolutely essential to understand. This has been built up over time, based on a slow adaptation of the initial rules of personnel management. This has tended to continually reduce the involvement of others in one's own work, as it has, little by little, nullified the powers of the hierarchy in terms of remuneration, grading, appraisal or career development for agents, yet again reinforcing their real autonomy. We can never repeat enough that, at least in the French case – but this is less isolated than one might think – it is not the general status of the public function which renders adaptation of administrations particularly arduous, but the use which has been made of it since the end of the Second World War. It is this internal constraint which has always been the second most important priority for administrative bodies.

So advantages for the agents, but disadvantages (and sometimes major ones) for tax- and rate-paying citizens and the community as a whole. Firstly, because this method of functioning badly affects the quality of the service: it produces slowness, waste, error and above all irresponsibility, to the extent that nobody is accountable for the end result to the customer. The latter must try to find his way through a jungle of tasks and segmentation, face up to the "monsters" which sometimes emerge after the thoughtless stringing together of actions that have been blindly carried out. In brief, he must follow the "bureaucratic path" of an organization which has shaped itself around its own needs instead of the needs of those whom it is supposed to serve. The example of the reimbursement of VAT credit, given in Chapter 5, is just one illustration. But we must repeat that all this is linked to the *bureaucratic form of the work and not the public nature of the organization*. This has only been involved through the policy of the employer-state, which has only rarely measured the impact, on the service and on its cost, of the successive advantages conceded to its employees, and even more so because long periods of political instability have not favoured an integrated vision of public action.[5] However, examples seen towards the end of the 1990s, particularly in the United Kingdom, have shown that the privatization of a state service is not in itself the guarantee of greater efficiency: changing the methods of functioning is not enough.

But alongside the poor quality of services offered by this type of organization, we also find the extra cost that it generates. Protection from others – the fierce desire not to be dependent upon them – always involves the consumption of additional resources: being autonomous presupposes the means for such autonomy and hence the multiplication of equipment and agents, offices, computers, photocopiers – in brief, everything that contributes to life in an autarchy, assimilated here to life free of all conditions. One might find it difficult to understand why, in the trading world in general and the car industry in particular, it is through a ceaseless concentration on transforming organizations – in the meaning given to this expression since the beginning of this book – and concretely by introducing always more in the way of cooperation, that production costs have been drastically reduced, but without the public organizations having to follow the same process in order to produce the same improvements. Or in other words, using an analogy which is dear to me, it is highly probable that the reduction in hospital spending, in countries such as France or Belgium, would doubtless be far more effective if it was based on a fundamental transformation of the working methods of hospital doctors amongst themselves and therefore on a reconstruction of the hospital around the patient, instead of on the strictly financial and bureaucratic control of medical treatment.

Doing more with less

What has been said here has never been properly understood by the civil servants themselves or by the political governing bodies. In a high proportion of countries, the equation of public services remains the same: if one wants a better quality of service, one must devote more resources to it – and always more resources for always more quality. It is of little consequence that pupil numbers are dropping – increasing the number of teachers is still a guarantee of quality for those who remain.

This logic has no end to it and it maintains a vicious circle that can paradoxically be observed in the most liberal as well as the most conservative countries in terms of state reform: as strong pressure is exerted in order to reduce public spending, cuts are made mechanically and often without discernment in the workforces. Such cuts are made without affecting the methods of functioning, that is, without using the levers which might lead actors to develop strategies other than those aimed to protect themselves, or to put it plainly, to cooperate more. The result is a deterioration in the services provided which increases not only the public's discontent but also and above all the frustration of agents who, taken individually, feel they are doing the best they can with the poor resources available to them. For it is true that, in administrations which do not understand the organizational dimension of quality and cost reduction, one is always obliged to call for greater goodwill and individual dedication – veritable safety valves for the system's inefficiency.

From this point, it is only by relying on public irritation that agents will obtain, as a matter of urgency and precipitation, the additional resources which will enable them to continue working in a segmented and uncooperative environment. Such unwillingness to understand is a paralysing situation in a country like France. In others, to the contrary – Australia, for example – it has led to a drastic reduction in the size of administrative entities, reconstructed around the customer–service duo, as well as to the introduction of a true logic for personnel management which has given true margins for manoeuvre to supervisors. One can also see that countries which are not in a position to offer the same margins for manoeuvre to their supervisory staff are starting to suffer from a veritable "vocation crisis", which is resulting in serious difficulties not only for recruiting but also for winning the loyalty of their managers, especially senior executives.[6]

What seems to be at cause is no longer the difference in remuneration between the public and private sectors, but rather the absence of prospects which characterizes the public sector and which is apparent on a day-to-day basis by the impossibility of introducing any reform whatsoever, while the trading sector shows evidence of extreme vitality. One encounters here the paradox of overprotection which characterizes such organizations: by trying to do too much in this context, they end up by only attracting or keeping people who have the greatest need for such protections – that is, to be quite clear, neither the best nor the most dynamic.

A general reappraisal

At the beginning of the twenty-first century, it is therefore this extra cost of poor service which makes the reform of public organizations so essential and indeed inevitable, just about everywhere in the world. The competition in allocating state resources is becoming increasingly keen, at the same time that new tax policies for reducing compulsory payments are making these same resources scarcer. Finally, the idea that only the public sector will be able to escape the general reappraisal of organizations, which has been a feature of recent years, is more and more untenable, even if, on this subject, people's feelings are sometimes ambiguous.[7] All this leads progressively to the idea that what has been possible in the trading sector, that is, *doing more and better with less*, should also be possible in the public sector.

We can add to this what was earlier termed the "capillarity effect", which means that the user/customer cannot continue to accept the ever-growing qualitative distance between the product and service offered to him by an increasing proportion of suppliers and what he obtains from everything to do with the public domain: individualization of service, immediateness of response, fair pricing, and so on, are today at the heart of taxpayer/customer expectations. If the gap between what is supplied by both domains were to grow any bigger, it would be the political market which would then sanction the administrative world, even if, for the time being, in countries such as France, it has demonstrated the greatest reluctance to do so.

Difficulty in changing public organizations

The forced privatization of whole sections of public services in the Anglo-Saxon countries falls within this type of sanction. But with a little hindsight, one might consider that this involves attempts similar, although more brutal and radical, to those that the de Gaullian reformism of the 1960s had tried to impose on France through the creation of semi-public agencies, for dealing with the most crucial problems in the country's modernization. The creation of the Agence Nationale pour l'Emploi (French national employment office) obeyed this logic. Its relative lack of success, at least in terms of imposing a new type of administrative action, shows that institutional intention is not, in itself, enough to produce change.

And indeed, if one lines up what have been identified as the dominant features of public bureaucracies and the new pressures which are exerted on them, one sees the first signs that these are the basic difficulties facing any true attempts at change in administrative areas. These are firstly *intellectual* and for the most part stem from the training received by public sector employees, dominated overwhelmingly by a narrow legalism which is truly the administrative version of Taylor's scientific organization of industrial work: the organization around a succession of tasks, as initially expounded by Taylor, is perceived by its practitioners as being of a virtually scientific nature, and hence the only one possible. The question which the reformer asks himself therefore becomes "Is it possible to do things differently?" However, this "differently" entails acceptance of the modes of action which for the most part are very distant from the culture and dominant practices of these bodies and from legalistic rhetoric. It is necessary to introduce some fuzziness into the definition of tasks, which is only possible if it is accompanied by methods of appraisal, individually or collectively, that prevent it from being a factor of increased irresponsibility; in the same way, redundancy and conflicts – in the sociological sense of the term – make their appearance, a situation which is poorly tolerated in organizations where the general interest should be to federate, at the same time as reducing any divergence.

From this point of view, this is indeed a transition from *legalism to management*, and certain countries have fully understood this, making it the predominant orientation of their strategies for reform.[8]

But the difficulties confronting change are just as practical and often more prosaic. *It is a matter of reversing the predominant habit of doing things, not necessarily better but always with more.* The link between quality and abundance of resources is at the heart of the problematic of public services. We will mention here the *abundance of resources consumed,* a situation not necessarily perceived by those who consume them, with segmentation and compartmentalization making everybody blind and producing virtually invisible effects of wastage: when the parents, teachers and pupils of a high school in the south of France were clamouring for an additional supervisor for their school, and were forced to occupy the premises in order to bring their problem to the attention of the authorities, no doubt they were aware of a cruel lack of resources; but at the same time, when one looks at the national education budget and the proportion of people in this administration who actually stand in front of the pupils, one cannot help a feeling of wastefulness and the impression of an organization which is going to the dogs in terms of managing its human resources.

Protection function and production function

Despite these examples which help one to understand that there is no contradiction between individual irritation and the formidable collective wastage, one can indeed speak of a *comfort relationship* with regard to these organizations, which makes it possible to promise more, on condition that the cost of this more is externalized onto the institution and not borne by the members of the organization itself, through new methods of work. If it is really necessary to do more with less, which is the predominant contemporary trend, it is a radical change, and there-fore no doubt costly in human terms, of the methods of functioning which is required.

One can understand from this that the reluctance of agents and their management is not a matter of abstract and theoretical resistance to change. It is one of the manifestations, more accentuated in the public sector for the reasons which have just been stated, of the transformation of work functions in our developed societies. The famous protection function is being gradually and *painfully* wiped out to the profit of the production function. This *mission logic*, forcing one to turn one's rout-ing operating methods towards the customer, towards the customer's expectations in terms of quality and cost, wins over the endogenous logic of the organization and its members. Under pressure from all the factors mentioned above, *precariousness* is gaining ground everywhere, including in the public sector.

In the case of administration employees, this does not mean a pre-cariousness on the job market, but rather a redefinition of the condi-tions of employment within these organizations; conditions which were until then very advantageous, since they were far more orientated towards the agents themselves than towards those at whom the services produced were aimed. We must see *simultaneity, cooperation, divergence of interest under the spotlight*, which cannot take place without some ups and downs. It is easy to understand that, if one is not in a position to offer an alternative, a "new deal" to those whose agreement linking them to their employer-state has just been brutally destroyed, it will be even more difficult to get them to accept the necessary reforms.

It is time to observe that this interruption of the link which, trad-itionally, used to connect organizations to their members around the theme of protection in all its shapes, is obviously not specific to public administrations. We have encountered it everywhere throughout this book – among teachers as well as in the transport company, in the bank as well as in that company that was focusing frenetically on perform-ance so as not to worry too much about the traditional importance of its protective systems. Quite simply, in the public world, the phenom-enon is amplified, blown up out of all proportion to the point of making even the most grotesque situation seem almost normal! And so, as we have seen for the other side of the coin, that makes change even more difficult. Let's move on.

However, the universality of this phenomenon has another conse-quence that we cannot silently pass by. If one destroys work in its traditional form, but without rebuilding an "offer" with meaning to the actors involved – a new deal, as has just been said – then it is the very value of work in our companies that is put in doubt – seriously and for a great length of time. Once again, common sense is not enough to get people to swallow a pill which, as we see every day, is becoming more and more bitter – but we are still lacking in hindsight even though the phenomenon now stretches back more than 30 years. In Western countries, work is an integral part of the social scene in terms of belonging and recognition. As soon as it loses its value, it is society itself that starts to disintegrate. The confusion of teachers confronted with this observation has already been mentioned – nothing, and especially not the immobilism of their organization, has prepared them for this.

What we really need to understand though is that it is not the *work value* that is gradually fading away in our companies – as if, little by little, what the old-timers used to consider important was now being excluded from the preoccupations of more recent generations. It is work itself that is destroyed, through the brutal and relentless change now taking place in organizations, while the value given to it can only follow such disintegration.

What strategy for change?

This raises the problem of the strategy for change, which here seems rather the same as that already mentioned for the transport company.[9] Until then, the dialogue – when it existed – had been reduced to only the representative organizations, real institutional relays for personnel management. However, the great majority of these are not and cannot be in favour of such reforms, to the extent that they are structured and organized in line with the conventional segmentations and working methods which are associated with them. Any reappraisal of any of these is a potential danger, including for implicit share-outs of territories, which are carried out over time between such organizations.[10]

The general main themes – sometimes abstract in their concrete consequences on daily life – which until now united public sector employees, whatever their job category, like public services or the general interest, are today paradoxically becoming more concrete, because the public is asking for accounts on their real meaning and their implications for the public. Because of this, not everything is defendable at the same time or for all. In the interest of citizens, it is more and more difficult not to match the opening hours of administrative offices with the times when people can go there; it is less and less legitimate to maintain a centralized personnel management when needs are becoming more and more qualitative and diversified. In brief, the traditional modalities of action for the most conservative union organizations have been hit head-on and made more rigid, even though experience shows that the agents themselves are far more aware of the transformations needed and certainly far more prepared to accept them – under certain conditions of course.

Starting from the agents themselves

This sends us back to the question of *trust* tackled in the previous chapter. It is still less in the traditions of the administrative world than in those of the trading sector. From a certain point of view, for the senior executives of public organizations, the professional reality of the agents does not exist. There are rules and procedures, which people are all the more willing to believe are applied since they are supposed to guarantee equality for all under the law. Apart from that, there are only the union organizations, reduced to a social dialogue which is becoming increasingly impoverished, occasionally puerile, and in any case dissociated from reality and without tangible results. Paradoxically, most actors are more or less in agreement on this observation, but do not see the means for getting out of the situation, which more and more resembles a zero-sum game, in which change becomes less and less playable for unions that are more and more strained over previous situations and where agents have an ingrained feeling that they are not being listened to.

It is those in charge of administration, whether elected or civil servants, who will be expected to break this vicious circle and lead all the actors towards another logic. This would make it necessary to start from cost and quality requirements, which are today part of the social system, *as well as from the agents themselves*. In-depth work explaining the new necessities and their translation into daily work, within the organization, accompanied by reasonable guarantees on employment, on development of qualifications, on opportunities which are likely to arise, will no doubt help to gradually unblock the situation. This would force the union organizations to take stock of themselves, by confronting them with the sole reality likely to get them to move because it is incontestable, that is, their principals who inevitably, at a given moment, become key actors in this process. At the moment, in the most conservative countries, there is nothing to indicate that those in charge are willing to make this break and run the risk of it influencing traditional balances.

Even with regard to the agents, this is another difficulty which must not be neglected, even if the general relaxation of the relationship, characteristic of these times, has made it less meaningful. It is *emotional* by nature and will give birth to change in the face-to-face relationship between the civil servant and the citizen who is now more a customer than a taxpayer. In the traditional system, such as that drawn up during the period of scarcity of offer, the public service agent was able to impose his own logic, his own pace, his own constraints on the public, who had no choice other than to accept them. This resulted in a very conventional dominator–dominated relationship between the expert and the requester, which is routinely expressed in submission to the waiting queue, to the opening times, to the uncertain routing of the file, as well as to the vocabulary used in the exchange. Real change in public organizations involves a reversal of this relationship and, as a minimum, its management on an equal footing between the partners. This will again inevitably reduce the possibilities of protection behind regulations, opening times and others in general. Increasingly, face-to-face contact with the public is going to take place on their terms, that is, individualized service, *and where the organization is not capable of meeting such requirements with suitable methods of collective functioning, the pressure exerted on the agents will be all the more heavy, conflictual, painful.*

Training, levers and structures

The real issue is therefore to change the methods of functioning with all the restrictive implications that have been described. This explains why certain countries balk at the task, while for others, reforming the state is not really even on the agenda if one gets past the abstract or incantatory speeches. Nonetheless, examples that are available open the way to discussing three strategies for change, such as used in recent times.

The first focuses on the training of public employees and, in particular, those holding functions of responsibility. The fact that, in most cases, they follow specific training courses – whether this is induction training or continued education – can only lead them to specific behaviours which have little relevance to the very real particularities and requirements of public management. Such behaviours are marked by conformism and the concern for self-protection, which dilute responsibility and prolong the time needed for any action and therefore add to the final cost. This conformism, reinforced by the veritable endogamy which, in a number of countries, characterizes the recruitment of public service employees, makes the very idea of reform unattractive to such agents: not only is it necessary to preserve the advantages acquired but also one sees the imposition of a dominant intellectual model, a way of

thinking, formulating and solving problems, which is never in competition with any other and which, because of this, has no difficulty in
being dominant.[11] It should be remembered, in counterpoint, that
when the United States in 1999 wanted to fundamentally change its tax
administration, it put at its head a consultant with a confirmed profile...
of consultant. Other countries attempt to offset the legal platitudes of
initial training courses by developing substantial continuing education
programmes, intended to introduce "managerial" thinking into these
organizations.

In this area, the results sometimes seem fairly poor in relation to the
resources engaged. There are two major reasons for this relative failure:
on the one hand, when the implementation of such programmes is
entrusted to specialized bodies in the administrations concerned, this is
quickly neutralized and ends up being a scarcely disguised repetition of
the predominant attitude; in addition, if one admits as a last resort *that
management is obtaining from actors that they do what one wants them to
do*, then one can understand that training can only be one element in
a strategy for change, as a backup for something else much more than
as a triggering factor. From this point of view, setting up "battle-training
schools" or "internal universities" comes to be a new windscreen for the
ambient immobilism. France had bitter experience of this in 1999 when
the reform of its tax administration was preceded by the introduction of
an ambitious training programme for senior managers in this Ministry.
This did not in any way prevent the resounding failure of a reform
which was to a great extent justified. For if one wants to change, it is of
course on the concrete levers that one must act, above and beyond
the management awareness to which the training programme can lay
claim.

Such levers, which must aim to put the actors of public administrations
into new contexts and thus change their behaviours – their strategies –
are mainly a matter for human resource management systems. However,
the very development of such systems over time has tended to neutral-
ize their impact on the differentiation of individuals and therefore to
deprive them of the managerial role originally attributed to them.

This leads to three observations. It has already been noted that, to
date, a change has never been seen in a bureaucracy's method of functioning, whether in the public or the private sector, without a fundamental change to its human resource management systems by
introducing randomness, differentiation, room for the manager's
appraisal – even subjective, of people of whom he is in charge, and
based on whose action he is himself assessed. The modification of such

systems and the sometimes fierce opposition that this arouses are indeed part of the movement to dilute the employment protection function which has been analysed above. Progress in this area can only be slow and negotiated with the agents themselves.

The privatization or subcontracting of public services is a way of getting round the obstacle which, as we have already seen, is not new. The acknowledgement that we find behind this strategy is in fact that the difference between the private and public sectors is based principally on the level of protection offered to employees, and hence on the degree of constraints that can be imposed on them, particularly in terms of working conditions. The wager which is made here is that change in public organizations is an illusion or at least that it requires so much time and effort that it does not fall within the deadlines that necessity demands. It is therefore necessary to go through the process of their disappearance and replacement. The consequence of this is sometimes to leave, in what is left of the traditional administrations, only the most insignificant tasks with low added value. Defenders of public services should reflect on this apparent paradox: the intransigent conservatism sometimes demonstrated by them has a chance of reducing this sector to what is least interesting, least valued, least lucrative.

This is why some countries – in France's case, some ministries – have chosen to negotiate, step by step, towards a development, even moderate, not of statutes but of their application, making it possible to re-introduce the idea and practice of management and responsibility in the management of agents. It is remarkable to see that, in a country so little open to the idea of administrative reform as France, it is in the Ministry of Public Works that the most significant progress has been accomplished. However, this Ministry is, at the same time, the one with the highest proportion of its activity taking place on the competitive market. Here again, necessity makes the rules.

The final key point which must be tackled in terms of change in administrative organizations is change in structures. This has not been dealt with until now because the thesis of this book is precisely that change in organization is not principally change in structures. But countries such as Australia or New Zealand have shown that there are alternative structures to those based on the strict succession of tasks, the adoption of which is a determining complement to the efforts which are made in terms of renewal and modernization of agent management. The operations and delivery services show that even an administrative world can be designed around a user logic and the translation of such a logic into routine methods of functioning. However, this involves abandoning the idea of integrated and undifferentiated "administrative mega-organizations".

And in fact, progress is made possible and obtained which does not consist simply of civil servants being more pleasant to the people they are dealing with – a poor vision of administrative change, reduced to the modification of individual behaviours in face-to-face contact with users. To return to the example of tax administration, it is not in giving the short-term satisfaction of not paying what is owed that they will become more efficient from the taxpayer's point of view; it is when their methods of functioning, during collection of the tax, no longer increase the amount of this tax. However, the differences which exist in this area, ranging from 1 for the most efficient or most "virtuous" countries – such as Sweden or the United States – to 3 for the bottom of the class – France, for example – show the progress which still remains to be achieved in the functioning of administrative organizations.

Conclusion

Public administrations are an extreme example of the paradox around which this book is built. It is precisely because these are the most difficult to change, because this is where the "bureaucratic meshing" is at its tightest and to which their members hang on sometimes so desperately, that they need to be trusted in order to make such changes possible. This requires vision, boldness and methodology. This book proposes to make its contribution to the third area. However, to conclude, a small amount of hindsight prompts us to ask three questions:

1. At the beginning of this book we talked about the enthusiasm of the revolution in organizations, their passage into "another time", the necessity and possibility for them to construct new customer-orientated methods of functioning. But at the end of the day, one can reasonably ask, is this in fact of any use, bearing in mind the difficulty of the task, the sacrifices and sometimes even the human suffering that such changes pull along in their wake?
2. Is this difficulty the same everywhere, or to put it differently, are there across the world any "cultures" that are less antagonistic, more accustomed to such movements and therefore making it possible to be managed more easily, maybe even more peaceably?
3. Lastly, if the process is truly under way, what do we see emerging? Can it already be those new organizations? And if the answer is yes, what shape are they taking, what can we expect that "work" will mean tomorrow?

The fragility of organizations

The first question gives rise to a twofold response. The question of the usefulness of change in organizations is asked in terms of survival, except when thinking that a country exists inside a "bubble", which would enable it to manage its affairs without taking the rest of the world into account. This kind of utopia has always led to totalitarianism. Once this hypothesis has been discarded, even in its "Rousseau-ist" version, it is indeed a matter of survival. One of the characteristics of the end of the twentieth century and the beginning of the twenty-first is that of having revealed to us that businesses, even those supposed to be the most robust, those that seemed to be real institutions, are in fact mortal. In the imaginary and mystique of air transport, Pan Am (Pan American Airlines) was an institution that seemed as inextinguishable to Americans as the SNCF is to the French. And yet it is dead – carried away by the whirlpool of deregulation. This was more a sudden accident that the consequences of a long illness.

Consequently, this inevitable change opposes two logics, or two "rationalities" as one might say when introducing the methods of analysis. It is of course the duty of the director to do everything, including things that are hard and painful, in order to save the company that has been put in his safekeeping. That being so, he does not always protect jobs, and one knows the despair caused by the sudden sacking of people who have worked in the company, *their* company, one of their reasons and purposes for living. And we have shown that saving the company is not easy, that it involves sacrifices and renunciations. Even if successful, everybody will be able to see that, in the new organization, work is no longer what it was. In its very substance – content of tasks, autonomy and non-dependency, protection in relation to the customer and others – it is comfort that has to be sacrificed. And that is what the actors anticipate from the start of the process. They resist it, debate becomes argumentative, without being able to tell, from the vantage point which is ours, whether one side or the other is right or wrong.

Finally, what has been suggested in this book is the *organization of this debate* by postulating that the intelligence of the actors enables them to have *at one and the same time* a strategy suited to their context *and* an understanding of the true nature of problems that occur, provided sufficient confidence is shown in sharing these with them. The case of Air France is a good example of this. There was no hue and cry. Attentive listening – that is, gaining an in-depth understanding of real-life working situations – made it possible to define the main lines of what is negotiable – and therefore acceptable – in terms other than those produced by ideological views (liberalism as opposed to social justice) or, worse, false common sense, the sort that hides biased rationality.

That does not mean that there was neither debate nor conflict. But at the very least, there was agreement on the real and organizational nature of problems, the resulting explicit attempt to find a "new deal" acceptable to all interested parties – and to find it together – considerably reduced the financial, but above all human, cost of the operation. Finally, and let us say fortunately, we are returned to the very purpose of this book – the question is not "Must it be done?" but "How must it be done?"

Are there places, environments, cultures, then, in which this "how" is made easier? All through our seminars, this is a question that is repeatedly asked by participants: is the grass of change greener somewhere else?

And in fact, putting forward a theory and a methodology for steering change in organizations cannot be concluded without tackling the question of their link with the cultural context in which they have been drawn up. Are they closely linked to this context – in this case that of developed countries in the Western world – and consequently relatively inadaptable and inoperative in very different surroundings? This question is based on the fact that, no doubt due to the globalization which characterizes the world at the start of the twenty-first century, executives and managers like tackling such "cultural" issues, sometimes according them an inordinate level of importance. There is no merger or acquisition which is not preceded by a harrowing interrogation on the "compatibility of cultures", a subject on which there is no hesitation in initiating in-depth research. All business schools have, in their international management programmes, courses that are devoted to such questions and each one proposes, in its continuing education programmes, seminars for familiarizing participants with the need to take action in very different environments.

What is at cause here is the well known "human factor" which, as already pointed out, most organizations consider to be a problem, in the primary sense of the term.

Two visions of culture which do not have the same consequences in terms of change

Not only is this fascination understandable, at a time when few companies can permit themselves the luxury of staying only in their domestic market and are launching themselves, sometimes at high speed, into internationalizing their operations, but also some countries are using it to protect themselves from an over-rapid invasion of foreign operators or to justify the existence, in such countries, of practices which would not be acceptable elsewhere. From this point of view, the opacity of the system built up in Japan by the producers, distributors, public authorities and consumer associations, and which has nothing in common with the commercial legislation in effect in that country, has long discouraged a high number of Western firms, from America in particular. This has enormously helped what is commonly called the "Japanese miracle". Similarly, today, the importance that the Chinese confer on relationships, or "*guanxhi*", once it is a question of venturing into this market, also leads many operators to favour "joint ventures" to the detriment of creating full-ownership subsidiaries.

Nevertheless, it must be emphasized that behind this passing craze there are two definitions of culture which do not have the same consequences on the subject that we are discussing. The first is general and focuses on a few major lines which characterize the living habits in the countries under consideration and, more particularly, the manner of grasping inter-individual relationships. We might say that this represents the *container* culture, which every visitor perceives at the outset and that a few specialists in management have absolutely insisted on theorizing. The word "container" refers here to the superficial aspect of this part of culture. It means that one perceives that which surrounds, that which may possibly attract or disturb. It indicates that one glimpses that part of the iceberg that is above the sea, which is striking because we are not used to icebergs, but which dissimulates beneath the water the full amplitude of the phenomenon. Thus one might explain that some of the difficulties experienced at EuroDisney when it first opened were due to the Americans refusing to allow alcohol to be served in the restaurants, a reflection of its emphasis on family values, even though the host country was celebrated above all for its wines; in the same way, one might say that the first Japanese industrials who established themselves in the United States had not understood the very special nature of labour relations in that country. Even if this is not a question of denying the extent of differences, or their occasional importance in the management of international operations, it is not an exaggeration to say that, in day-to-day management, a whole series of *romantic stereotypes* have been developed which, at the end of day, have little to do with the action.

This is why we need to reach a second dimension of culture which is more practical, and above all more operative once it is a question of steering organizations in general and introducing change in particular. You will remember for this that we have defined an organization as a set of actor strategies, as opposed to a definition based on organization charts, rules or procedures. When such strategies, which are in fact behaviours, solutions found by the actors, to solve the problems which present themselves, appear repetitively, we might say that they constitute the organization's culture. A rougher, although more illustrative, way of stating the same idea would be to say that culture is what *everybody must do in a human population in order to be accepted and survive in that population*. This is not the set of actor strategies, which would lead to a tautological vision assimilating organization and culture, but the redundant strategies that the actors use when faced with the key questions that collective life asks of them. Thus, under this heading, one will put *a decision process*.

The best example of this would be the cosmetics company, the undisputed world leader in its market, which, at least in its marketing and commercial spheres, has for many years cultivated "fuzzy" and divided responsibilities, even going so far as to forbid any organization chart or definition of function. A decision – such as a product launch, for example – could only result from the *confrontation* of viewpoints, that is, interest, with market knowledge as the principal resource to be mobilized in winning the day. The result was a situation in which nobody could take advantage of the slightest monopoly and everybody depended on others to undertake any action. The environment created in this way was characterized by its hardness – offering not the slightest intra-organizational protection – and by the need for restrictive performance appraisal systems as well as conciliation boards before which actors had only a small interest in presenting themselves in order to settle their disputes. Such a decision process is as far as it can be from that identified in the transport company, where it was primarily a question of being able to present, to higher levels of the hierarchy, a well reasoned *dossier* which guaranteed to whoever had drawn it up that they were *covered* in the event of a problem. We might call what we have just described as the "*content*" culture.

Here the word "content" indicates that we are close to the essential, to what is most important, to what it is necessary to grasp before launching oneself into action. The container is the fruit's outer husk, the content is the fruit itself. Moving from the first to the second presupposes that one is no longer fascinated by the form, the beauty, the originality of appearance, that one agrees to remove the outer protection in order to reach the inner flesh. We rediscover the theme of investment in knowledge, which we have used as one of the major orientations for leading change. But it is also the distinction between symptoms and problems which returns to mind. The container culture is the one that remains at the level of the symptom, the sign, the warning, the "misunderstood information". The content culture stems from the problem, that is, the real mechanisms which are at work. It is indeed this which must be the subject of all attentions, at least in terms of management.

The consequences of the distinction between the container culture and the content culture

These two visions lead to a better understanding of why, in most cases, we overestimate the importance and concrete impact of cultural phenomena. In the case of the container culture, the tree hides the forest and the capacity for action generally finds itself penalized. Fascinated by *attitudes*, we tend to see only them, to find in them a root system with a thousand years of history, and to think that their reappraisal is an impossible exploit.

This was how it was in the myth of life employment in Japan, which has resulted in the elaboration of sophisticated theories on the constraints of human resource management in this country ... although this was a recent phenomenon, linked to the present economic climate, that the Japanese themselves did not hesitate to question, at the end of the 1980s, when difficult economic circumstances justified this.[1] In 2000, the senior executive sent by Renault to Nissan in order to save the company from bankruptcy, had no hesitation in reappraising the family-like links, which, apparently, united the company and its most favoured suppliers, and drastically reducing the number ... without this appearing to pose major problems but, what is more, doing the greatest good to the companies.[2]

This simple idea that, at least in terms of management, necessity to a great extent makes its own rules, is the basis for what we have called the content culture and is going to open interesting perspectives in terms of leading change and the transferability of methodologies and approaches, even if nobody will dispute all the nuances and cautions needed. This in fact implies that actors placed in a similar context are going to have, on *content*, roughly the same reactions, are going to find the same solutions, develop strategies that are close to each other in order to face up to identical managerial situations, while the *form* that such reactions will take can, in appearance, be very varied and, at first sight, exotic and surprising. An example will help to illustrate this proposal.

Differences in attitudes and communities of strategy

In the 1980s, we had the opportunity to carry out an in-depth survey on "white" goods,[3] in the United States, Japan and France.[4] The purpose of this work was to understand, from a sociological point of view, the way in which the different operators making up a market – producers, distributors, consumers and their associations, public authorities – managed their relationships. Starting from this analysis, it became possible to understand the strength of the Japanese producers and the weakness of their French counterparts, not in terms of how the industrial apparatus functioned, an interpretation that was very popular at the time, but based on an understanding of the strategies developed by these different actors and of the relationships of power and dependency which held them together.

This survey was carried out in an empirical fashion, on the basis of interviews conducted in the three countries with the main parties concerned. Among the questions asked during these interviews, there was one which showed itself to be particularly fruitful and revealing in terms of the day-to-day reality of the so-called "differences of culture". This was addressed to producers of household electrical equipment and consisted of asking them, based on a situation that was painful to them, particularly in France, what their reactions were when a distributor took over one of their best known brands or products and "broke" the price in a logic of sales drift or shelf drift.[5]

The French replies were always embarrassed, hesitant and blamed the legislation in force at the time (prohibiting refusal to sell) which placed them in a situation of extreme dependency with regard to distributors, to whom they were not allowed to refuse their products. They therefore appealed to the good sense of public authority to re-establish a healthy balance between the players. Nevertheless, when driven into a corner, they finally admitted that they did have some possibilities of retaliation, even if very unofficial and consisting either of refusing to deliver the goods with a total disregard for regulations, or, when they had been trapped into it, of buying back, themselves and in bulk, the stock of products purchased by the distributor, or, even more brutally, making available to the distributor a batch that had been "inadvertently" damaged during transport.

The same question addressed to an American provoked outright hilarity. It was a situation he said he knew well, describing it humorously as "Mickey Mouse business". He did not need much time or many pointless oratorical precautions to explain that, once such a distributor had been identified, he was subjected to an immediate and strict boycott, and that if, by mistake, delivery had been made, the products were bought back on opening, which did not prevent the culprit sometimes being sanctioned by surreptitiously procuring damaged equipment for him.

The Japanese immediately showed themselves to be extremely shocked by the question, emphasizing its brutal character, finally very "Western", and putting the interpreter in an uncomfortable situation in which he vigorously manifested his agreement with the interviewees' reaction. The latter, with ostensibly reproachful patience, were explaining that this type of behaviour was impossible in Japan, where producers and distributors were connected by close links, built up over time, and such behaviour was certainly quite alien to the Japanese. And anyway, they added, if that did happen, there was a "committee of honest trading" which supervised the legality and good faith of transactions. This affirmation was manifestly intended to put an end to the interview. But this had been carefully prepared and we had a few examples in mind which showed that similar cases could have occurred. At the end of a good two hours of very disagreeable discussion, during which we had the feeling of adding, every moment, to our impoliteness and boorishness, it was admitted, without really spelling things out, that such a situation could have existed in times and places that nobody could remember clearly. Looking back, somebody remembered that, faced with this problem, one of the producers (but which one?) had refused to deliver, had eventually bought back offending stock and had even taken retaliatory measures which, we were led to understand, were the same as those mentioned above for France and America.

And so we find a new illustration of the distinction between the *container culture* and the *content culture*. Each of the speakers reacted to the question asked in a totally different way and replied to it with an openness or goodwill that revealed a wide diversity, if not total opposition, in the management of inter-individual relationships. Evidently, the social codes defining what can be said and what cannot, and determining the fashion of conducting an interview (the possibility for the interviewer to insist when he considers that the speaker has not answered the question), had little in common with each other. Even the goal pursued by means of the answer was not the same: the French disclaimed their responsibility and passed on a message to the public authorities, the Americans immediately discharged what they considered to be a naivety, while the Japanese preferred to maintain good relations with their usual long-term partners.

But apart from that, the *practices* which ended up being revealed, what throughout this book we have referred to as strategies, were more or less the same, expressing concrete methods of adaptation that were to all intents and purposes identical. This observation makes no inference regarding the mechanisms of differentiation which are far deeper and could affect social life in general, family or friends, the processes of integration or rejection. It simply indicates that, in daily working life, there are proximities which are certainly stronger than one thinks, especially when one allows oneself to be impressed by methods of expression, language used, including body language, which can be observed during a conversation of the type which has been mentioned. But the management of organizations is not a form of tourism.

The universality of the theory of limited rationality

It is essential to draw all the consequences in terms of steering change. One of the guiding ideas in this book is to show that, since actors are intelligent – in the sociological sense of the term – there is no point in trying to convince them to act differently from how they are acting now, as long as one maintains them in an identical context. It is better to act on the levers to make their behaviour change and hence change the organization. *This seems to be able to be applied in contexts that are very different at first sight.* In fact, while the concept of lever covers a *mechanism*, this infers nothing regarding the *nature* of the lever used which, no doubt, is itself susceptible to major adaptations, in line with the most important issues for the actors.

In this way, at the time of a survey carried out at Wuhan in central China and focusing on the management of a "joint venture" between an American company and the Chinese Ministry of Mail and Telecommunications, we were asking an expatriate in charge of managing this unit about the reward system that he used to differentiate local managers and valorize their performances. He replied seriously that the length of the siesta was the most appropriate mechanism, to the extent that, for financial reasons, most of the managers in question carried out a second job during the evening/night and that, because of this, the possibility of recovering slightly during the day was crucial! Nobody disputed the need to use a *lever*, but emphasis was placed on the necessity to find one that was suited to local reality, which only a good integration in the environment would no doubt make it possible to understand.

This is why, although remaining cautious, one can consider that what in previous chapters has been called *"the problematic and the methodology of change" is largely transferable into contexts perceived in principle as very dissimilar.* In fact, in the same way that the strategic analysis of organizations and systems in particular, and the theory of limited rationality in general, do not in any way prejudice the substance of the subject being studied, the theory of change which is deduced from it, and which has been talked about in this book, is only marginally influenced by what are habitually called cultural contexts. This time, these relate more to the container than to the content.

Adapting the strategy

And yet one cannot say the same for what relates to the *strategy for change*, precisely because it is itself a container. We have already seen that this is the subject of discussions between the specialists on the precise point of knowing whether it is necessary to associate all the actors with the process or if, to the contrary, it is necessary to act quickly and strongly, creating a shock, without worrying too much about human considerations.[6]

All the restructuring, downsizing and other practices of the 1980s and 1990s have taught us that not all countries had the same capacity to survive their brutal and devastating effects. Some writers even think this capacity to be an important success factor in the competition for adaptation of economies and companies to the new realities.[7]

For ourselves, we have seen that the difficulty in consenting to instant sacrifices, renouncing advantages, or *protections* as we have said, severely compromises the possibility of operating the necessary transformations of the public sector in a country such as France, where the reform of the administration is continually put off until tomorrow, that is, until the next government. There is therefore a great temptation not to use participative strategies such as those for which we have pleaded, but to use more radical actions in which the parties concerned submit or resign.

We continue to believe that the remedy would be worse than the disease, in the same way that we do not dispute the fact that the Americans would be wrong to ask questions that those who suffer the brutal changes imposed on them do not ask themselves. As in the proverb, *"When in Rome, do as the Romans do."*

All through this book, right up to the end, one thesis has been defended – that of profound transformation – sometimes violent, almost always painful – of technical bureaucracies, generally constructed on Taylor's model of the scientific management of work. Once again, it must be emphasized that this is a fundamental trend and one found virtually everywhere, even if the problem is tackled in relatively varied fashions depending on the different national contexts. The thing that differentiates between countries, as has already been said, is less the rigidity of their bureaucracies – and, once again, extreme rigidity is not always found on the side of the Atlantic that one expects – than their capacity to reappraise them, whatever the cost in social and human terms. This is, it will be said once again, a dominant and fundamental movement that goes far beyond companies or administrations.

And yet if one looks at matters on a day-to-day or routine basis in this organizational revolution in which we are all involved, trends are as usual less clear, movements are not linear and easily discernible, sometimes they are even contradictory. And if, over the long term, everything seems to be going in the same direction, it seems possible to pick a few trends that allow us today to make one or two assumptions on what things may be like in tomorrow's world in which we ourselves – or our children – will be working.

The disappearance, or rather disintegration of borders between organizations and their environment

With their customers first of all, businesses renegotiate the creation of value, or more precisely that part of value that the customer him- or herself intends to create. However, if one accepts that a company is in fact a machine for creating value, the contours of this machine then become elastic, even though, here again, the organization charts continue to give the illusion of clarity. This trend is encountered in sectors as varied as furniture-making[8] or hotel-keeping: leaving the customer to "construct" the content of his/her stay in the hotel, based on a range of available choices, is today, in this industry, the key ingredient in the policy of service quality. One can even observe, to take another very contemporary example, that the concept of the Smart car (Swatch-mobile) obeys the same logic: car production is getting away from the narrow limits of the manufacturing business and entering into the domain of services, revolving around the use made of the vehicle, but with a far greater scope. It's up to the customer to decide what he or she wants to buy or produce, and what he or she expects from the supplier. Such an evolution, although still only in a minority, calls to mind two things.

1. As already discussed in this book, one cannot attain a level of versatility, of "flexibility", by simultaneously keeping the same work habits and the same job content as before. Technical specializations – often overvalued – disintegrate and disappear even while others emerge elsewhere, such as around computer technologies in particular.

   As far as traditional bureaucracies are concerned, their regulations, their working hours, their various and varied advantages are all negatively affected – a situation which, as we have seen, goes some way towards explaining the fierce resistances that express themselves, and where it is no longer enough to say that these are rearguard actions in order to manage them. Once again, what is being described here from a specific viewpoint is the way in which the victorious customer profits from his victory, as the producer profited from his, in the preceding period. The two key words for the approach proposed in this book are "fuzzy" and "cooperation". Fuzzy, because new organizations need to accept that the configurations that they adopt can be very quickly transformed,[9] and even that, at a given moment, nobody really knows any more, or at any rate only marginally, what relates strictly speaking to the company and what does not. Cooperation, because one cannot achieve a high degree of adaptability and flexibility in verticality, traditional segmentations and processes without it. In other words, it is not ISO standards – today's version of Taylorism – and their lack of trust in the ability of those involved to do things and do them together that will make it possible to produce the type of quality that is looked for here.

2. But it is also important to observe that the producer's own borders are also tending to evolve. Here again, this is a problem of the distribution of value creation. By means of strategies, still minority certainly, but increasingly well established on the market – total facilities management, multi-services – one radically redefines what is meant by the trades. A trade is no longer just catering, or cleaning, or maintenance – but the management of a building, a place, with all the activities that are associated with the management of this place. The consequences of such an evolution are many and no doubt still not all clearly perceived. Before mentioning a few, let me vigorously emphasize one point. This use of what can be called integrated outsourcing obeys the general logic expounded throughout this book – one seeks to obtain more from one's suppliers but at a lower cost. More means integration of what, to give an example, the individual who wants to "have something built" knows so well – the fragmentation of trade associations, of their day-to-day contact on the site, for which the customer finally pays the cost in terms of quality and delivery time. The riposte to that is the search for a supplier who takes responsibility and at the end of day reduces the overall cost of the services. This logic – which has appeared in the building trade in response to the customer's need for cross-functionality in relation to a product (the house) with complex components – extends nowadays to a whole range of services that companies no longer want to carry out themselves, on the one hand, and no longer wish to manage through a multitude of scattered interlocuteurs, on the other.

The most important consequence of this evolution is without any doubt the reduced number of suppliers, which will result in the disappearance of some and the integration of others into units with variable contours, under the aegis of the principal service provider, whose role will be precisely that of an "overseer". The whole automobile sector today – and it is not alone – applies the twofold strategy of drastic reductions in the number of service providers at the same time as their integration, which sends us back once again to fuzzy borders, and to changes in jobs and their content. At the time of writing, Ford had stated its intention of reducing the number of its suppliers by 95 per cent by 2000, and certain customers will even go so far as offering to share with their service providers any savings that these new forms of organization and their relationships will make possible. Decidedly, it is indeed the question of value sharing which is central to this. Here as you will have understood, the key word is "integration", and without doubt this is characterized by multi-services. It is at the heart of the complex, one might even say sophisticated, customers' requirement – not necessarily institutional customers, but, for example, multi-route plane passengers who, like Smart-car buyers, also claim this integration and a new arrangement of tasks and jobs, placing them at the heart and not the periphery of the production of a service or merchandise.

A future world, one might say, not only in which there is no more room for our bureaucrats, but also in which their emergence will be accompanied by the "liberalization"[10] of a high number of activities and the "nomadism" of jobs. Here we are not very far from the thesis, proposed as an introduction, on the radical tendency towards the disappearance of work in its most traditional forms.

And yet the "Taylorian" choice still exists

A few years ago in the United States, we took part in a debate – focusing specifically on change in organizations – during which the CEO of a business specializing in consumer credit and debt restructuring, with 800 branches spread over the whole of the United States territory, delivered this profession of faith: "I am certainly one of the last true believers in Taylorism!" The explanation that he gave, reasoned and convincing, is well worth reproducing. It emphasizes the statistical rather than individual knowledge of the customer; it highlights the development of simple products, in accordance with the most industrial processes possible, the only way to cut costs; it emphasizes the need to segment customers into main categories with homogeneous behaviours and with which one can associate a risk value. In other words, it takes back all the ingredients of mass production. However, not only is this still current practice, but indeed managing it in the bureaucratic manner well and truly involves a choice which is structured around a twofold problematic – reducing the risk, reducing the cost, and thereby reducing individual knowledge of the customer as well as some leeway for the organization's members, thanks, in particular, to the sophistication of computer technology. This is what Alvin Toffler, going back to one of George Orwell's ideas, calls "trying to turn one's employees into electronic plebs".[11]

This choice is becoming widespread today because, once again, it appears as an alternative to massive investment in the transformation of operating methods in organizations. One thing is obvious – when, during inter-company training seminars being run in Europe as well as the United States, one asks managers the question "Do you have the feeling that, in your organization, there are always more rules and procedures being produced?", the response is generally positive. It seems to me that this results from two things:

1. The hope that the segmentation of routine tasks can make it possible to achieve a sufficient degree of quality for a customer whose interest focuses primarily on price, and who would therefore be prepared to accept sacrifices on condition that the product is indeed available. The company's risk and investments would at the same time find themselves minimized. Why not? This is the strategy chosen by most – but not all – banks in the retail banking sector (network banks), because they do not know another way of managing their relationship with a customer in whom, basically, they have no confidence;
2. The consequence of hiring staff who are increasingly less qualified, another solution found for reducing production costs. This drop in the level of qualifications, that is encountered, for example, in the medium-size American airlines, automatically leads to less confidence (again!) in the ability of employees to manage problems, without resorting to a precise and detailed specification. But this is also, and here is the paradox, a movement which is affecting small businesses. When we get our American students to write their end-of-term papers so that we can grade them, they analyse ad nauseam the organizations in which they are working to pay for their education, that is, most often local restaurants. The recurrence of what they

describe is impressive – work organized down to the last millimetre, scientifically calculated intervals between courses, menu presentation speeches learned by rote; in brief, scenarios in which nothing is left to chance or individual initiative, everything is calculated down to the last detail so that production can be carried out without requiring the slightest previous know-how. Once again, why not? even if, otherwise, the fatality rate for these small organizations is impressive and if, at the end of the day, the only survivors are those that are capable of introducing a little extra organizational "soul" into this well oiled process.

The emergence of a differentiation between organizations based on their product/customer strategy, or in other words based on the wager that they make on the changing requirements of their customers

There is no such thing as determinism here. Those that remain in mass production are not necessarily condemned to bureaucratic Taylorism – in the consumer credit sector, as in mail order distribution (the two are linked), we are seeing the appearance of fascinating attempts to use the definite advantage of information technologies. Proletarianization is not intrinsically associated with this. Such technologies enable sales advisors to instantly view not only the customer's profile and "purchase history", but also their physical appearance – so that, in terms of dress taste, for example, they will be able to provide a customized and suitable recommendation without wasting any time. What is more, advisors find themselves given "room for manoeuvre", that is, the possibility – although limited – of offering discounts, or some other advantage. This, in a way, is a return to confidence and, for the time being, results are excellent. Here we are not far away from the case already mentioned of the American business banks which preferred to assess their managers on their ability to cooperate rather than on the amount of business that they were generating – possibly to the detriment of overall results.

As we can see, at least in the short term, nothing is written in stone. The managers and members of organizations are returned not only to their perception of the future, to their choices, but above all to their reciprocal confidence – an essential condition for introducing a process of change into organizations – while at the same time offsetting the most severe aspects of the crisis, the drama or the ever-renewed pressure.

We have seen that such confidence is found neither in Taylorian traditions nor in elite cultures, which is self-explanatory. It therefore needs to build itself up around the sharing of knowledge, the increased ability of each individual to play the game – which is a necessity if one wants individuals to accept a little more confrontation, and therefore a little more cooperation. And, at the end of the day, if pressure from the customer, a wider range of choice, its growing maturity can bring the members of organizations closer together in the true sense of the term, to listen to each other as defined above, then this victory will not have been in vain.

Notes

Introduction

1. Michael Beer, Russell A. Eisensat and Bert Spector, "Why change programs don't produce change". *Harvard Business Review*, November–December 1990.
2. John P. Kotter, "Leading change: why transformation efforts fail". *Harvard Business Review*, March–April 1995.
3. Peter F. Drucker, *Management Challenges for the 21st Century*. Harper Business, New York, 1999.
4. Ibid.
5. This is a recurrent theme in organizational sociology, which has been developed in France by Michel Crozier. See in particular *La société bloquée*. Editions du Seuil, Paris, 1971. This theme is today once again up with the times, due to the extreme difficulty in getting public bodies to evolve: cf. Chapter 12.
6. We will return to this particular case in more detail at the end of this book.
7. We should – amongst others – add Chris Argyris, *Savoir pour agir: Surmonter les obstacles á l'apprentissage organisationnel*. Interéditions, Paris, 1995.
8. Chris Argyris, "Teaching smart people how to learn. Every company faces a learning dilemma: the smartest people find it the hardest to learn". *Harvard Business Review*, May–June 1991, pp. 99–109.
9. Robert B. Reich, *The Work of Nations: Preparing Ourselves for 21st Century Capitalism*. Vintage, New York, 1992.
10. In the meaning given to this expression by Herbert Simon. See James G. March and Herbert A. Simon, *Organizations*, J. Wiley, New York, 1958.
11. The expression comes from Peter Drucker, *Management Challenges for the 21st Century*, Harper Business, New York, 1999.

Chapter 1   An Uncertain World

1. Cf. Chapter 2.
2. See for example Robert H. Waterman Jr, *What America Does Right*. Plume-Penguin, New York, 1995.
3. Edgar Morin and Sami Naïr, *Une Politique de civilisation*. Arléa, Paris, 1997, p. 194.
4. Ibid.
5. Viviane Forrester, *Economic Horror*, Fayard, Paris, 1996.
6. Robert Castel, *Les métamorphoses de la question sociale, une chronique du salariat*. Fayard, Paris, 1995. Note that this extremely well documented book provides a useful and fruitful way of looking at all that has been said and written about work in general and salaried employment in particular.
7. Jeremy Rifkin, *The End of Work: The Decline of the Global Labor Force and the Dawn of the Post-Market Era*. Putnam Group, 1996.
8. Morin and Naïr, *Une Politique*, p. 89.

9. On the United States, see F. Leseman, *La politique sociale Américaine*. Synos, Paris, 1988. On Great Britain, see L. Ville, "Grand Bretange: le chomage diminue, l'emploi aussi". *L' Expansion*, No. 478, 2–15 June 1994. These works are cited in Castel, *Métamorphoses*.
10. It is true that one has to work with some of the huge public or para-public French monsters to find even today weak union organizations, artificially maintained in a dominant role since the "fear of social concerns" has a strong impact on company strategy.
11. Robert B. Reich, *The Work of Nations: Preparing Ourselves for 21st Century Capitalism*. Vintage, New York, 1992, p. 6.
12. Castel, *Métamorphoses*, p. 436.
13. Jean-Maric Thievenard.
14. For a quick review of the literature concerning this debate, see *Le Monde Économie*, 28 January 1997.
15. Michel Crozier, *L'enterprise á l'écoute*. InterÉditions, Paris, 1994.
16. Much of the executive class at the time thought that France could escape the widespread paralysis and it consequences thanks to the strength of its agricultural sector.
17. Alvin Toffler, *Le Nouveaux pouvoirs*. Fayard, Paris, 1991.
18. This is moreover a noteworthy reversal. Robert Castel shows that for many centuries, within the Catholic tradition, outcasts were not really a constraint for the wealthy, but rather a resource. Castel, *Métamorphoses*.
19. The upsets seen in France during spring 2003 on the issue of pensions or casual workers in the performing arts are the "irrational impact" of such profound transformations.
20. Morin and Naïr, *Une Politique*, p. 100.
21. Dear to Jeremy Rifkin (see Rifkin, *The End of Work*; in particular chapter 17; for France, see the preface written by Michel Rocard for this book, pp. i–xvii). This is also a theme of which Jacques Delors is very fond.
22. See, for example, the analysis presented by Sami Naïr in Morin and Naïr, *Une Politique*.
23. One example of this can be found in the slightly different but mostly very optimistic analysis of Jean-Paul Fitoussi and Pierre Rosanvallon, *Le Nouvel Âge des inégalités*. Le Seuil, Paris, 1996.
24. See Part II of this book.
25. See the case of privatization of the railways in Great Britain or electricity in the United States.
26. This term was popularized by Michael Hammer and James Champy, *Reengineering the Corporation*. Harper Business, New York, 1993. On page 40 the authors write: "If we had to define reengineering of a company in a few words, we would offer the following 'to start from scratch'. Reengineering … does not involve reworking what already exists, no more than modifying for an nth time some system without getting at its fundamental structure. It is not redistributing existing systems in the hope of getting them to run more smoothly … Reconfiguring a business means getting rid of previous systems and starting over."
27. Gary Hamel and C. K. Prahalad. *Competing for the Future*. Harvard University Press, Cambridge, MA, 1994. See also Jacques de Bandt, "Renault, un triste cas d'école". *Libération*, 12 March 1997, and Jacques de Bandt and F. de Bandt-Flouriol, *La descente aux enfers du travail*. ADST, Paris, 1996.

28. Morin and Naïr, *Une Politique.*
29. Rifkin, *The End of Work*, especially Part 2 and Part 3.
30. Which is, by the way, the main point discussed by Reich, *The Work of Nations.*
31. Rifkin, *The End of Work*, chapter 5.
32. "The 6.8% illusion". *New York Times*, 8 August 1993, p. 15; "Into the dark: rough ride ahead for American workers". *Training*, July 1993. Quoted by Rifkin, *The End of Work*, pp. 229–33.
33. Reich, *The Work of Nations*, p. 7.
34. Rifkin, *The End of Work*, p. 230.
35. We will return to this concept later in the book.
36. Waterman, *What America Does Right*, p. 17.
37. See for example Luc Lampiere, "États-Unis: pourvu que ça dure…". *Libération*, 8 and 9 February 1997.
38. Erik Izraëlewicz, "Oú va le monde?" *Le Monde Économie*, 18 March 1997.
39. Viviane Forrester, *Economic Horror.*
40. Philippe Thureau-Dangin, *La Concurrence et la mort.* Sifros, Paris, 1995.
41. Alain Duhamel, *Les Peurs françaises.* Flammarion, Paris, 1993.
42. De Bandt and de Bandt-Flouriol, *La descente.*
43. Roger Cohen, "A somber France, racked by doubt". *International Herald Tribune*, 12 February 1997.
44. Edgar Morin writes that "Religious fundamentalism, ethnic nationalism and differentialism are at once the manifestation of conservatism and the dark side of liberalism erected in a system for the world. Be this as it may, one Satan cannot take the place of another. Liberalism is not responsible for everything…It is just that is radical victory engenders is radical reverse side. And it is a reverse side headed in a backward direction." Morin and Naïr, *Une Politique*, p. 194.
45. Viviane Forrester, *Economic Horror*, p. 57.
46. See for example *Le Monde Initiatives*, 19 February 1997. Alain Lebaube writes: "Whereas companies have obtained everything they want, they continue to demand the easing of restrictions. Just how far can they go?"
47. See for example "La France en marge de la société en réseau". *Libération*, 7 February 1997.
48. Ethan B. Kapstein, "Capital mobile, travailleurs immobiles". *Le Monde*, 4 March 1997. The author (professor of political economics at the University of Minnesota) writes: "European leaders are in the process of tackling the problem of welfare benefits, as much within as outside their own borders… In fact, the crisis of European public finance gives each government the chance to reform the social contract which binds it to its citizens."
49. See, in the same issue of *Le Monde*, the article by Alain Henriot, "Quand la flexibilité modifie les comportements économiques". The author notes that out of 959,000 net jobs created between 1986 and 1996, three-quarters are either of a short-term nature, are temporary jobs, or paid internships, reminding us of the words of Robert Reich and Jeremy Rifkin concerning the United States.
50. François Dupuy and Jean-Claude Thoenig. *L'Administration en miettes.* Fayard, Paris, 1986. See also, following exactly the same logic, but eleven-year, "Les auxiliaires de l'État patron". *Le Monde Initiative*, 5 February 1997.
51. Michel Crozier, *La Crise de l'intelligence: Essai sur l'incapacité des élites á se réformer.* InterÉditions, Paris, 1995. See also De Bandt, "Renault, un triste cas d'école".

52. Alain Lebaube, "Pratiques syndicales flexibles en Europe". *Le Monde Initiative*, 19 March 1997.

53. For example, François Gave, "Le modèle allemand est-il en crise?" Centre d'études et de recherches internationales – FNSP, No. 19, September 1996; Serge Milano, *Allemagne: la fin d'un modèle*. Aubier, Paris, 1996.

54. Henri Duisbourg, "Le coup de grâce de la réunification". *Libération*, 24 February 1997.

55. Michel Drancourt. "Révolution chez les managers". *Sociétal*, No. 4, January 1997.

56. "Volkswagen relance ses innovations sociales pour résoudre ses surcoûts de production", *Le Monde*, 6 March 1997.

57. Rifkin, *The End of Work*, p. 154.

58. See *Le Monde Initiatives*, 19 March 1997.

59. An interesting example are the two major labour unions in France: the CGT (Confédération générale du travail) associated with the Communist Party, and the CFDT (Confédération française démocratique du travail). The infamous economic crisis in France provided opportunity for the CFDT, which underwent transformation, but was taken poorly by the CGT, which has been particularly resistant to change.

60. François Dupuy and Jean-Claude Thoenig, *La Loi du marché: étude sur les marchés de l'électroménager blanc en France, aux États-Unis et au Japon*. L'Harmattan, Paris, 1986.

61. Rifkin, *The End of Work*, p. 195. Rifkin writes: "New technology is starting to make the clothing industry of the industrialized nations just as competitive as the manufacturing companies of the low-wage nations. As manufacturing processes begin to bow to reconfiguration and automation, even exporters from the third world countries such as China or India will be forced to shift from the current methods requiring a large labour force, to the faster and more cost-effective techniques of mechanized production."

62. Jean-Raphaël Chaponniére, "Les leçons de la crise en Corée du Sud". *Le Monde*, 28 January 1997.

63. See Erik Israëlewicz, "Ombres et réalités chinoises". *Le Monde Économie*, 25 February 1997.

Chapter 2　The Customer's Victory

1. For example, Kenichi Ohmae, *The End of the Nation State: The Rise of Regional Economics? De l'État-nation aux États-régions*. Dunod, Paris, 1996.

2. Robert Reich, *The Work of Nations: Preparing Ourselves for 21st Century Capitalism*. Vintage, New York, 1992.

3. Robert Castel, *La métamorphoses de la question sociale, une chronique du salariat*. Fayard, Paris, 1995.

4. Michel Drancourt, for example, writes: "A lot of fun has been poked in France at the re-engineering movement from which we have only retained the 'nuts and bolts'. We did not understand that it was a management and business organization revolution, directed no longer just at the huge American market, but at the conquest of global markets as well" ("Révolution chez les managers". *Sociétal*, No. 4, January 1997, p. 33).

5. Michael Hammer and James Champy, *Reengineering the Corporation*. Harper Business, New York, 1993, p. 27.
6. Edgar Morin and Sami Naïr, *Une Politique de civilisation*. Arléa, Paris, 1997, p. 45.
7. Jeremy Rifkin, *The End of Work: The Decline of the Global Labor Force and the Dawn of the Post-Market Era*. Putnam Group, 1996, p. 150.
8. Louis Uchitelle, "The rehabilitation of morning in America". *New York Times*, 23 February 1997.
9. Viviane Forrester writes: "We can truly count on a good deal of cheerful deception, such as the one which eliminated between 250 000 and 300 000 unemployed workers from the statistics in a single blow ... by striking from the lists those who do at least 78 hours of work per month, in other words, less than two weeks, and without any benefits. It was a solution waiting to be found! Bear in mind the unchanged fate of bodies and souls hidden behind the statistics, of little importance as compared to how a particular calculation is carried out. Numbers are what count, even if they reflect no real value, nothing organic, no result, even if they only signify deception." Viviane Forrester, *Economic Horror*. Fayard, Paris, 1996, pp. 12–13.
10. Morin and Naïr, *Une Politique*, p. 21.
11. For more definitive proof, consider investment banking products and related services, each one more immaterial than the last, each one more complex, but never really any different.
12. What is being challenged here is not the goodwill of individuals, nor some intentionally manipulative endeavour on the part of the organization. The problem is the mode of reasoning employed.
13. Richard Normann and Rafaël Ramirez, "From value chains to value constellation: designing interactive strategy". *Harvard Business Review*, July 1993, pp. 65–75.
14. Pierre Grémion, *Le Pouvoir périphérique, bureaucrates et notables dans le système politique français*. Le Seuil, Paris, 1976.
15. Robert H. Waterman Jr, *What America Does Right*. Plume-Penguin, New York, 1995; see chapter 5.
16. See the analysis presented in François Dupuy, "The bureaucrat, the citizen and the sociologist", *French Politics and Society*. Harvard University Press, Cambridge, MA, 1990, volume 8.
17. Hammer and Champy, *Reengineering the Corporation*.
18. Ibid.

Chapter 3   What is a Bureaucracy?

1. Warren Bennis and Burt Nanus, *Leaders: Strategies for Taking Charge*, 2nd edition. HarperCollins, London, 1997, p. 40.
2. Robert H. Waterman Jr, *What America Does Right*. Plume-Penguin, New York, 1995, p. 283.
3. Robert B. Reich, *The Work of Nations: Preparing Ourselves for 21st Century Capitalism*. Vintage, New York, 1992.
4. Jeremy Rifkin, *The End of Work: The Decline of the Global Labor Force and the Dawn of the Post-Market Era*. Putnam Group, 1996, p. 137.
5. Henry Mintzberg, *Structure et dynamique des organisations*. Éditions d'Organisation, Paris, 1982.

6. T. Burns and G. M. Stalker, *The Management of Innovation*. Tavistock, London, 1961.

7. Henri Fayol, *Administration industrielle et générale*. Dunod & Pinot, Paris, 1917.

8. François Dupuy and Jean-Claude Thoenig, *Sociologie de l'administration française*, collection U. Armand Colin, Paris, 1983.

9. Michel Crozier, *The Bureaucratic Phenomenon*. University of Chicago Press, Chicago, 1964; but also Michel Crozier, Erhard Friedberg, Pierre Grémion, Catherine Grémion, Jean-Claude Thoenig and Jean-Pierre Worms, *Où va l'administration française?* Éditions d'Organisation, Paris, 1974.

10. Michel Crozier and Erhard Friedberg, *Organizations and Collective Action: Our Contribution to Organizational Analysis, Research in the Sociology of Organizations*, Vol. XIII. Volume editors Samuel P. Bacharach, Pasquale Gagliardi and Bryan Mundell. JAI Press, Greenwich, CT, 1994.

11. Frederick W. Taylor, *La Direction scientifique des entreprises*. Dunod, Paris, 1957. A certain number of Taylor's writings have been assembled and published by the Institut Renault de la Qualité. On the link between Weber, Taylor and democracy, see Jean-Pierre Rouze, "Frederick W. Taylor, inventeur de la démocratie moderne?" *Gérer et Comprendre*, March 1993, No. 30, pp. 97–105.

12. A simple and accurate presentation of this can be found in Erhard Friedberg, *L'analyse sociologique des organisations*, POUR, les dossiers pédagogiques du formateur. L'Harmattan, Paris, 1988.

13. Rifkin, *The End of Work*.

14. See Crozier, *The Bureaucratic Phenomenon*.

15. When they speak out against the "mania for meetings", the members of bureaucracies probably do not realize they are hitting an organization's soft spot. The unending, ever-increasing succession of meetings – today's meetings in preparation for tomorrow's – reveals the contradiction between the increasingly important need to work together (to cooperate) and the impossibility of cooperating in traditional bureaucracies.

16. With some differences however. To paraphrase Henry Ford, customers can choose any colour car they want, so long as it's black.

17. On this topic, see Christopher Midler, *La Voiture qui n'existait pas*. InterÉditions, Paris, 1993.

18. See Thierry Weil, "Provoquer les conflits: une pratique de bon management?", about two articles by Kathleen M. Eisenhardt, Jeannie L. Eisenhardt and L. J. Bourgeois III. *Le Journal de l'École de Paris*, No. 1, January 1997.

19. Waterman, *What America Does Right*, p. 16.

20. This is also what Rosabeth Moss Kanter says in *L'Entreprise en éveil*. InterÉditions, Paris, 1992.

21. See for example Patrick Hassenteufel, *Les Médecins face á l'État: une comparaison européenne*. Presses de Sciences Po, Paris, 1997. Quoted by Philippe Arnaud in "Le pouvoir contesté des médecins". *Le Monde*, 25 February 1997.

22. As is the case in Waterman, *What America Does Right*, pp. 80–6.

23. Edgar Morin and Sami Naïr, *Une Politique de civilisation*. Arléa, Paris, 1997, p. 128.

24. On this subject see Thomas Schelling, *La Tyrannie des petites décisions*. Presses Universitaires de France, Paris, 1974.

25. In a section entitled "Un new-deal de civilization", Edgar Morin writes: "The tremendous advances in health care, especially in the reduction of infant mortality, have nonetheless a dark side. Medical hyper-specialization, the treatment of organs rather than organisms and organisms rather than persons, the declining role of the generalist, the bureaucratization of hospital services, the increase in iatrogenic illnesses caused by side effects of medicine or by the spread of infections within hospitals, all of this adds a great deal to the cost of health care. Real reform of the medical establishment that entails at the same time reform in the way the biomedical world thinks (avoiding errors and waste) would help to decrease health costs as well." Morin and Naïr, *Une Politique*, p. 15.

26. France experienced the catastrophic results of this approach during the "crisis" linked to the heatwave in the summer of 2003.

Chapter 4   A Requiem for Bureaucracy

1. Thomas Schelling, *La Tyrannie des petites décisions*. Presses Universitaires de France, Paris, 1974.
2. Anne-Marie Bisaoui-Baron, "Origine et avenir d'un rôle balzacien: l'employé aux morts", *L'Année balzacienne*. Garnier, Paris, 1978, pp. 63–74.
3. Robert Reich, *The Work of Nations: Preparing Ourselves for 21st Century Capitalism*. Vintage, New York, 1992.
4. François Dupuy and Jean-Claude Thoenig, *L'Administration en miettes*. Fayard, Paris, 1985.
5. Pierre Birnbaum et al., *La Classe dirigeante française*. PUF, Paris, 1978; also Jean-Claude Thoenig, *L'Ère des technocrates*. Éditions d'Organisation, Paris, 1973; and Ezra Suleiman, *Les Élites en France: Grands corps et grandes écoles*. Le Seuil, Paris, 1979.
6. This is taken from an actual experiment conducted as part of consulting work requested by a large cosmetics company. We will return to this example in Part II.
7. Just as many are beginning to realize; see for example Erik Israëlewicz, "Big, small, beautiful". *Le Monde Économie*, 11 February 1997.
8. Michel Crozier went so far as to claim a few years ago that this organization was so very turned in upon itself and incapable of self-reform that nothing short of a change in the environment was required (the customer's victory suggested by this book, I might add) before there could be any hope of change; see Michel Crozier, *On ne change pas la société par décret*. Grasset, Paris, 1979.
9. This is, moreover, what happens when a bureaucracy is attacked. A good example occurred in France when a Prime Minister called state employees "spoiled brats", referring to their job security. See for example "La sécurité de l'emploi est absolument indispensable au bon fonctionnement de l'État". Interview with Professor Piquemal. *Le Monde*, 8 March 1984.
10. Edgar Morin writes: "Our democracies are correlatively confronted with a huge problem, resulting from the growth of the enormous machine in which science, technology, and bureaucracy are intimately connected. This enormous machine does not only produce knowledge and education, it also produces ignorance and blindness. The development of various scientific

disciplines has brought with it not only the advantages of the division of work, but also the problems of overspecialization, of compartmentalization, and of the partitioning of knowledge." Edgar Morin and Sami Naïr, *Une Politique de civilisation*. Arléa, Paris, 1997, p. 160.

11. "Tough schedule for take off". *Financial Times*, 16 January 1995.
12. This presentation stems from work carried out in 2003 by Mercer Delta Consulting France. I take this opportunity to thank the directors of this firm for having allowed me to use part of the results of this work.
13. Jeremy Rifkin, *The End of Work: The Decline of the Global Labor Force and the Dawn of the Post-Market Era*. Putnam Group, 1996.
14. Reich, *The Work of Nations*. Also cited in Morin and Naïr, *Une Politique*.
15. Christer Karlsson and Pär Ahlström. "The difficult path to lean product development". *Journal of Product Innovation Management*, Vol. 13, No. 4, July 1996, pp. 283–95.
16. Nevertheless, as we have argued, there still exists a great deal of confusion between coordination and cooperation. See for example X. Michael Song, Mitzi M. Montoya-Weiss and Jeffrey B. Schmidt, "Antecedents and consequences of cross-functional cooperation: a comparison of R&D, manufacturing and marketing perspectives". *Journal of Product Innovation Management*, Vol. 14, No. 1, January 1997, pp. 35–47.
17. Oliver E. Williamson, *Markets and Hierarchies: Analysis and Antitrust Implications*. The Free Press, New York, 1975. See also W. G. Ouchi, "Review of Williamson's 'Markets and hierarchies'". *Administrative Science Quarterly*, Vol. 22, 1977, pp. 541–4; Oliver E. Williamson and W. G. Ouchi, "The markets and hierarchies program of research: origins, implications, prospects", in A. Van De Ven & W. F. Joyce (eds) *Perspectives on Design and Behavior*. Wiley, New York, 1981, pp. 347–70; Michel Moulet, "Modes d'échange et coûts de transaction: une approche comparative de la firme et du marché". *Sociologie du travail*, Vol. 4, 1982, pp. 484–90.
18. Kagono et al., *Strategic versus Evolutionary Management: A U.S./Japan Comparison of Strategy and Organization*. New York, North Holland, 1985, pp. 112–13, quoted by Rifkin, *The End of Work*.
19. See Mike Parker and Jane Slaughter, "Management by stress". *Technology Review*, October 1988, p. 37.
20. Morin and Naïr, *Une Politique*.

Chapter 5   Change, Yes, but Change What?

1. On this subject, see the excellent dossier presented by *Le Monde* (5 February 1997) on the ability of French administration to recreate margins of freedom despite the constraints that the public authorities seek to impose on it. On this same capacity of resistance in organizations, one can also consult Jeremy Rifkin, *The End of Work: The Decline of the Global Labor Force and the Dawn of the Post-Market Era*. Putnam Group, 1996.
2. This was, for example, the position developed by the French President at the beginning of 1997. For an answer – in anticipation – to this vision, one can refer to Jean-Paul Fitoussi and Pierre Rosanvallon, *Le Nouvel Âge des inégalités*. Le Seuil, Paris, 1996, in particular the section on rethinking reformism (*repenser le réformisme*), pp. 185–95.

3. Chris Argyris, *Savoir pour agir: surmonter les obstacles á l'apprentissage organisationnel*. InterÉditions, Paris, 1995, pp. 30–65.

4. Robert A. Waterman Jr, Thomas J. Peters and Julien R. Phillips, "Structure is not organization". *Business Horizons*, Vol. 23, No. 3, June 1980.

5. Such literature is particularly well developed in the United States. Let us quote a few important titles: R. Tannenbaum et al., *Human Systems Development*. Jossey-Bass, San Francisco, 1985; Rosabeth Moss Kanter et al., *The Challenge of Organizational Change: How Companies Experience It and Leaders Guide It*. The Free Press, New York, 1992; D. Nadler et al., *Discontinuous Change: Leading Organizational Transformation*. Jossey-Bass, San Francisco, 1995; Michael Hammer and James Champy, *Reengineering the Corporation*. Harper Business, New York, 1993; N. Tichy, *Managing Strategic Change: Technical, Political and Cultural Dynamics*. John Wiley & Sons, New York, 1983; Argyris, *Savoir pour agir*.

6. Erhard Friedberg, *Le Pouvoir et la règle: dynamiques de l'action organisée*. Éditions du Seuil, Paris, 1993, p. 337.

7. "On continue à ne gouverner que dans l'urgence". Interview with Jacques Chereque by Laetitia Van Eeckhout. *Le Monde*, 12 March 1997.

8. Jean-Luc Rougé, "On change une équipe qui gagne". *L'Équipe*, 19 July 1996.

9. Ibid.

10. Rosabeth Moss Kanter, *When Giants Learn to Dance*. Unwin, London, 1989.

11. Pascale Marie Deschamps, "Pourquoi tout changer quand tout va bien". *L'Expansion*, No. 496, 6–19 March 1995.

12. Cf. Chapter 6.

13. Michel Crozier, *La Crise de l'intelligence: Essai sur l'incapacité des élites à se réformer*. InterÉditions, Paris, 1995. Note this passage at the beginning of the book: "Our elites are getting stressed. The less efficient they are, the less they can take criticism. It is absolutely inconceivable that people in power, directors of institutions should be able to declare without compunction that they are incapable of making the slightest change due to the rigidity, compartmentalization and conservatism of the company or organizations that they are in charge of. ... For it is indeed at the summit of the State, of the administrations, of the system of *grandes écoles* and senior civil servants that one discovers the reason for such rigidities and compartmentalizations" (p. 8).

14. Michael Beer, Russell Eisenstadt and Bert Spector, "Why change programs don't produce change". *Harvard Business Review*, November–December 1990.

15. See, in Chapter 8, the case of the European Development Bank.

16. Beer et al., "Why change programs don't produce change".

17. For example see R. Quinn, *Deep Change: Discovering the Leader Within*. Jossey-Bass, San Francisco, 1996.

18. Fitoussi and Rosanvallon, *Le Nouvel Âge*, p. 187.

19. This vision is somewhat generalized and optimistic. It will be discussed and enlarged upon throughout this book.

20. Jerry Stermin and Robert Choo, "The power of positive deviancy". *Harvard Business Review*, January–February 2000, pp. 14–15.

21. When teaching in business schools, it frequently happens that we are called upon to pronounce ourselves in favour of one "system" or another for the reason that it really is necessary to make choices.

22. In the sociological meaning of "control over what is important for other actors or for the organization itself". See Chapter 6.

23. François Dupuy and Jean-Claude Thoenig, *L'administration en miettes*. Fayard, Paris, 1986.
24. This discussion will be continued in the second part of Chapter 11, focusing on implementation.
25. We will return to this topic in Chapter 11 when analysing the Air France case study.
26. Michael Hammer and Steven Stanton, "How process enterprises really work". *Harvard Business Review*, November–December 1999, pp. 108–18.
27. The concept is borrowed from Donald N. Sull, "Why good companies go bad". *Harvard Business Review*, July–August 1999, pp. 42–52.
28. There is plentiful reading on the difference between behaviours and attitudes. This is far more scientific than managerial, showing the progress that organizational management has yet to achieve. See Michel Crozier and Erhard Friedberg, *Actors and Systems*. University of Chicago Press, Chicago, 1990.
29. French writer, Georges Moinaux Courteline, 1858–1929.
30. This is the case in particular of public organizations, for which this can sometimes be the start of a true revolution. Cf. Chapter 12.
31. This complexity is outlined and analysed in Chapter 7.
32. In fact, they only occupy the space that they are allowed to take, or rather that the mechanisms of lack of knowledge leave them.

Chapter 6   Review of Pure Reasoning: The Frame of Reference

1. For example: J. G. March, *Decisions and Organizations*. Basil Blackwell, London, 1981; J. G. March and J. P. Olsen (eds), *Ambiguity and Choice in Organizations*. Universitetsforlaget, Bergen, 1976; Graham T. Allison, *Essence of Decision: Explaining the Cuban Missile Crisis*. Little Brown, Boston, 1971.
2. For an explanation of systemic analysis and its scientific foundations, see Michel Crozier and Erhard Friedberg, *Actors and Systems*. University of Chicago Press, Chicago, 1990.
3. See the discussion on this concept in Chapter 7.
4. J. G. March and H. A. Simon, *Organizations*. J. Wiley, New York, 1958.
5. An extensive bibliography is presented in Erhard Friedberg, *Le Pouvoir et la règle: dynamiques de L'action organisée*. Éditions du Seuil, Paris, 1993, pp. 387–405.
6. This study was conducted under the author's direction by Hélène Bovais, a member of Stratema Consulting.
7. The entire theory of motivation should be under the gun here, not only from a theoretical point of view (see Crozier and Friedberg, *Actors and Systems*) but from a practical point of view: since it represents a rather substantial approach to human behaviour in organizations, it regularly draws from models which are necessarily reductionist in respect both to the complexity of this behaviour and the complexity of the organizations. Yet taking into account – accepting – this complexity is one of the conditions for successful change. History has shown that the alternative is totalitarianism.
8. March and Simon, *Organizations*, p. 141.
9. Something Durkheim had already affirmed.

10. Quoted in "Des experts soulignent les effets pervers des politiques uniquement répressives". *Le Monde*, 26 August 2003.
11. Alan Ehrenhalt, "Keepers of the dismal faith. How economists outwit common sense". *New York Times*, 23 February 1997.
12. See Robert Reich's discussion of this in *The Work of Nations: Preparing Ourselves for 21st Century Capitalism*. Vintage, New York, 1992.
13. This case will be developed in Chapter 7.
14. This case was studied by Dominique Thomas, working with the Association pour le Développement des Sciences Sociales Appliquées (ADSSA).
15. It should be clear now that within organizations, there is no such thing as the "irrational". To suggest that an actor's behaviour is irrational simply reveals how difficult it is to piece back together the logic of his or her behaviour.
16. There is a superb discussion of the problems of uncertainty and of power in Michel Crozier's *The Bureaucratic Phenomenon* (University of Chicago Press, Chicago, 1964). His example, the "industrial monopoly", which he uses again in *Actors and Systems* (Crozier and Friedberg), is today as valid as ever. It is unfortunate that some unenlightened minds do not realize that examples retain their heuristic value with age, considering them "too old" to be used for pedagogical purposes. Is the prisoner dilemma too old?
17. This is a recurrent theme in the sociology of organizations. For an in-depth discussion, see Friedberg, *Le Pouvoir*.

Chapter 7   The Process: From Symptom to Problem

1. "The next frontier: Edgard Schein on organizational therapy". *The Academy of Management Executive*, Vol. 14, No. 1, February 2000, pp. 31–48. It is very interesting to read the commentary on this article written by Manfred Kets de Vries in the same issue.
2. "Citygroup's John Reed and Standford's James March on management research and practice". *The Academy of Management Executive*, Vol. 14, No. 1, February 2000, pp. 52–64.
3. Chris Argyris, *Savoir pour agir: Surmonter les obstacles à l'apprentissage organisationnel*. InterÉditions, Paris, 1995.
4. Cf. Chapter 10 focusing on the "moment of change".
5. "The next frontier".
6. Ryan K. Sahti and Michael M. Beyerlein, "Knowledge transfer and management consulting: a look at 'the Firm'". *Business Horizons*, Vol. 43, No. 1, January–February 2000, pp. 65–74.
7. The +, − or = signs form a simple assessment, based on what the actors are saying, of the relationships that they have, whether positive, negative or neutral. This involves starting from "feelings" expressed by these actors in order to trace out a sort of "map of the human heart" for the organization. It is up to each person to build his or her own ladder, to make the simplest possible sociogram (this is not a scientific tool). The basic assumption is that from behind the interviews will appear the strategies. This first representation, based on the direct expression of the parties concerned, therefore allows a first interrogation on the alliances, the conflicts, the closeness of

interests, and so on. This is why, methodologically speaking, the sociogram must precede the analysis grid presented in Chapter 6.

8. The author made a first presentation of this case in François Dupuy and Jean-Claude Thoenig, "Public transportation policy making in France as an implementation problem". *Policy Sciences*, Vol. 11, 1979, pp. 1–18.

9. The problem is framed differently today – for an update on these cases see Frédéric Ocqueteau and Jean-Claude Thoenig, "Mouvements sociaux et action publique: le transport routier de marchandises". *Sociologie du travail*, Vol. IV, 1997, pp. 397–423.

10. Or at least prior to 1992/93.

11. See François Dupuy, "Personne n'écoute". *Le Monde*, 17 July 1992.

12. "Industrial monopoly" had already been the subject of study in the 1960s by Michel Crozier. It subsequently became one of the most classic case studies in organizational sociology. We had the opportunity to study this same company at the beginning of the 1990s, just before it was privatized. It is on this second study that we are basing ourselves, but the continuity of situations – even 30 years apart – is amazing. See Michel Crozier, *The Bureaucratic Phenomenon*. University of Chicago Press, Chicago, 1964.

Chapter 8   The Process: From Problem to Priorities

1. See amongst others the example on change in a car company given by G. Roth and A. Kleiner, "Car launch: the human side of managing change", in G. Roth and A. Kleiner (eds), *The Learning History Library*. Oxford University Press, New York, 2000.

2. This case has already been presented in another form in François Dupuy, *The Customer's Victory: From Corporation to Cooperation*. Macmillan Business, London, 1999.

3. This is what one might call a "paradoxical cooperation": people help each other to avoid the involvement of third parties, but never for the advantage of the organization in its entirety.

4. Here we can understand the vanity of the "common-sense speech" in these organizations. Explaining to account executives that they should communicate their information and that it is vital for the survival of the bank of which they are part, that is common sense. And yet, in an identical context, this has no sense for them, to the extent that it would result in giving up their principal resource.

5. This observation is not new. It has already been shown by Beer et al. See Michael Beer, Russell Eisensat and Bert Spector, "Why change programs don't produce change". *Harvard Business Review*, November–December 1990.

Chapter 9   The Process: From Priorities to Levers

1. The Taylorist concept of the universal rule which, because it ensures a system that is optimal, fair, legitimate, in relation to the goals to be achieved, would be imposed on all without discussion, is still very much alive. In recent times, this has been rediscovered in job descriptions, of course, but also in quality certifications. These have had to undergo profound changes in their philosophy, integrating the strategic dimension of human behaviour.

2. In Chapter 10, we will have the opportunity to return to problems of implementation which are more difficult to deal with in other ways than the definition of programmes and strategies.
3. Like culture, values only take on meaning in action, through concrete acts by actors. They then show themselves to be far more homogeneous than they appeared to start with.
4. On the subject of project management, its advantages and its difficulties, see "Où en est la gestion de projet?" *Le Journal de l'École de Paris*, No. 1, January 1997, pp. 17–26.
5. One can see that, historically, coercion has always been the counterpart to utopia. When societies have tried to define utopian projects (from each according to their possibilities, to each according to their needs, for example) they have always come up against resistance from those involved, precisely because such projects did not correspond to any practical or indeed practicable reality. It was therefore necessary to "force" this reality. Certain businesses have this same tendency towards utopian projects (being the preferred customer of their suppliers). Fortunately, the environment intervenes to limit – but only limit – their capacity to resort to coercion.
6. On the importance of managing human resources when conducting change, see Dave Ulrich, "A new mandate for human resources". *Harvard Business Review*, January–February 1998, pp. 125–34; also Thomas M. Begley and David P. Boyd, "Articulating corporate values through human resource policy". *Business Horizon*, Vol. 43, No. 4, July–August 2000.
7. This is the case in the transport company – as soon as a delay is seen, a code is attributed to it, indicating clearly which team is involved in this delay. But allocating this code does not incur any consequence for those that it puts at cause. It is therefore not a lever and the person who controls it gains no power from it.
8. Peter Drucker, *Management Challenges for the 21st Century*. Harper Business, New York, 1999.

Chapter 10   Implementation: The Moment of Change

1. Charles H. Noble, "Building the strategy implementation network". *Business Horizons*, Vol. 42, No. 6, November/December 1999, pp. 19–28.
2. In such circumstances, companies adopt a logic of action which is close to that of politics: it is programmatic, that is, turned towards the intentions, towards what must be achieved, the desirable, but takes little interest in implementation. However, everything shows that, in the political domain as in management, the main difficulty does not lie in drawing up programmes but in their effective implementation.
3. Donald N. Sull, "Why good companies go bad". *Harvard Business Review*, July–August 1999, pp. 42–52.
4. Michael Hammer and Steven Stanton, "How process enterprises really work". *Harvard Business Review*, November–December 1999, pp. 108–18.
5. John Daniels and Lee H. Radebaugh, *International Business Environments and Operations*, 9th edition. Prentice Hall, New Jersey, 2001, p. 759.
6. A survey conducted in 1999 by the General Inspectorate of this Ministry established that not one of the actors in the conflict had protested: tax

collection in France is carried out at a cost which is sometimes three times higher than that observed in comparable countries such as Spain or the United States. The complexity of the tax system is not enough to explain this differential. It is indeed the methods of functioning and therefore the organization which are at cause.

7. On the function of work protection and its reappraisal under the effects of globalization and new economic logics, see Robert Castel, *Les métamorphoses de la question sociale, une chronique du salariat.* Fayard, Paris, 1995.

8. See François Dupuy, *The Customer's Victory: From Corporation to Cooperation.* Macmillan Business, London, 1999.

9. See Chapter 12 devoted to the specific case of public organizations which correspond best to this definition.

10. This issue will be discussed at length in Chapter 11.

11. This was the CFDT (Confédération Française Démocratique du Travail).

12. Cf. the description given on p. 64.

13. Dominique Thomas has given a perfect analysis of the phenomenon in "Les employés d'assurance face au changement". PhD dissertation, Institut d'Études Politiques de Paris, 1979.

14. Nigel Nicholson, "How Hardwired is Human Behavior". *Harvard Business Review*, July–August 1998, pp. 135–47.

Chapter 11   Implementation: Playing on Trust

1. "Unit revenue" is the name used for average revenue earned on the sale of a seat. When an airline is in difficulty, it tends to leave tour operators free to offer its seats at whatever price they want in order to be sure of filling the aircraft. In this way, it gradually gains control over its pricing policy and, finally, its turnover.

2. There appears to be a lot to say on the need, in this type of listening operation, to use interviewers who have been well trained and well prepared. This means collaborators who know the sociological usage that will be made of the material they are collecting and who, in particular, understand that the problem is not knowing whether or not the person replying to the question is telling the truth, but understanding that he is saying something interesting because he is the one saying it, from where he is in the organization. This is the condition for developing the empathy necessary for the creation of an atmosphere of trust which will provide the interview with its best input. This is something which cannot be improvised.

3. There were at the time 14 union organizations in the company, representing both central labour bodies and an impressive number of sectional unions.

4. This is an approach which was greatly inspired by the example of British Airways where it has been quickly forgotten that a few years ago the situation here was hardly more brilliant than that at Air France. The highlighting of the concept of "seamless travelling" and its interpretation into the organization's day-to-day methods of functioning were, together with drastic cost reductions, one of the main factors for this company's success. The problems that it lived through later do not in any way contradict the very positive lessons that can be drawn from this experience.

5. This penchant for abstraction commences very early, right from the start of training for managers in general and senior executives in particular, even in the best business schools where the fear of taking risks leads to making students and managers work on theoretical and stereotyped situations, on stylized case studies which will only be encountered extremely rarely in reality. It is very satisfying to see that once one accepts a little more uncertainty in the teaching process by making participants reflect on real-life situations – their own, in fact – they begin to take real pleasure in this. They discover that reality is not a threat, that one can talk about it, discuss it, provided one has the right tools to bring it to light.

6. In "The next frontier: Edgar Schein on organizational therapy". *The Academy of Management Executive*, Vol. 14, No. 1, February 2000, p. 38.

7. Jean-François Manzoni and Jean-Louis Barsoux, "The set-up-to-fail syndrome". *Harvard Business Review*, March–April 1998, pp. 101–13.

8. These have been presented and developed by Michael Beer and Nitin Nohria in "Cracking the code of change". *Harvard Business Review*, May–June 2000, pp. 133–41. I summarize here the main points of their statement, even if I do not necessarily share their optimism when it concerns the possibility of combining the two approaches.

9. Cf. Chapter 12 on the specific case of public organizations.

10. Cf. François Dupuy, *The Customer's Victory: From Corporation to Cooperation*. Macmillan Business, London, 1999.

Chapter 12   The Particular Case of Public Organizations

1. This chapter is based on a presentation to the OECD symposium "Government of the Future, from Here to There" held in Paris on 14 and 15 September 1999, entitled "Why is it so difficult to change public organizations?".

2. François Dupuy, *The Customer's Victory: From Corporation to Cooperation*. Macmillan Business, London, 1999.

3. Robert Castel, *Les métamorphoses de la question sociale, une chronique du salariat*. Fayard, Paris, 1995.

4. See Jeremy Rifkin, *The End of Work: The Decline of the Global Labor Force and the Dawn of the Post-Market Era*. Putnam Group, 1996, and Robert Reich, *The Work of Nations: Preparing Ourselves for 21st Century Capitalism*. Vintage, New York, 1992.

5. Patrice Duran, *Penser l'action publique*. LGDJ, Paris, 1999.

6. See for example Alexandre Garcia, "La 'crise des vocations' accentue le malaise des hauts fonctionnaires". *Le Monde*, 2 November 2000.

7. This was the case during the famous "strikes by proxy" at the end of 1995 in France against the reforms proposed by the Juppé government.

8. This is the case in Ireland, Sweden, New Zealand or the Netherlands.

9. Cf. Chapter 7.

10. We have already mentioned in Chapter 5 the probability that the main obstacle in France to the merger between the General Tax Division and Public Accounting is the sharing out of these two entities between Syndicat Unifié des Impôts on one side, and Force Ouvrière on the other.

11. It is here that the word "culture" takes on all its practical meaning. If one uses it to designate not just a few abstract norms, but routine ways of dealing

with questions which return most frequently on the agenda, then the administrative culture is very strong. Often this starts to be learned in family life, then continues to be developed within the educational establishments attended. Its adoption, in this context more so than anywhere else, is necessary for a good integration in the environment, and therefore for a successful career in it. Here there are a number of areas in which one does not succeed against the system, but with it, that is, with others.

Conclusion

1. See for example Kazutoshi Koshiro, "Life employment in Japan". *Monthly Labour Review*, August 1984; or Yoshi Tsurumi, "Executive commentary". *The Academy of Management Executive*, Vol. 7, No. 4, 1993.
2. "Sous la houlette de Renault, Nissan renoue avec les profits". *Le Monde*, 30 October 2000.
3. This is what one calls electrical kitchen appliances (cooker, microwave, dishwasher, and so on) as opposed to "brown" goods for the living room (television, hi-fi, and so on).
4. François Dupuy and Jean-Claude Thoenig, *La Loi du Marché. L'électroménager en France aux Etats-Unis et au Japon*. Collection Logiques Sociales. L'Harmattan, Paris, 1986.
5. Current practice, especially in France.
6. Cf. Chapter 11.
7. This is the case of Robert H. Waterman Jr in *What America Does Right*. Plume-Penguin, New York, 1995.
8. Richard Normann and Rafaël Ramirez, "From value chains to value constellation". *Harvard Business Review*, July 1993, pp. 65–75.
9. For example, the alliances that are made and then unmade in the chemical industry, the co-management by two groups of a single production unit, and so on.
10. In the sense of the so-called "liberal" professions.
11. Alvin Toffler, *Les Nouveaux pouvoirs*. Fayard, Paris, 1991, p. 255.

Glossary

Note: The definitions given in this glossary are not academic in nature. They make reference to what has been developed in this book and are intended to facilitate reading. It is for teaching purposes that we have preferred to keep to simple and practical definitions.

actor(s)
The actor can be individual or collective; it is defined by its *relevance* in relation to the organization being studied, that is, by the necessity to take it into consideration in order to understand the reality of this organization. The overall set of stable relationships between relevant actors forms a system.

analysis grid
One of two tools in the strategic analysis of organizations. Makes it possible in a simple format to make links between the context, the problems to be solved and the strategies of actors. It is only useful when accompanied by an excellent understanding of the conceptual context underpinning it.

arrangement(s)
Solution(s) found by actors through the confrontation of their divergent interests. All arrangements have a cost, not only financial. It is easier for actors to find an arrangement where they externalize the cost onto third parties.

attitudes
The most apparent way in which an actor reacts or expresses itself. Assumed to depend on the actor itself and its intention, attitudes are understood in opposition to behaviours which are themselves of a contextual nature. The distinction between the two is the subject of endless debates between sociologists.

autonomy
Situation in which an actor succeeds in avoiding any situation of dependence on others. The search for autonomy appears empirically to be the most widely found problem in organizations.

bureaucracy
An organization which is characterized by the endogenous nature of all the criteria that it uses and which builds its methods of functioning on its own constraints and not on those of its relevant environment. In managerial language, it contrasts with customer-organization.

change
Substantial and durable modification from the strategies of actors, such as those expressed in their daily behaviour. In contrast to the modification of structures.

concrete
Close to "reality". Designates what exists effectively, as opposed to what should exist. Taking it into account is one of the conditions for a successful action of change. Methods of functioning are concrete, structures are not.

confidence
Acknowledgement of the capacity of actors to accept reality such as it is. Involvement of such actors in looking for solutions.

constraints
One of the elements in the context of actors: what they must face up to in order to resolve their problems. Can be material elements or other actors. Are never fixed once and for all. In contrast to resources.

context
The actor's relevant environment, made up of a set of resources and constraints, including rules, procedures or other actors. The actor's intelligence allows it to adapt by seeking to obtain what can be obtained in the context such as it is. It is the change of context which allows change in the strategy of actors, and therefore in the organization.

cooperation
Designates the direct confrontation of the diverging interests of actors and the immediate search for a negotiated solution acceptable to them. Is neither natural nor spontaneous since it reduces autonomy. Must therefore be constructed with the help of levers. Involves simultaneity and thus makes it possible to reduce costs and lead-times. In contrast to coordination.

coordination
Both an activity and a function. Consists of getting a third-party actor to manage the logics, timings, decisions and the actions of actors who

are not cooperating. The multiplication of coordination functions is one of the characteristics of bureaucratic organizations.

Culture (company)
Package of strategies which are found recurrently in an organization. Predominant way in which actors in this organization resolve their problems.
"Containing" culture: appearance, speech, external signals.
"Contained" culture: concrete practices, strategies.

dependence
Situation in which an actor sees another actor controlling something of importance for it. In contrast to autonomy.
Inverse dependence: situation in which real dependence is in contrast to hierarchical. Characteristic of bureaucratic organizations.

empowerment
Action of giving actors the intellectual and methodological means allowing them to go beyond their partial view of reality. Giving the means of knowledge and not just the knowledge itself.

implementation
Device adopted in order to bring envisaged solutions into effect. Concerns both the conditions of associating actors with the process and bringing overall management systems into concordance with what one wishes to obtain from these actors.

intelligence
Capacity of any actor to find an acceptable solution for itself, in the context in which it exists. Basic postulate in the theory of limited rationality.

knowledge
Apprehension or organizational mechanisms which are at work and which characterize the system on which analysis is focusing. Is identified with the understanding of problems. Refers to reality and concreteness.
Knowledge sharing: circulation of what has been updated to all actors concerned. Is identified with "listening". Involves confidence.

levers
Component parts of the context of actors on which one can play in order to achieve progress in their problem solving and strategies. The systems for managing human resources are the levers that are most frequently used. We talk of "leverage effect".

limited rationality
Calculation (conscious or unconscious) made by an actor in a given context in order to find a solution acceptable to it. In contrast to absolute rationality which presupposes the existence of a single good solution.

listening
Action consisting of putting feelings expressed by actors to the evidence of their reality, beyond the partial and partisan perception that they have of them. Listening is not asking actors what they want, it is saying it to them based on an understanding of their concrete working world.

management
Obtaining from actors for whom one is responsible that they do what one wants them to do.

margin(s) for manoeuvre
Area of freedom possessed by an actor allowing it to act on the context of other actors in order to cause them to change strategies. Often underestimated by the actors themselves. Can only be identified by knowledge.

method
Arrangement of the different phases of a process of change. Concerns the way of proceeding and not the content. In contrast to model.

method of reasoning
Set of notions and concepts arranged in relation to one another enabling an understanding of the reality. The strategic analysis of organizations and systems is a method of reasoning. In contrast to model.

method of functioning
Expression used to differentiate between organization and structure. Concrete and day-to-day way in which actors organize themselves to ensure the sustainability of the environment in which they are developing.

methodological realism
Postulate which means that an action (of change) can only be controlled and effective if it is based on a thorough knowledge of reality.

monopoly
Organization where the dominant actors have a strong capacity to make their environment – which has no choice – bear the cost of their internal arrangements. Within an organization, an overly precise definition of functions and territories leads to the formation of internal monopolies.

opportunity(ies)
Designates here the possibility for an actor to succeed in transforming a constraint into a resource, for itself or for another actor. The play of actors with their resources and constraints is known as management of opportunities.

organization
Designates the overall strategies of actors, what they do, the way in which they work and resolve their problems. Must be differentiated from the structure which is only one of the elements in the context of such actors. Relates to concreteness and reality.

outsourcing (of costs)
Organizational mechanism through which the actors in a system cause actors outside this system to bear the costs of arrangements that they have organized. The same mechanisms exist within organizations on behalf of actors who are dominant and/or in a situation of monopoly.

perverse effects
Result different from that expected, or uncontrolled result of an action or a decision for change. Occur generally when investment in knowledge has not been adequate.

play
Stable arrangement of the strategies of relevant actors, leading to the permanence and stability of a system.
Play with: use, employ.

power
An actor has power when it controls something important for another actor or for the organization in general. Power is not an attribute. It only exists in the relationship with others. Different from hierarchy.

priority(ies)
Part of a system, either a field, or a category, which an action of change will attack first, to the extent that it makes it possible to unbalance the system. Does not necessarily cover the most important problem. Is found at the junction of the desirable with the possible.

problem(s)
Used here with two meanings:

Information understood, meaning organizational mechanisms making it possible to interpret the symptoms which have drawn attention;

Problem to be resolved: what an actor seeks to achieve in the context in which it finds itself. Different from task or assignment. Does not mean that the actor "has a problem" in the usual sense of the term, but that it wishes to obtain something.

protection (function of)
Expression used with regard to work in developed countries. Organizations have a natural tendency to develop this function to the detriment of that of production turned towards the environment. Market pressure inverses this tendency.

reality
Designates the concrete conditions in which actors find themselves and which explain why they do what they are doing. The starting point for initiating an action of change. In contrast to appearance and generally to structure, rules and procedures.

resources
One of the elements in the context of actors. What they can activate in order to solve the problems they are seeking to solve. Can be material elements (rules and procedures) or other actors. Are never fixed once and for all. In contrast to constraints.

Principal resource of the most powerful actor: the "hard" point of an organization. The point that must generally be attacked in order to obtain true change.

site
Part or activity of an organization which has been identified as being sufficiently important to be the subject of special treatment, in the context of a project for change.

sociogram
One of two tools in the strategic analysis of organizations. Visualization of relationships between actors, such as can be perceived by getting them to express their feelings about one another. Is built on a simple qualification: positive, negative or neutral. Must be considered as a dynamic tool which makes it possible to ask the questions that the analysis grid will help to elucidate.

strategic analysis of organizations
Method of reasoning (concepts) and tools (sociogram and analysis grid) which make it possible to understand organizations as a set of rational actor strategies. "Strategic reasoning" will be spoken of.

strategy

Acceptable solution – but not necessarily the best – found by an actor in a given context in order to achieve what it is seeking to achieve. Concrete expression of the actor's intelligence.

Rational strategy: in the meaning of limited rationality (Herbert Simon). Does not mean either that the actor is right, or approved. In contrast to irrationality, stupidity, dishonesty, which are not sociological concepts.

symptom(s)

Term borrowed from medical language which designates what appears, what gives the alarm signal: defects, excessive delays, financial losses. It is "not understood information" that analysis will help to transform into "understood information", that is, into an identified problem.

system

Overall strategies of actors only understood in relation to one another. A system presupposes a certain degree of stability. Sociology uses the phrase "concrete action system" to indicate that this is a reality which has meaning for the actors.

uncertainty

Important element for an actor, but which is not dependent on the actor. Whoever controls an uncertainty has power; whoever is subject to this control is in a situation of dependence. Conventional sociology talks of the "area of uncertainty" to express the idea that uncertainty is generally poorly defined.

Relevant uncertainty: refers to the idea that, in order to give power, the uncertainty being controlled must be significant for another actor or for the organization itself.

References

The Academy of Management Executive. "The next frontier: Edgard Schein on organizational therapy". Vol. 14, No. 1, February 2000, pp. 31–48.

The Academy of Management Executive. "Citygroup's John Reed and Stanford's James March on management research and practice". Vol. 14, No. 1, February 2000, pp. 52–64.

Allison, Graham T. *Essence of Decision: Explaining the Cuban Missile Crisis.* Little Brown, Boston, 1971.

Argyris, Chris. "Teaching smart people how to learn. Every company faces a learning dilemma: the smartest people find it the hardest to learn". *Harvard Business Review*, May–June 1991, pp. 99–109.

Argyris, Chris. *Savoir pour agir: Surmonter les obstacles à l'apprentissage organisationnel.* InterÉditions, Paris, 1995.

Arnaud, Philippe. "Le pouvoir contesté des médecins". *Le Monde*, 25 February 1997.

Beer, Michael, Russell A. Eisensat and Bert Spector. "Why change programs don't produce change". *Harvard Business Review*, November–December 1990.

Beer, Michael and Nitin Nohria. "Cracking the code of change". *Harvard Business Review*, May–June 2000, pp. 133–41.

Begley, Thomas M. and David P. Boyd. "Articulating corporate values through human resource policy". *Business Horizon*, Vol. 43, No. 4, July–August 2000.

Bennis, Warren and Burt Nanus. *Leaders: Strategies for Taking Charge*, 2nd edition. HarperCollins, London, 1997.

Birnbaum, Pierre et al. *La Classe dirigeante française.* PUF, Paris, 1978.

Bisaoui-Baron, Anne-Marie. "Origine et avenire d'un rôle balzacien: l'employé aux morts", *L'Année balzacienne.* Garnier, Paris, 1978, pp. 63–74.

Burns, T. and G. M. Stalker. *The Management of Innovation.* Tavistock, London, 1961.

Castel, Robert. *Les métamorphoses de la question sociale, une chronique du salariat.* Collection "L'espace du politique". Fayard, Paris, 1995.

Chaponnière, Jean-Raphaël. "Les leçons de la crise en Corée du Sud". *Le Monde*, 28 January 1997.

Cohen, Roger. "A somber France, racked by doubt". *International Herald Tribune*, 12 February 1997.

Crozier, Michel. *The Bureaucratic Phenomenon.* University of Chicago Press, Chicago, 1964.

Crozier, Michel. *La société bloquée.* Le Seuil, Paris, 1971.

Crozier, Michel. *On ne change pas la société par décret.* Grasset, Paris, 1979.

Crozier, Michel. *L'enterprise à l'écoute.* InterÉditions, Paris, 1994.

Crozier, Michel. *La Crise de l'intelligence: Essai sur l'incapacité des élites à se réformer.* InterÉditions, Paris, 1995.

Crozier, Michel and Erhard Friedberg. *Actors and Systems*, University of Chicago Press, Chicago, 1990.

Crozier, Michel and Erhard Friedberg. *Organizations and Collective Action: Our Contribution to Organizational Analysis, Research in the Sociology of Organizations,*

Vol. XIII. Volume editors Samuel P. Bacharach, Pasquale Gagliardi and Bryan Mundell. JAI Press, Greenwich, CT, 1994.

Crozier, Michel, Erhard Friedberg, Pierre Grémion, Catherine Grémion, Jean-Claude Thoenig and Jean-Pierre Worms. *Où va l'administration française?* Éditions d'Organisation, Paris, 1974.

Daniels, John D. and Lee H. Radebaugh. *International Business Environments and Operations*, 9th edition Prentice Hall, New Jersey, 2000.

de Bandt, Jacques. "Renault, un triste cas d'école". *Libération*, 12 March 1997.

de Bandt, Jacques and F. de Bandt-Flouriol. *La descente aux enfers du travail*. ADST, Paris, 1996.

Deschamps, Pascale Marie. "Pourquoi tout changer quand tout va bien". *L'Expansion*, No. 496, 6–19 March 1995.

Drancourt, Michael. "Révolution chez les managers". *Sociétal*, No. 4, January 1997.

Drucker, Peter F. *Management Challenges for the 21st Century*. Harper Business, New York, 1999.

Duhamel, Alain. *Les Peurs françaises*, Flammarion, Paris, 1993.

Duisbourg, Henri. "Le coup de grâce de la réunification". *Libération*, 24 February 1997.

Dupuy, François "The bureaucrat, the citizen and the sociologist", in *French Politics and Society*. Harvard University Press, Cambridge, MA, 1990, Vol. 8.

Dupuy, François. "Personne n'écoute". *Le Monde*, 17 July 1992.

Dupuy, François. "Why is it so difficult to change public organisations?" OECD colloquium "Government of the Future, from Here to There". Paris, 14 and 15 September 1999.

Dupuy, François. *The Customer's Victory: From Corporation to Cooperation*. Macmillan Business, London, 1999.

Dupuy, François and Jean-Claude Thoenig. "Public transportation policy making in France as an implementation problem". *Policy Sciences*, Vol. 11, 1979, pp. 1–18.

Dupuy, François and Jean-Claude Thoenig. *Sociologie de l'administration française*, collection U. Armand Colin, Paris, 1983.

Dupuy, François and Jean-Claude Thoenig. *L'administration en miettes*. Fayard, Paris, 1986.

Dupuy, François and Jean-Claude Thoenig. *La Loi du Marché. L'électroménager en France aux Etats-Unis et au Japon*. Collection Logiques Sociales. L'Harmattan, Paris, 1986.

Duran, Patrice. *Penser l'action publique*. LGDJ, Paris, 1999.

Ehrenhalt, Alan. "Keepers of the dismal faith. How economists outwit common sense". *New York Times*, 23 February 1997.

Fayol, Henri. *Administration industrielle et générale*. Dunod & Pinot, Paris, 1917.

Financial Times. "Tough schedule for take off". 16 January 1995.

Fitoussi, Jean-Paul and Pierre, Rosanvallon. *Le Nouvel Âge des inégalités*. Le Seuil, Paris, 1996.

Forrester, Viviane. *Economic Horror*. Fayard, Paris, 1996.

Friedberg, Erhard. *L'analyse sociologique des organisations*, POUR, les dossiers pédagogiques du formateur. L'Harmattan, Paris, 1988.

Friedberg, Erhard. *Le Pouvoir et la règle: dynamiques de l'action organisée*. Éditions du Seuil, Paris, 1993.

Garcia, Alexandre. "La 'crise des vocations' accentue le malaise des hauts fonctionnaires". *Le Monde*, 2 November 2000.

Gave, François. "Le modèle allemand est-il en crise?". Centre d'études et de recherches internationales – FSNP, No. 19, September 1996.

Grémion, Pierre. *Le Pouvoir périphérique, bureaucrates et notables dans le système politique français*. Le Seuil, Paris, 1976.

Hamel, G. and C. K. Prahalad. *Competing for the Future*. Harvard University Press, Cambridge, MA, 1994.

Hammer, Michael and James Champy. *Reengineering the Corporation*. Harper Business, New York, 1993.

Hammer, Michael and Steven Stanton. "How process enterprises really work". *Harvard Business Review*, November–December 1999, pp. 108–18.

Hassenteufe, Patrick. *Les Médecins face à l'État: une comparaison européenne*. Presses de Sciences Po, Paris, 1997.

Henriot, Alain. "Quand la flexibilité modifie les compartements économiques". *Le Monde*, 4 March 1997.

Izraëlewicz, Erik. "Big, small, beautiful". *Le Monde Économie*, 11 February 1997.

Izraëlewicz, Erik. "Ombres et réalités chinoises". *Le Monde Économie*, 25 February 1997.

Izraëlewicz, Erik. "Où va le monde?" *Le Monde Économie*, 18 March 1997.

Kagono et al. *Strategic versus Evolutionary Management: A U.S./Japan Comparison of Strategy and Organization*. North Holland, New York, 1985.

Karlsson, Christer and Pär Ahlström. "The difficult path to lean product development". *Journal of Product Innovation Management*, Vol. 13, No. 4, July 1996, pp. 283–95.

Kanter, Rosabeth Moss. *When Giants Learn to Dance*. Unwin, London, 1989.

Kanter, Rosabeth Moss. *L'Enterprise en éveil*. InterÉditions, Paris, 1992.

Kanter, Rosabeth Moss et al. *The Challenge of Organizational Change: How Companies Experience It and Leaders Guide It*. The Free Press, New York, 1992.

Kapstein, Ethan B. "Capital mobile, travailleurs immobiles". *Le Monde*, 4 March 1997.

Koshiro, Kazutoshi. "Life employment in Japan". *Monthly Labor Review*, August 1984.

Kotter, John P. "Leading change: why transformation efforts fail". *Harvard Business Review*. March–April 1995.

Lampiere, Luc. "États-Unis: pourvu que ça dure". *Libération*, 8 and 9 February 1997.

Lebaube, Alain. "Pratiques syndicales flexibles en Europe". *Le Monde Initiative*, 19 March 1997.

Le Journal de l'École de Paris. "Où en est la gestion de projet?" No. 1, January 1997, pp. 17–26.

Leseman, F. *La politique sociale Américaine*. Synos, Paris, 1988.

Manzoni, Jean-François and Jean-Louis Barsoux. "The set-up-to-fail syndrome". *Harvard Business Review*, March–April 1998, pp. 101–13.

March, James G. *Decisions and Organizations*. Basil Blackwell, London, 1981.

March, James G. and J. P. Olsen (eds). *Ambiguity and Choice in Organizations*. Universitetsforlaget, Bergen, 1976.

March, James G. and Herbert A. Simon. *Organizations*. J. Wiley, New York, 1958.

Midler, Christopher. *La Voiture qui n'existait pas*. InterÉditions, Paris, 1993.

Milano, Serge. *Allemagne: la fin d'un modèle*. Aubier, Paris, 1996.

Mintzberg, Henry. *Structure et dynamique des organisations*. Éditions d'Organisation, Paris, 1982.

Le Monde. "La sécurité de l'emploi est absolument indispensable au bon fonctionnement de l'État". Interview with Professor Piquemal. 8 March 1984.

Le Monde. "On continue à ne gouverner que dans l'urgence". Interview with Jacques Chereque by Laetitia Van Eeckhout. 12 March 1997.

Le Monde. "Sous la houlette de Renault, Nissan renoue avec les profits". 30 October 2000.

Le Monde. "Des experts soulignent les effets pervers des politiques uniquement répressives". 26 August 2003.

Morin, Edgar and Sami Naïr. *Une Politique de civilisation.* Arléa, Paris, 1997.

Moulet, Michel. "Modes d'échange et coûts de transaction: une approche comparative de la firme et du marché". *Sociologie et travail*, Vol. 4, 1982, pp. 484–90.

Nadler, David et al. *Discontinuous Change: Leading Organizational Transformation.* Jossey-Bass, San Francisco, 1995.

New York Times. "The 6.8% illusion". 8 August 1993.

Nicholson, Nigel. "How hardwired is human behavior". *Harvard Business Review*, July–August 1998, pp. 135–47.

Noble, Charles H. "Building the strategy implementation network". *Business Horizons*, Vol. 42, No. 6, November–December 1999, pp. 19–28.

Normann, Richard and Rafaël Ramirez. "From value chains to value constellation: designing interactive strategy". *Harvard Business Review*, July 1993, pp. 65–75.

Ocqueteau, Frédéric and Jean-Claude Thoenig. "Mouvements sociaux et action publique: le transport routier des marchandises". *Sociologie du travail*, Vol. IV, 1997, pp. 397–423.

Ohmae, Kenichi. *The End of the Nation State: The Rise of Regional Economics? De l'État-nation aux États-régions.* Dunod, Paris, 1996.

Ouchi, W. G. "Review of Williamson's 'Markets and hierarchies'". *Administrative Science Quarterly*, Vol. 22, 1977, pp. 541–4.

Parker, Mike and Jane Slaughter. "Management by stress". *Technology Review*, October 1988, p. 37.

Quinn, R. *Deep Change: Discovering the Leader Within.* Jossey-Bass, San Francisco, 1996.

Reich, Robert B. *The Work of Nations: Preparing Ourselves for 21st Century Capitalism.* Vintage, New York, 1992.

Rifkin, Jeremy. *The End of Work: The Decline of the Global Labor Force and the Dawn of the Post-Market Era.* Putnam Group, 1996.

Roth, G. and A. Kleiner. "Car launch: the human side of managing change", in G. Roth and A. Kleiner (eds), *The Learning History Library.* Oxford University Press, New York, 2000.

Rougé, Jean-Luc. "On change une équipe qui gagne". *L'Équipe*, 19 July 1996.

Rouze, Jean-Pierre. "Frederick W. Taylor, inventeur de la démocratie moderne?" *Gérer et Comprendre*, March 1993, No. 30, pp. 97–105.

Sahti, Ryan K. and Michael M. Beyerlein. "Knowledge transfer and management consulting: a look at 'the firm'". *Business Horizons*, Vol. 43, No. 1, January–February 2000.

Schelling, Thomas. *La Tyrannie des petites décisions.* Presses Universitaires de France, Paris, 1974.

Song, X. Michael, Mitzi M. Montoya-Weiss and Jeffrey B. Schmidt. "Antecedents and consequences of cross-functional cooperation: a comparison of R&D,

manufacturing and marketing perspectives". *Journal of Product Innovation Management*, Vol. 14, No. 1, January 1997, pp. 35–47.

Stermin, Jerry and Robert Choo. "The power of positive deviancy". *Harvard Business Review*, January–February 2000, pp. 14–15.

Suleiman, Ezra. *Les Élites en France: Grand corps et grandes écoles*. Le Seuil, Paris, 1979.

Sull, Donald N. "Why good companies go bad". *Harvard Business Review*, July–August 1999, pp. 42–52.

Tannenbaum, R. et al. *Human Systems Development*, Jossey-Bass, San Francisco, 1985.

Taylor, Frederick W. *La Direction scientifique des enterprises*. Dunod, Paris, 1957.

Thomas, Dominique. "Les employés d'assurance face au changement". PhD dissertation, Institut d'Études Politiques de Paris, 1979.

Thoenig, Jean-Claude. *L'Ère des technocrates*. Éditions d'Organisation, Paris, 1973.

Thureau-Dangin, Philippe. *La Concurrence et la mort*. Sifros, Paris, 1995.

Tichy, N. *Managing Strategic Change: Technical, Political and Cultural Dynamics*. John Wiley & Sons, New York, 1983.

Toffler, Alvin. *Le Nouveaux pouvoirs*. Fayard, Paris, 1991.

Training. "Into the dark: rough ride ahead for American workers". July 1993.

Tsurumi, Yoshi: "Executive commentary", *The Academy of Management Executive*, Vol. 7, No. 4, 1993.

Uchitelle, Louis. "The rehabilitation of morning in America". *New York Times*, 23 February 1997.

Ulrich, Dave. "A new mandate for human resources". *Harvard Business Review*, January–February 1998, pp. 125–34.

Ville, L. "Grand Bretagne: le chomage diminue, l'emploi aussi". *L'Expansion*, No. 478, 2–15 June 1994.

Waterman, Robert H. Jr, Thomas J. Peters and Julien R. Phillips. "Structure is not organization". *Business Horizons*, Vol. 23, No. 3, June 1980.

Waterman, Robert H. Jr. *What America Does Right*. Plume-Penguin, New York, 1995.

Weber, Max. *Wirtschaft and Gesellschaft*. Berlin Kieperrhalten & Witsch, Cologne, 1964.

Weil, Thierry. "Provoquer les conflits: une pratique de bon management". *Le Journal de l'École de Paris*, No. 1, January 1997.

Williamson, Oliver E. *Markets and Hierarchies: Analysis and Antitrust Implications*. The Free Press, New York, 1975.

Williamson, Oliver E. and W. G. Ouchi. "The markets and hierarchies program of research: origins, implications, prospects", in A. Van De Ven and W. F. Joyce (eds) *Perspectives on Design and Behavior*. Wiley, New York, 1981, pp. 347–70.

Index

Compiled by Sue Carlton